Loan and Security

A Negotiating Handbook

Second Edition

James Dakin (Partner, Nabarro Nathanson)

Consulting editors

Gavin Rabinowitz (Director, Credo Property Group Limited)

Vanessa Beattie-Jones (Head of UK Asset Management, GE Capital Real Estate)

JORDANS
2002

NabarroNathanson

Published by
Jordan Publishing Limited
21 St Thomas Street
Bristol BS1 6JS

British Library Cataloguing-in-Publication Data
A catalogue record for this book is available from the British Library.

ISBN 0 85308 592 7

Typeset by Mendip Communications Ltd, Frome, Somerset
Printed in Great Britain by MPG Books Ltd, Bodmin, Cornwall

PREFACE

This book, like the first edition, is not intended to be an encyclopaedic tome on the state of banking law. Nor is it intended to be a comprehensive precedent source. Its aim is to provide an introduction to banking law through the practical examination of the key banking documents. It will serve as a negotiating tool and provide a general overview of a very complex area of law and practice. While having the luxury of specialising in this area, the author appreciates that most of the practitioners referring to this book will not. It is really to them, and to those beginning to specialise in banking, that this book has been addressed.

The documents in this book, set out clause by clause, are not intended to be used as precedents but are provided as examples typical of the layout and content of most of the loan and security documents seen in the market today. The book covers the three principal banking documents: the loan agreement, the debenture and the guarantee, and also contains a glossary of commonly used finance terms and a short overview of the legal pitfalls arising in this area.

Since the publication of the first edition in 1996 there have been many changes in the banking market and to the documentation typically used in it. Chief among these has been the emergence of the Loan Market Association recommended forms of primary document. Although designed chiefly for unsecured syndicated credits, the architecture and boilerplates of these documents have been enthusiastically adopted and adapted by practitioners to the full range of banking transactions. Within the documentation are embodied developments taking account of the Euro, changes to the taxation of interest, assignability and a host of other matters.

There have also been a number of legal developments which have had an impact on banking documentation since 1996, particularly in the taking of security over certain types of asset. Real Estate Banking has also been affected by the introduction of tougher environmental legislation. On the horizon, and referred to in these pages, are the Government's intended changes to insolvency law which promise to have a profound effect on secured lenders in the UK.

I would like to thank all those at Nabarro Nathanson who have helped me in the production of this book, particularly Marika Chalkiadis and Anna Marshall for their contributions on insolvency and environmental matters, Darren Kent for his work on the debenture, and Naoko Yasutake and Saffi Rayman for their tireless assistance in checking the copy as it was produced. I would also like to express my gratitude to the original authors, Vanessa Beattie-Jones and Gavin Rabinowitz, without whom this book could not have been written.

JAMES DAKIN
December 2001

CONTENTS

PREFACE   v
TABLE OF CASES   xi
TABLE OF STATUTES   xiii
TABLE OF STATUTORY INSTRUMENTS AND CODES OF PRACTICE   xv
TABLE OF EUROPEAN MATERIALS   xvii
TABLE OF FOREIGN ENACTMENTS   xix

GLOSSARY OF TERMS   1

INTRODUCTION   15
   1   The Loan Agreement   15
   2   The Debenture   16
   3   The Guarantee   16
   4   Pitfalls   17

DOCUMENT 1: THE LOAN AGREEMENT   19
   1   Definitions and Interpretation   21
   2   The Facility   35
   3   Purpose   35
   4   Conditions of Utilisation   36
   5   Utilisation   38
   6   Repayment   39
   7   Prepayment and Cancellation   39
   8   Interest   43
   9   Interest Periods   46
  10   Changes to the Calculation of Interest   48
  11   Bank Accounts   49
  12   Fees   52
  13   Tax Gross-up and Indemnities   53
  14   Increased Costs   58
  15   Other Indemnities   60
  16   Mitigation by the Lender   61
  17   Costs and Expenses   61
  18   Representations   62
  19   Information Undertakings   69
  20   Financial Covenants   72
  21   General Undertakings   74
  22   Property Undertakings   78
  23   Events of Default   81
  24   Changes to the Lenders   88

25 Changes to the Borrower 89
26 Conduct of Business by the Lender 91
27 Payment Mechanics 91
28 Set-off 93
29 Notices 93
30 Calculations and Certificates 95
31 Partial Invalidity 96
32 Remedies and Waivers 96
33 Counterparts 96
34 Governing Law 96
35 Enforcement 97
Schedule 1 Conditions Precedent 98
Schedule 2 Requests 101
Schedule 3 Mandatory Cost Formulae 103

DOCUMENT 2: THE DEBENTURE 105
1 Definitions and Interpretation 107
2 Covenant to Pay 117
3 Interest 118
4 Security 118
5 Negative Pledge 125
6 Conversion of Floating Charge 125
7 Further Assurance 126
8 Intellectual Property 127
9 Deposit of Documents and Title Deeds 128
10 The Book Debts Account 129
11 The Rental Account 131
12 Dividends, Voting Rights and Nominees 134
13 Representations and Warranties 135
14 Undertakings 136
15 Costs Indemnity 139
16 Enforcement 140
17 Statutory Power of Sale 140
18 Receiver 141
19 Protection of Third Parties 146
20 No Liability as Mortgagee in Possession 146
21 Release and Reassignment 147
22 Power of Attorney 147
23 Cumulative and Continuing Security 148
24 Avoidance of Payments 148
25 Prior Charges 150
26 Opening a New Account 150
27 Suspense Account 151
28 Payments and Withholding Taxes 151
29 Set-off 152
30 Assignment 152
31 Waivers 152
32 Severability 153

33   HM Land Registry   153
34   Notices   153
35   Governing Law and Jurisdiction   154
Schedule 1   Scheduled Property   156
Schedule 2   Form of Notice to Tenant   157
Schedule 3   Part 1: Notice to Bank   159
             Part 2: Acknowledgement from Bank   160

DOCUMENT 3: THE GUARANTEE   165
  1   Definitions and Interpretation   167
  2   Guarantee and Indemnity   170
  3   Continuing Security   173
  4   Protective Clauses   174
  5   Powers of the Lender   177
  6   Termination   178
  7   Expenses   179
  8   Set-off and Lien   180
  9   Payments, Currencies and Taxes   180
 10   Miscellaneous   181
 11   Notices   183
 12   Governing Law   184
 13   Counterparts and Delivery   184

PITFALLS   185
  1   Unfair Terms in Consumer Contracts Regulations 1999   187
  2   Environmental Liability   189
  3   Loans to Directors   190
  4   Financial Assistance   194
  5   Insolvency Act 1986   198
        5.1 Transactions at an undervalue   198
        5.2 Preferences   199
        5.3 Avoidance of certain floating charges   200
        5.4 Extortionate credit transactions   201
        5.5 Generally   201
  6   Registration of Charges   201
        6.1 Charges created by English and Welsh companies   201
        6.2 Charges created by overseas companies   202
        6.3 Other forms of registration   203

INDEX   205

TABLE OF CASES

References are to page numbers.

Bache and Co (London) Ltd v Banque Vernes et Commercial de Paris SA
    [1973] 2 Lloyd's Rep 437, (1973) 117 SJ 483, CA   173
Bank of Credit and Commerce International SA (No 8), Re [1998] AC 214,
    [1997] 3 WLR 909, [1997] 4 All ER 568, HL   120
Barclays Bank v O'Brien [1994] 1 AC 180, [1993] 3 WLR 786, [1993] 4 All ER
    417, HL   167
Brightlife Ltd, Re [1986] Ch 200, [1987] 2 WLR 197, [1986] 3 All ER 673   130
Brumark Investments Ltd, Re [2001] 3 WLR 454, [2001] Lloyd's Rep 251, PC   130

CIBC Mortgages plc v Pitt [1994] 1 AC 200, [1993] 3 WLR 802, [1993] 4 All
    ER 417, HL   167
Carney v Herbert [1985] AC 301, [1984] 3 WLR 1303, [1985] BCLC 140, PC   195
Charge Card Services Ltd, Re [1987] Ch 150, [1986] 3 WLR 697, [1986] 3 All
    ER 289   120
Cope (Benjamin) & Sons Ltd, Re; Marshall v Benjamin Cope & Sons Ltd
    [1914] 1 Ch 800, 83 LJ Ch 699, 21 Mans 254   126
Cryne v Barclays Bank plc [1987] BCLC 548, CA   117

Dearle v Hall (1828) 3 Russ 1, [1824–34] All ER Rep 28   124
Denton's Estate, Re; Licences Insurance Corporation and Guarantee Fund v
    Denton [1904] 2 Ch 178, 73 LJ Ch 465, 52 WR 484, CA   171
Devaynes v Noble (Clayton's Case) (1816) 1 Mer 529, 35 ER 781, [1814–23] All
    ER Rep 1   148, 150
Dunlop Pneumatic Tyre Co Ltd v New Garage and Motor Co Ltd [1915] AC
    79, [1914–15] All ER Rep 739, 83 LJKB 1574, HL   46

Ellis v Emmanuel (1876) 1 Ex D 157, 46 LJQB 25, 24 WR 832, CA   172

General Produce Co v United Bank Ltd [1979] 2 Lloyd's Rep 255   171
Griffiths and Another v Yorkshire Bank and Others [1994] 1 WLR 1427, (1994)
    91(36) LS Gaz 36, ChD   126
Guinness Mahon & Co Ltd v Kensington and Chelsea Royal London Borough
    Council [1999] QB 215, [1998] 3 WLR 829, [1998] 2 All ER 272, CA   176

Heald v O'Connor [1971] 1 WLR 497, [1971] 2 All ER 1105, (1970) 115
    SJ 244   171, 172, 195

Lordsdale Finance plc v Bank of Zambia [1996] QB 752, [1996] 3 WLR 688,
    [1996] 3 All ER 156, QBD   46

New Bullas Trading Ltd, Re [1994] BCC 36, [1994] 1 BCLC 485, CA   130

Perry v National Provincial Bank of England [1910] 1 Ch 464, 79 LJ Ch 509,
    102 LT 300, CA   175

Selangor United Rubber Estates Ltd v Craddock (No 3) [1968] 1 WLR 1555,
    [1968] 2 All ER 1073, [1968] 2 Lloyd's Rep 289   195
Siebe Gorman & Co Ltd v Barclays Bank Ltd; Same v McDonald (RH) and
    Barclays Bank Ltd [1979] 2 Lloyd's Rep 142   130
Slavenburg's Bank NV v International Natural Resources Ltd and Others
    [1980] 1 WLR 1076, [1980] 1 All ER 955   202
South Western Mineral Water Co v Ashmore [1967] 1 WLR 1110, [1967] 2 All
    ER 953, 111 SJ 453   195

Victor Battery Co Ltd v Curry's Ltd [1946] Ch 242, [1946] 1 All ER 519, 115 LJ
    Ch 148   195

Yorkshire Woolcombers' Association Ltd, Re; Houldsworth v Yorkshire
    Woolcombers' Association Ltd [1903] 2 Ch 284, 72 LJ Ch 635, 88 LT 811,
    CA   130

TABLE OF STATUTES

References are to page numbers.

Ancient Monuments and
 Archaeological Areas Act
 1979 — 111

Bank of England Act 1998 — 104

Companies Act 1948
 s 54 — 195
Companies Act 1985 — 202
 Pt XXI — 202
 s 35A — 155
 s 36A(4) — 155
 ss 151–158 — 194
 s 151 — 195, 196, 197
  (1), (2) — 194
 s 152(1)(a) — 194
 s 153(1), (2) — 194
  (3) — 194, 196, 197
 s 154 — 196, 197
 s 155 — 195, 196, 197
 s 330 — 190, 191, 192, 193
 s 331(6) — 191
 s 335(2) — 193
 s 337(3) — 192, 193
 s 338 — 191, 192, 193
 ss 341, 342 — 191
 s 395 — 68, 201
 s 396 — 180, 202
 s 399 — 202
 s 401(2) — 202
 s 404 — 202
 s 409 — 202
 s 691(1) — 202
 s 736 — 33, 116
 s 744A — 191
Contracts (Rights of Third
 Parties) Act 1999 — 35

Environment Act 1995 — 189, 190
 s 57 — 190

Environmental Protection Act
 1990 — 109, 189
 s 78F — 190
 ss 79–82 — 189
 s 157(1) — 189
European Communities Act 1972 — 2

Finance Act 2001 — 56
Financial Services Act 1986 — 2

Health and Safety at Work etc
 Act 1974 — 190

Income and Corporation Taxes
 Act 1988 — 33
 s 11(2) — 53
 s 349 — 10, 55
 s 349B — 56
 s 840A — 10, 56
Insolvency Act 1986 — 144, 148, 198
 s 9(3) — 122
 s 11 — 122
 s 29 — 142
  (2) — 122
 s 123 — 198, 201
  (1)(a)–(e) — 198
 s 238 — 198
  (1)(a), (b) — 199
  (3) — 199
  (5)(a), (b) — 199
 s 239 — 199
  (4)–(6) — 200
 s 240 — 199
  (1)(a) — 199, 200
  (b) — 200
  (2) — 198
 s 241(1) — 199
 s 244 — 201
 s 245 — 200
  (2) — 201

Insolvency Act 1986 – *cont*
  s 245(3), (4)   200
  s 249   199
  s 251   189
  s 339   201
  s 340   201
  s 343   201
  s 386   67
  Sch 1   142
Insolvency Act 2000   122
  s 1   122
  Sch 1   122

Land Registration Act 1925   68
Land Registration Act 1986   68
Landlord and Tenant Act 1927
  s 3(1)   30, 112
  s 18(2)   6
Landlord and Tenant Act 1954
  s 24(A)   112
  s 24A   30
Landlord and Tenant
    (Covenants) Act 1995   79
  s 17(2), (3)   78, 79
Law of Property Act 1925   112, 141
  s 85(1)   154
  s 93   140
  ss 99–109   145
  s 99   140
  s 100   141
  s 101   140, 154
    (1)   117, 146
  s 103   140, 141
  s 104   146
  s 109   117, 142, 146
    (2)   145
    (8)(i), (ii)   146
  s 117   118
  s 136   123
  s 146   6
  Sch 5   118
Law of Property (Miscellaneous
  Provisions) Act 1989
  s 1   147
Law of Property (Miscellaneous
  Provisions) Act 1994
  s 1   119

Law Reform (Miscellaneous
  Provisions) Act 1971
  s 2   155
Local Government Planning and
  Land Act 1980   111

Mercantile Law Amendment Act
  1856
  s 5   177
Mines and Quarries Act 1954
  s 181   190

Occupiers Liability Act 1957   190

Planning (Hazardous
  Substances) Act 1990   111
Planning (Listed Buildings and
  Conservation Areas) Act
  1990   111
Planning and Compensation Act
  1991   111
Powers of Attorney Act 1971
  s 1   147, 154

Statute of Frauds Act 1677
  s 4   17

Town and Country Planning Act
  1990   111
Trustee Act 1925
  s 10(3), (4)   134
Trustee Investments Act 1961
  s 9   134

Unfair Contract Terms Act 1977   187
Unfair Contract Terms Act 1982   187

Value Added Tax Act 1994   34

Water Resources Act 1991
  s 85   190
  s 161   190
  s 217(1)   190

TABLE OF STATUTORY INSTRUMENTS AND CODES OF PRACTICE

References are to page numbers.

Banking Supervision (Fees) Regulations 1999   104

Insolvency Rules 1986, SI 1986/1925
   r 4.90   93

RICS Guidance Notes   34
RICS Statements of Asset Valuation Practice   34

Unfair Terms in Consumer Contracts Regulations 1994, SI 1994/3159   96, 187, 188
   Sch 3, para 2(b)   46
Unfair Terms in Consumer Contracts Regulations 1999, SI 1999/2083   175, 187, 188
   reg 3   188
   reg 5   188
      (1)   188
      (2)–(4)   187
      (5)   188
   reg 6(1)   188
      (2)(b)   188
   reg 8(1), (2)   188
   reg 13(1), (2)   188
   reg 15(3)   188
   Sch 1   188
   Sch 2   188
      para 1(b)   188
        (i)   188
        (q)   188
Uniform Customs and Practice No 500 – ICC Publication 516, 1993   5

TABLE OF EUROPEAN MATERIALS

References are to page numbers.

Draft EC Directive for Civil Liability Caused by Waste (1989) OJ C251/3
  (4.10.1989)   189

European Capital Adequacy Directive; Council Directive 93/6/EEC of 15
  March 1993; on the capital adequacy of investment firms and credit
  institutions (1993 OJ L141/1)   2

TABLE OF FOREIGN ENACTMENTS

References are to page numbers.

US Comprehensive Environmental Response Compensation and Liability Act   189

GLOSSARY OF TERMS

Administrative Receiver

A person who is appointed by or on behalf of a creditor over all of the assets of a company pursuant to a floating charge, to realise a security. His principal duty is to the appointing debenture holder. He has wider powers than a receiver.

Administrator

A person appointed by the court to manage an insolvent company, as an alternative to that company being wound up. The purpose of the appointment may be to achieve the survival of the company and all or part of its undertaking as a going concern, or to achieve a more advantageous realisation of the company's asset than would be effected on a winding-up.

Advance

A loan payment by the lender to the borrower. It could be the whole of the loan or part of the loan.

Agent

In a syndicated loan, a financial institution which is responsible for administering the loan and which acts as a conduit for all payments.

Amortisation

A loan is 'amortised' where principal is repaid over a period of time by a number of instalments.

Availability Period

This is also known as the 'commitment period' and is used to describe the period in which borrowings may be made.

Balloon Repayment

A single repayment instalment, usually at the end of a series, which is much larger than the others.

Base Rate

A rate of interest which is published by UK banks and building societies from time to time as a basis for determining their individual lending rates. This is the simplest interest rate to draft into a document.

Basis Point or 'bps'	100th of 1 percentage point (0.01%), used to express differentials in interest rates, for example:

130 Basis points = 1.3%
100 Basis points = 1.0%
 90 Basis points = 0.9%

Basle Agreement	An agreement first drawn up in 1975, in the wake of the Herstatt Bank collapse, by the Bank for International Settlements to improve the supervision and monitoring of banking operations. It is the only international pact in respect of banking supervision and is concerned, inter alia, with setting capital adequacy requirements. It is now largely absorbed into the European Capital Adequacy Directive[1] which was implemented in the United Kingdom.[2]
Breakage Costs	The cost to the lender of terminating a loan prematurely.
Bullet Loan	A single repayment loan with no instalments.
Cap	A limit or ceiling, usually setting the maximum interest that may be charged on a loan.
Capital Adequacy Ratios	These ratios stipulate the amount of its own money which a bank needs relative to its total assets. Such ratios are not a simple calculation: the Bank of England will look at the make-up of a bank's business and decide whether the risks which need to be covered are higher for some types of business than for others.
Clearing Banks	Banks which are part of the clearing system which significantly reduces the number of interbank payments.
Certificate of Non-Crystallisation	A certificate issued by a lender confirming that, as of any given date, a floating charge granted by a borrower over its assets has not crystallised into a fixed charge over any of those assets.
Certificate of Title	A certificate given by solicitors that a specified party has acquired or will acquire 'good

---

1   Council Directive 93/6/EEC of 15 March 1993.
2   Implemented by a series of regulations and orders made under the European Communities Act 1972 and the Financial Services Act 1986.

marketable title' to specified real property subject to the matters disclosed within the certificate. Such certificates are usually given to a party who is not the solicitor's own client and are often provided to a lender by a borrower's solicitors in respect of properties to be used as security for a loan. Certificates of title are particularly useful in relation to portfolios of investment properties. Where the borrower's solicitors are already familiar with the relevant title, certificates can potentially save on legal costs as the lender's solicitors will not themselves review the original title documents but will only review the certificate. The disadvantage is that the lender and its solicitors will be less familiar with the details of the title to the property being taken as security, and certificates are therefore less suitable for unusual or development properties. By convention, certificates of title (as distinct from reports on title) only recite the facts of title as revealed by the relevant documentation but do not offer advice or opinions on any of the issues present in the documentation. In relation to investment properties, such a certificate would usually be based upon the form produced by the City of London Law Society Land Law Sub-Committee (4th edition).

Clearing House

Any institution which settles mutual indebtedness between a number of organisations. The London Bankers' Clearing House was set up to net-out interbank indebtedness by offsetting cheques drawn on each other's accounts and presented by each clearing bank on a daily basis.

Clog on the Equity of Redemption

A provision preventing the borrower from getting back what it was charged once it has repaid all the outstanding indebtedness.

Collar

A combination of an interest rate cap and an interest rate floor, limiting exposure to changing interest rates within a defined range.

Collateral

An American expression meaning assets pledged as security for a loan.

Commitment

An obligation by a lender to make funds available for a loan. By extension, the amount

	a lender is obliged to make available under a loan facility.
Commitment Fee	A fee payable by a borrower to a lender in return for the lender's undertaking to make a loan to a borrower or to keep an undrawn portion of a loan available.
Commitment Period	See 'Availability period'.
Conditions Precedent	The conditions which have to be met before a borrower will be allowed to draw down any funds under a loan agreement. These are mostly documents and information which will be listed in the loan agreement or facility letter.
Covenant	A legally binding agreement by a borrower contained in loan or security documents to perform certain acts ('positive covenants') or to refrain from performing certain acts ('negative covenants').
Cross-collateralisation	The use of security for one loan as security for another loan from the same lender.
Cross-default	Where an event of default under any other loan agreement to which the borrower is a party will constitute an event of default in relation to the loan in question.
Debenture, Debenture Stock	Fixed-interest securities issued by limited companies in return for long-term loans. Debentures are usually secured against specific assets of the company (mortgage debentures) and debenture stock and debentures which are freely transferable and listed on the London Stock Exchange. 'Debenture' is also commonly used as a generic term to describe any security document comprising fixed and floating charges over all the undertaking and assets of a company.
Deed of Priority	A document which regulates the rights and priorities of creditors and usually displaces the common law rules of priority in relation to debt owed by a debtor.
Default Interest	A financing document generally provides that any payment which is not paid on its due date will itself bear interest. Usually, this is at a higher rate than the basic contractual rate.

Documentary Credit	Also called a 'letter of credit'. An irrevocable undertaking to pay a specified amount to a beneficiary upon presentation of certain documents including a written demand. Governed by the Uniform Customs and Practice No 500.[3] It is used as a method of financing trade whereby the buyer is substituted by the lender as the party which will make payment to the seller.
Drawdown	The actual advance of funds made available to the borrower by the lender.
Equity of Redemption	The right which a mortgagor has to redeem the mortgaged estate, even after the legal right of redemption terminated or passed, on payment of the mortgage debt with interest and costs.
Event of Default	One of a series of events or circumstances (which will be stipulated in the loan agreement) which gives the lender the right to call for immediate repayment of the loan. This may include non-payment of principal or interest, non-compliance with a covenant, insolvency or liquidation.
Facility	A generic term denoting a bank loan in various forms.
Facility Letter	A document setting out the terms of a Facility in the form of a letter from the lender to the borrower, differing from a loan agreement only in terms of length, layout and complexity. Facility letters tend to be used in smaller transactions and for uncommitted working capital facilities.
Fixed Exchange Rates	Currencies with set values against each other which vary only in times of crises when one or more currencies will revalue or devalue.
Floating Exchange Rates	Currencies whose values against each other are set by market forces.
Fixed Charge	An encumbrance over an asset identified at the date of creation of the encumbrance.
Fixed Rate	An interest rate which remains a constant specified percentage of the principal amount

---

3   UCP500 – ICC Publication 516, 1993.

of the loan throughout the life of the loan. Some lenders may refer to LIBOR as a fixed rate as it is, in effect, a rate which is constant for a certain period of time, in contrast to base rate which could technically change each day.

Floating Charge
A charge on a class of assets, present and future, which is changing from time to time in the ordinary course of business. When the lender takes steps to enforce his security, the floating charge is said to 'crystallise' and until that time the borrower is free to carry on its business in the usual way.

Floating (or Variable) Rate
A rate of interest on a security or loan which is not fixed for the term of the loan, but which is changed at intervals in accordance with fluctuations in market rates of interest, generally by reference to LIBOR or base rate.

Foreclosure
The forfeiture by a mortgagor of its equity of redemption by reason of its default in payment of the principal or interest of the mortgage debt. A method of enforcing security which is not much used because of technical restrictions. Also used non-technically to mean 'enforcement'.

Forfeiture
A punishment annexed by law to some illegal act, negligence or breach of covenant, on the owner of certain interests in land, whereby it loses all its interest in them and they pass to the injured party. The law provides relief against forfeiture.[4]

Guarantee
An undertaking given by a third party (guarantor) that, if the borrower does not pay or perform, the guarantor will pay and perform in place of the borrower. It imposes a secondary obligation.

Hedging
The process of buying or selling financial instruments in order to offset the risk of the price of another financial instrument rising or falling. The most common example is the purchase of an interest rate swap to protect against fluctuations in the interest rate accruing on a variable rate loan.

---

4   Section 146 of the Law of Property Act 1925; s 18(2) of the Landlord and Tenant Act 1927.

Income Cover Ratio

The ratio of anticipated or existing rental income (gross of tax) to interest payable to the lender. This is one of the measures used by lenders when assessing the financial viability of a project.

Indemnity

An agreement to protect a person against the consequences (specifically financial loss) of particular circumstances such as an increase in costs to the lender. It imposes a primary obligation.

Intercreditor Agreement

An agreement ranking the right of creditors to payments from a borrower and providing junior creditors to be subordinated to senior creditors. A cross between a deed of priority and a subordination deed.

Interest

A payment made in return for the use of money.

Interest Period

In respect of LIBOR loans, the period by reference to which each successive interest rate is determined.

Lead Bank

In a syndicated loan, this is the bank which organises the syndication.

Leasing

An alternative to secured lending as a means of raising finance. Instead of making a loan to the borrower to finance the purchase of an asset and taking a security interest over the asset to secure the borrower's obligations under the loan, a lender may buy the asset and lease it to the borrower (lessee). The lessee has the right to possession and use of the asset in return for making a series of rental payments. The borrower may also have an option to purchase the asset at the end of the period.

Letter of Credit

A method of financing trade. A form of documentary credit, substituting a lender for the buyer as the party which will make payment to the seller. See 'Documentary Credit'.

LIBID

London Interbank Bid Rate – the rate at which a bank is prepared to borrow from another bank.

LIBOR

London Interbank Offered Rate – the rate at which a bank will lend to good credits in the London interbank market.

LIMEAN

The mean of LIBID and LIBOR.

Limited Recourse Finance	This is a loan similar to Non-recourse finance but here there is some recourse to other assets of the borrower, although this recourse is generally limited to a percentage of the original amount borrowed.
Liquidity	The degree of ease with which an asset can be bought or sold. For example, real estate is relatively illiquid whereas quoted shares are relatively liquid.
Loan	An agreement whereby one party gives another use of money for a set period in return for the payment of interest.
Loan Market Association or LMA	The Loan Market Association is a trade association for banks operating in London. It was founded in 1996 with the objective of boosting the development of loan trading. Since then, the LMA has expanded its activities to include all aspects of the primary and secondary syndicated loan markets. For banking lawyers, its most significant achievement has been the creation of standard form unsecured syndicated loan agreements which, since their launch in 1999, have been used increasingly as the basis of much of the loan documentation used in the London market. There are, however, at present no secured or bilateral LMA primary documents. Further information can be found at the LMA website, at www.loan-market-assoc.com or www.lma.eu.com.
Loan Portfolio	A group of loans.
Loan to Value	The ratio that the loan sum bears to the value of the property charged as security for it.
Manager	A person appointed by the court to carry on the business of a company, usually in order to sell it as a going concern.
Margin	The difference between the rate at which a lender borrows and the rate at which a lender lends. The lender's profit element. Also referred to as the 'spread', particularly in the context of bonds.
Maturity	The length of time before a loan or bond will be repaid.

Mezzanine Finance

A term signifying an intermediate ranking in a financing operation. It usually refers to debt which stands between secured debt and equity in ranking for payment in the event of default (see also 'Subordinated'). The margin on mezzanine debt will be significantly higher than the margin on senior debt because of the additional risk borne by the mezzanine lender.

Minimum Lending Rate

The interest rate which the Bank of England will charge in its role as lender of last resort. This is used by the Bank of England to influence the level of interest rates in the economy.

Mortgage

A conveyance, assignment, or demise of real or personal estate as security for the repayment of money borrowed.

Mortgagee in Possession

A mortgagee who, in exercise of his rights under a mortgage, has taken actual possession of the mortgaged property.

Multi-currency Loan

A loan where the borrower has the option to choose to make borrowings in more than one currency.

Negative Pledge

An undertaking by a borrower to a lender not to grant security in favour of other lenders, although the term is now also used in the market to cover restrictions against the disposal of assets.

Non-recourse Finance

Finance with no recourse to the assets of the borrower other than the asset charged. The loan is thus secured only by charging an asset acquired with the money borrowed. The loan would usually be repaid out of the income produced by that asset or, on default, out of the proceeds of sale of that asset. Used to describe a loan where the lenders are looking to a particular revenue-generating asset of the borrower to fund payments of interest or repayments of principal. If that stated source is insufficient, the lenders will not be entitled to claim against the general assets or revenues of the borrower. Used in project finance.

Off Balance Sheet Items

Covers a range of items – usually potential liabilities – which do not appear in the balance sheet of the company concerned. Examples of off balance sheet financing are leasing (although companies are now meant to show leased assets and the corresponding obligation to make payments), factoring, sale and leaseback finance for property development, non-recourse loans in joint venture companies, etc. Can cause concern when it disguises the extent of the commitments the company has entered into.

On Demand A loan such as an overdraft which must be repaid immediately on the demand of the lender. Also referred to as an uncommitted facility.

Pari Passu Ranking equally in right of payment. This is used in the context of unsecured debt securities which are said to rank equally with each other or with other unsecured debt.

Participating Loan A loan which entitles the lender to a specified share in the profits of the borrower beyond the normal interest.

Penalty A provision requiring payment of a sum which is not designed to be merely compensatory in nature. As a matter of contract law, it may be unenforceable in whole and not just as to the penal element.

Pledge The security interest created by actual or constructive delivery to the lender of an asset.

Power of Sale The right of the mortgagee to sell the property at the best price reasonably obtainable.

Principal The capital lump sum lent under a facility.

Project Finance Lending (usually for a major capital or infrastructure project) which is structured so that the lenders rely on the income stream from the project (once it has been established) to pay interest on and repay the loan.

Qualifying Bank Generally means, in the United Kingdom, a bank which is authorised by the Inland Revenue to receive payments of interest gross[5] (ie without deduction of tax). May well be a defined term in a loan agreement with a slightly different meaning (see Document 1 for further details).

---

5   Sections 349 and 840A of the Income and Corporation Taxes Act 1988. See also Document 1: Clause 13.

Receiver

An officer appointed to receive the rents and profits of property, and to account for them to the court or the appointer. If there is a business to be carried on temporarily the receiver may also be appointed as manager.

Redemption

The liquidation of a debt by repayment by the borrower.

Reference Bank

A bank which is consulted to indicate the prevailing rate of LIBOR at any given time, often used where the lender is small and not a 'prime' bank and the borrower considers a more favourable LIBOR would be obtained by seeking the LIBOR offered to the large reputable banks. Also used in syndicated facilities as a back-up to a screen rate where it would be impracticable to use LIBOR for each lender.

Report on Title

A summary of material title issues prepared by the lender's solicitors in connection with real property.

Representations and Warranties

A representation is a statement made prior to entering into the loan agreement. Warranties are made as part of the terms of the contract and may be repeated on a regular basis during the life of the loan.

Repurchase Agreement

A deal in which one financial institution sells a security to another and agrees to buy it back at a future date.

Reserve Asset Costs

Financing costs which a bank incurs because of regulatory requirements (see 'Capital Adequacy Ratios'). A bank will seek to claim any increase in these from the borrower.

Revolving Credit

Credit providing short-term funds up to a specified limit for a stipulated period of time, all or part of which can be repaid and, if the borrower wishes, re-borrowed as required.

Roll-over

(i) The notional repayment and relending of a revolving credit loan at the expiry of the current interest period.

(ii) The process by which the date of maturity of a loan or deposit is extended by agreement between the parties.

Secured Loan   A loan where the borrower's obligations can be enforced more usually against specific assets of the borrower or of someone other than the borrower (generally a guarantor) (over which the lender is given a security interest) in which case the claims of the lender against those assets generally rank ahead of the claims of any other creditors. A guaranteed loan is not a secured loan (in the absence of supporting security) because a guarantee is simply an unsecured claim against a third party.

Securities   A generic term for tradeable financial assets such as bonds, bills and shares.

Securitisation   The process of issuing marketable securities on the security of loans or other assets, usually taking the loans or other assets off the originator's balance sheet and enabling the originator to use the funds so realised to make further loans or acquire other assets.

Security Interest   A right granted by the owner of an asset to a lender to apply the asset (and its earnings) to satisfy the borrower's obligations. In the event of non-payment by the borrower, the asset can be sold and the proceeds used to repay the debt, provided any surplus proceeds are paid back to the borrower. The borrower has what is called an 'equity of redemption'.

Senior Debt   A term referring to loans which rank ahead of ordinary creditors and mezzanine or subordinated lenders to the borrower.

Set-off   The process whereby the liabilities of the borrower to the lender can be offset against the liabilities of the lender to the borrower. The amount held in a bank account is technically a debt owed by the bank to the account holder.

Special Purpose Vehicle or SPV   A special purpose vehicle (SPV) is a company set up to carry out a particular transaction, for example to hold a property which is being acquired for investment purposes. It will not have any assets or liabilities other than those associated with the transaction it was set up for. This arrangement is attractive to the owners of the SPV because they are able to limit their exposure to the extent of the equity contributed and the failure of the project in the SPV will not affect other investments outside the vehicle. For banks there is, in some senses, additional risk associated with lending to an SPV because it has no other assets than those which the bank is funding. In contrast, more traditional loans to large companies would have the benefit of the strong covenant (ie creditworthiness) of the substantial borrower. On the other hand, the bank at least has the comfort of knowing that the SPV will not have any liabilities other than those associated with the transaction being financed. Generally, a loan to an SPV will carry more risk than a loan to a substantial company and will therefore attract a higher margin.

Spot Rate

Rate at which currencies are bought and sold at a particular time on a particular day.

Standby Letter of Credit

Performs the function of a guarantee and is commonly used where the giving of a guarantee is prohibited. Enables a party to obtain money from the issuing bank in relation to the performance of a contract between that party and the party who has arranged the opening of the credit. A form of Documentary Credit.

Structured Finance

A tailor-made financial package usually intended to achieve a particular tax or accounting treatment.

Subordinated

Of a liability, means ranked below another liability in order of priority for payment. By virtue of subordination, junior debt may rank after senior debt for repayment in the event of default.

Substitution

The ability of the borrower to substitute alternative assets for the assets covered by the security.

Swap

A contract under which two parties exchange (in economic terms) financial rights and obligations. The two most common swaps are interest rate swaps and currency swaps. In an interest rate swap, A will pay B at regular intervals amounts representing interest at a pre-determined fixed rate on a notional principal sum and B will pay A at regular intervals amounts representing interest at a floating rate on the notional principal sum. In a currency swap, A will pay B one currency in return for B paying A an amount in another currency. At the end of a pre-determined period the operation will be reversed.

Syndicate

In the banking context, a group of banks severally agreeing to lend money on like terms.

Syndicated Loan

A means of packaging a series of individual loans by a group of lenders into a single transaction governed by a common set of terms and conditions and administered by an agent bank.

Term Loan

A loan granted for a specific period of time.

Unsecured Loan

A loan made without collateral or any charge on the assets of the borrower.

Withholding Tax

A tax which is collected by deduction by the debtor from the sum of money which he is to pay to the creditor. The debtor then passes the balance to the Inland Revenue. Generally, the tax is levied upon the creditor's income (interest). See also 'Qualifying Bank'. Since the 2001 Budget, the scope of withholding tax in UK domestic lending is much reduced.

INTRODUCTION

1 The Loan Agreement

There are many different types of debt finance and their availability and form depends very much on the type of borrower, the purpose of funding, the security available and the prevailing market conditions.

At its simplest, a bank loan involves a bank advancing a sum of money to a borrower on certain terms and conditions for a certain period of time. Due to the increase in competition and sophistication amongst banks and borrowers alike, however, the basic bank loan can become very complex, offering the borrower a multitude of facilities in different currencies, at different interest rates, over different time periods, for different purposes and using different banks in different countries.

Also, certain borrowers will be able to access the capital markets to raise their debt finance in the form of commercial paper, medium-term note issues, bonds and debenture stocks.

The type of debt finance available is endless. However, irrespective of whether the finance facility is a straightforward overdraft from the local high street bank, or a syndicated acquisition facility involving numerous banks, the principles and concepts are the same and almost all debt finance documentation will contain similar clauses.

This book has used as its model a simple secured Sterling loan from a bank to a company. Until the advent of the LMA primary documents, there was generally no fixed or determined order for clauses in a standard loan agreement and the content varied significantly. This was the case even of the boilerplate clauses, ie the provisions that are intended to be mechanical and standard. There has been something of a sea change since then. Notwithstanding that the LMA documents are not intended to fit all circumstances, the general layout and, often, the boilerplate clauses have been adopted enthusiastically and tend to form the spine of many firms' standard documents. In this book, the loan document forming the basis of our commentary is a secured bilateral facility which is about as far as one can get from an unsecured syndicated facility. Nonetheless, its architecture follows that of the LMA documents, reflecting the state of the market today.

Generally, the borrower's main concerns are the cost of borrowing, the availability of funds and the ability to retain a degree of autonomy in the day-to-day running of its own business. Where the borrower is a special purpose vehicle, the lender is more likely to insist on a greater degree of control.

The lender wants to be repaid its principal advance together with interest and wants to protect its profit margin at a minimal risk. Unlike a provider of equity, a senior lender will not run any risk of losing its money. It receives a low return for the use of its money without sharing in the success of the enterprise being funded and this low return is agreed solely on the basis that it runs minimal risk of loss.

2   The Debenture

The market is awash with different forms of security documents, many known by different and often confusing descriptions. This book focuses on the most typical, the debenture, which consistently comprises a number of fixed and floating charges over all the assets and undertaking of the mortgagor divided into a number of broad categories. As transactions become more complex, however, tailor-made debenture documents have become sophisticated and may now include the whole range of security types, from legal mortgages over land, to equitable assignments of debts.

A debenture is therefore a good basis for discussing security documents generally, and the form set out in Document 2 below is in the shorter market standard format rather than in a more complex one.

Security documents vary in two principal respects:

(a) the range of assets intended to be covered by the security; and
(b) the degree of control over these assets vested in the lender both before and after enforcement of the security.

Most standard debentures take a common middle ground on both issues, but for security documents such as mortgages of land or charges over shares, the question of control over the asset becomes the negotiable point and even the description of the type of security may become contentious in this regard.

Nevertheless, and aside from the provisions on enforcement which tend to be standard, there are half-a-dozen 'boilerplate' clauses in all types of security document which rarely vary between transactions or between documents.

3   The Guarantee

Most commercial transactions incorporate guarantees in some form or other as part of the general security package. A guarantee can have various functions in a transaction. The principal function is to provide credit enhancement; if the borrower does not have sufficient funds there is another party (generally with a larger pocket) to whom the lender can look. Personal guarantees can also have a psychological function; the provision of a guarantee ensures that the person behind the borrowing entity is committed personally to the transaction. Parent company guarantees are a way of ensuring that a parent does not simply abandon a failing subsidiary.

Guarantees are used in a wide variety of transactions including simple household mortgages, loans to start up businesses, lease agreements, international trade, property finance and project finance. The function of the guarantee in all these diverse areas is the same, although the type and effect of the agreement will differ and can include 'guarantees', 'indemnities', 'third party charges', 'performance bonds', 'rent guarantees', 'demand guarantees' and 'standby letters of credit'.

The most common confusion which arises in dealing with guarantees is the distinction between guarantees and indemnities. This is probably the fault of the lenders and lawyers who incorporate both guarantee and indemnity provisions and sometimes use the terms interchangeably in their standard documents.

The fundamental distinction between guarantees and indemnities is that in a contract of guarantee the liability of the guarantor is always contingent or secondary to that of the principal debtor (normally the borrower), whereas a contract of indemnity is a primary obligation independent of the underlying principal debtor/lender relationship. In contrast, the term 'bank guarantee' is a misnomer, for, in practice, the term is used to describe a primary obligation imposed on a bank.

A guarantor is only liable to the extent that the principal debtor is liable to the lender. This principle of 'co-extensiveness' flows from the guarantor's secondary liability and does not apply to an indemnifier whose obligation is primary and independent of any underlying contract.

Guarantees are governed by s 4 of the Statute of Frauds Act 1677 which states that a guarantee must be in writing and signed by the guarantor. This section applies only to guarantees and not to indemnities.[1]

The apparent simplicity and brevity of some lenders' standard form guarantees (sometimes little more than three pages long) does not mean that this is a simple area of law. In fact, quite the contrary. The interpretation and enforcement of guarantees has given rise to a large amount of litigation in all forms of commercial transactions including, for example, rent guarantees, construction/completion guarantees, bonds, performance bonds, personal guarantees and mortgage indemnity guarantees.

It is an intricate and complicated area of law and the subject of many academic works.[2] We have provided a basic guide to the most common clauses in a standard guarantee in an attempt to explain their incorporation.

Unfortunately, most lenders will not accept amendments to their standard form agreements other than those necessary to reflect the commercial terms of the transaction (ie limitation of amounts, termination provisions, etc). Nevertheless, it is most important from the guarantor's perspective to understand its liability, when it arises, and how long and under what circumstances it will continue.

4   Pitfalls

The final section of this book aims to provide a very general indication of the legal trouble spots emerging in financing transactions every day. The topics covered are by no means exhaustive, either in their number or their detail, but are intended to be described sufficiently to ring 'alarm bells' when the situations arise in practice.

The flow charts which make up part of the sections on loans to directors and financial assistance are intended as basic route maps through the topics and not as detailed town plans.

---

1   For more information on indemnities see Lingard *Bank Security Documents* 3rd edn (Butterworths, 1993).

2   Ibid, also Andrews and Millett, *Law of Guarantees* 3rd edn (Sweet & Maxwell, 2000).

The text and the diagrams in this section together provide a useful checklist, but it is important to remember that they are not designed to act as a substitute for detailed consideration of the facts and the relevant law.

DOCUMENT 1: THE LOAN AGREEMENT

CONTENTS

1	Definitions and Interpretation	21
2	The Facility	35
3	Purpose	35
4	Conditions of Utilisation	36
5	Utilisation	38
6	Repayment	39
7	Prepayment and Cancellation	39
8	Interest	43
9	Interest Periods	46
10	Changes to the Calculation of Interest	48
11	Bank Accounts	49
12	Fees	52
13	Tax Gross Up and Indemnities	53
14	Increased Costs	58
15	Other Indemnities	60
16	Mitigation by the Lender	61
17	Costs and Expenses	61
18	Representations	62
19	Information Undertakings	69
20	Financial Covenants	72
21	General Undertakings	74
22	Property Undertakings	78
23	Events of Default	81
24	Changes to the Lenders	88
25	Changes to the Borrower	89
26	Conduct of Business by the Lender	91
27	Payment Mechanics	91
28	Set-off	93
29	Notices	93
30	Calculations and Certificates	95
31	Partial Invalidity	96
32	Remedies and Waivers	96
33	Counterparts	96
34	Governing Law	96
35	Enforcement	97
Schedule 1	Conditions Precedent	98
Schedule 2	Requests	101
Schedule 3	Mandatory Cost Formulae	103

DOCUMENT 1: THE LOAN AGREEMENT[1]

DATE

PARTIES

(1)   [   ] (the **'Borrower'**); and

(2)   [   ] (the **'Lender'**).

IT IS AGREED AS FOLLOWS:

1   Definitions and Interpretation

1.1   Definitions

Purpose: The definitions cannot be read in isolation but must be looked at in the context of the operative provisions. Words will normally bear their everyday meaning unless they are given a specified meaning. Any specified meaning will usually be given in the definitions and interpretation provision though some definitions appear in the clauses in which they are used. Depending on the word and its meaning in the context of the operative provision, amendment may be necessary. As well as listing here certain definitions which are common to each of the precedent documents in this book, others which are often amended will be analysed within the context of their operative provisions.

In this Agreement:

'Account'	means the General Account and the Rent Account;
'Account Bank'	means, subject to Clause 11.5 (*Change of Bank Accounts*), [ ];
'Affiliate'	means, in relation to any person, a Subsidiary of that person or a Holding Company of that person or any other Subsidiary of that Holding Company;
'Agreement for Lease'	means an agreement to grant an Occupational Lease of all or part of any Property;

---

1   This loan agreement is based on the recommended form of primary document published by the Loan Market Association which owns the copyright in it. The author and publisher are grateful to the Association for permission to publish this version of it.

'Authorisation'	means an authorisation, consent, approval, resolution, licence, exemption, filing or registration;
'Availability Period'	means the period from and including the date of this Agreement to and including [ ];
'Available Facility'	means the Facility Commitment less any outstanding Loans;
'Break Costs'	means the amount (if any) by which:

(a) the interest which the Lender should have received for the period from the date of receipt of all or any part of a Loan or Unpaid Sum to the last day of the current Interest Period in respect of that Loan or Unpaid Sum, had the principal amount or Unpaid Sum received been paid on the last day of that Interest Period

exceeds:

(b) the amount which the Lender would be able to obtain by placing an amount equal to the principal amount or Unpaid Sum received by it on deposit with a leading bank in the London Interbank Market for a period starting on the Business Day following receipt or recovery and ending on the last day of the current Interest Period;

Purpose: see Clause 7.7.2 at page 42 which contains ancillary provisions relating to prepayment.

'Business Day'	means a day (other than a Saturday or Sunday) on which banks are open for general business in London;
'Debenture'	means a debenture executed or to be executed by the Borrower in favour of the Lender, substantially in the agreed form;
'Default'	means an Event of Default or any event or circumstance specified in Clause 23 (*Events of Default*) which would (with the expiry of a grace period, the giving of notice, the making of any determination under the Finance Documents or any combination of any of the foregoing) be an Event of Default;

Purpose: *This definition describes not only Events of Default but also 'potential events of default', in other words events which would amount to Events of Default on satisfaction of the technical conditions listed. It is important to understand that a potential event of default might never become an Event of Default and therefore should not by itself trigger repayment of the loan. However, it is legitimately used as a trigger for the following:*

1. *to bar drawings (because it is unreasonable to expect a lender to lend into a situation which is only a technicality away from a full Event of Default);*
2. *to require the borrower to inform the lender of the occurrence of the event; and*
3. *to block payments out of security accounts (because the lender may well want recourse to those monies if a potential event of default becomes a full Event of Default).*

'Event of Default'	means any event or circumstance specified as such in Clause 23 (*Events of Default*);
'Facility'	means the term loan facility made available under this Agreement as described in Clause 2 (*The Facility*);
'Facility Commitment'	means £[ ];
'Facility Office'	means the office or offices through which the Lender will perform its obligations under this Agreement;
'Finance Document'	means this Agreement, the Debenture, any Hedging Arrangement, the Subordination Deed and any other document designated as such by the Lender and the Borrower;
'Financial Indebtedness'	means any indebtedness for or in respect of:

(a) moneys borrowed;
(b) any amount raised by acceptance under any acceptance credit facility;
(c) any amount raised pursuant to any note purchase facility or the issue of bonds, notes, debentures, loan stock or any similar instrument;

(d) the amount of any liability in respect of any lease or hire purchase contract which would, in accordance with GAAP, be treated as a finance or capital lease;

(e) receivables sold or discounted (other than any receivables to the extent they are sold on a non-recourse basis);

(f) any amount raised under any other transaction (including any forward sale or purchase agreement) having the commercial effect of a borrowing;

(g) any derivative transaction entered into in connection with protection against or benefit from fluctuation in any rate or price (and, when calculating the value of any derivative transaction, only the marked to market value shall be taken into account);

(h) any counter-indemnity obligation in respect of a guarantee, indemnity, bond, standby or documentary letter of credit or any other instrument issued by a bank or financial institution; and

(i) the amount of any liability in respect of any guarantee or indemnity for any of the items referred to in paragraphs (a) to (h) above;

'GAAP'	means generally accepted accounting principles in the United Kingdom;
'General Account'	means the account referred to in Clause 11.1.1(a) (*Designation of Accounts*);
'Group'	means the Borrower and its Subsidiaries for the time being;
'Headlease'	means any lease under which the Borrower holds a Property;
'Hedging Arrangements'	means any interest hedging arrangements entered into by the Borrower in connection with, or otherwise relating to, interest payable under this Agreement;
'Holding Company'	means, in relation to a company or corporation, any other company or corporation in respect of which it is a Subsidiary;

'Interest Payment Date'	means each date on which interest is payable in accordance with Clause 8.2 (*Payment of interest*);
'Interest Period'	means, in relation to a Loan, each period determined in accordance with Clause 9 (*Interest Periods*) and, in relation to an Unpaid Sum, each period determined in accordance with Clause 8.4 (*Default interest*);
'Lease Document'	means any Occupational Lease or any Agreement for Lease;
'LIBOR'	means, in relation to any Loan:

    (a) the applicable Screen Rate; or

    (b) (if no Screen Rate is available for the currency or period of that Loan) the arithmetic mean of the rates (rounded upwards to four decimal places) as supplied to the Lender at its request quoted by the Reference Banks to leading banks in the London interbank market,

as of 11.00 am on the Quotation Day for the offering of deposits in the currency of that Loan and for a period comparable to the Interest Period for that Loan;

Purpose/Lender/Borrower: see Clause 8 at page 43.

'Loan'	means a loan made or to be made under the Facility or the principal amount outstanding for the time being of that loan;
'Mandatory Cost'	means the percentage rate per annum calculated by the Lender in accordance with Schedule 3 (*Mandatory Cost formulae*);

Purpose/Lender/Borrower: see Clause 8 at page 43.

'Margin'	means [ ] per cent per annum;

Purpose/Lender/Borrower: see Clause 8 at page 43.

'Material Adverse Effect'	means anything which in the opinion of the Lender, has had or could reasonably be expected to have a material adverse effect on:

(a) the consolidated financial position of the Group; or

(b) the ability of the Borrower to perform its payment or other material obligations under the Finance Documents;

Purpose: This definition is used throughout the Finance Documents as a qualification to Events of Default, covenants and representations.

Lender: Where (b) refers to all obligations under all the Finance Documents, the borrower is likely to negotiate to limit them. The most usual compromise is reached with 'any financial obligations under the Finance Documents' and if the borrower has any doubt that covenants as to repair or insurance, for example might indirectly constitute financial obligations, the parties should be able to agree some wording on the subject such as 'for the avoidance of doubt, it is hereby agreed that the obligations comprised in Clauses [   ] (repair [   ] insurance) [etc] do not constitute financial obligations for the purpose of this clause'.

Borrower: The borrower will usually argue that the only obligations with which the lender should be concerned for these purposes are payment obligations. Arguably, a failure to repair a property, for example, only affects the lender if it means the borrower cannot continue to service the loan. Other specific concerns, such as the maintenance of the value of the property, are dealt with specifically, in this case in the loan to value covenant.

'Month'

means a period starting on one day in a calendar month and ending on the numerically corresponding day in the next calendar month, except that:

(a) if the numerically corresponding day is not a Business Day, that period shall end on the next Business Day in that calendar month in which that period is to end if there is one, or if there is not, on the immediately preceding Business Day; and

(b) if there is no numerically corresponding day in the calendar month in which that period is to end, that period shall end on the last Business Day in that calendar month.

The above rules will only apply to the last Month of any period;

'Net Rental Income'	means Rental Income other than:

(a) any amount (together with any value added tax or similar taxes charged thereon) due to the Borrower and any tenant under an Occupational Lease or other occupier of the Property, by way of contribution to insurance premia, the cost of an insurance valuation or by way of service charge in respect of costs incurred or to be incurred by the Borrower under any repairing or similar obligation, or in providing services to the tenants of the building;

(b) any contribution to a sinking fund paid by any tenant or other occupier; and

(c) any value added tax or similar taxes payable on any items listed in paragraphs (a) and (b) above, and paragraphs (a)–(k) of the definition of 'Rental Income';

'Occupational Lease'	means, in relation to any Property, any occupational lease or licence or other right of occupation to which that Property may be subject from time to time;
'Original Financial Statements'	means the audited consolidated financial statements of the [Group] for the financial year ended [ ];
'Participating Member State'	means any Member State of the European Communities that adopts or has adopted the Euro as its lawful currency in accordance with legislation of the European Union relating to European Monetary Union;
'Party'	means a party to this Agreement;
'Permitted Disposals'	means any sale, lease, transfer or other disposal:

(a) made in the ordinary course of trading of the disposing entity;

(b) of assets in exchange for other assets comparable or superior as to type, value and quality;

(c) [   ]; or

(d) where the higher of the market value or consideration receivable (when aggregated with the higher of the market value or consideration receivable for any other sale, lease, transfer or other disposal, other than any permitted under paragraphs (a) to (c) above) does not exceed [   ] (or its equivalent in another currency or currencies) in any financial year;

Purpose/Lender/Borrower: see Clause 21.5 (Disposals) at page 77.

'Permitted Financial Indebtedness'	means [ ];
'Permitted Security'	means

    (a) [specific security interests];

    (b) any netting or set-off arrangement entered into by the Borrower in the ordinary course of its banking arrangements for the purpose of netting debit and credit balances;

    (c) any lien arising by operation of law and in the ordinary course of trading;

    (d) any Security over or affecting any asset acquired by the Borrower after the date of this Agreement if:

        (i) the Security was not created in contemplation of the acquisition of that asset by the Borrower;

        (ii) the principal amount secured has not been increased in contemplation of, or since the acquisition of that asset by the Borrower; and

        (iii) the Security is removed or discharged within [   ] months of the date of acquisition of such asset;

    (e) [   ]; or

(f) any Security securing indebtedness the principal amount of which (when aggregated with the principal amount of any other indebtedness which has the benefit of Security other than any permitted under paragraphs (a) to (e) above) does not exceed [   ] (or its equivalent in another currency or currencies);

Purpose/Lender/Borrower: *see Clause 21.3 (Negative pledge) at page 74.*

'Property'	means the property at [ ] as more particularly described in schedule 1 to the Debenture;
'Qualifying Lender'	has the meaning given to it in Clause 13 (*Tax Gross-up and Indemnities*);
'Quotation Day'	means, in relation to any period for which an interest rate is to be determined the first day of that period unless market practice differs in the London Interbank Market for a currency, in which case the Quotation Day for that currency will be determined by the Lender in accordance with market practice in the London Interbank Market (and if quotations would normally be given by leading banks in the London Interbank Market on more than one day, the Quotation Day will be the last of those days);
'Reference Banks'	means, in relation to LIBOR, the principal London offices of [ ], [ ] and [ ] or such other banks as may be appointed by the Lender in consultation with the Borrower;
'Rent Account'	means the account referred to in Clause 11.1.1(b) (*Designation of Accounts*);
'Rental Income'	means the aggregate of all amounts payable to or for the benefit or account of the Borrower in connection with the letting of the Property or any part of it, including (without limitation) each of the following amounts:

(a) rent (and any amount equivalent to it) payable whether it is variable or not and however or whenever it is described, reserved or made payable;

(b) any increase of rent payable by virtue of an offer falling within the proviso of s 3(1) of the Landlord and Tenant Act 1927;

(c) any rent payable by virtue of a determination made by the Court under s 24A of the Landlord and Tenant Act 1954;

(d) any sum received from any deposit held as security for performance of any tenant's obligations;

(e) a sum equal to any apportionment of rent allowed in favour of the Borrower under the contract for the purchase of any Property;

(f) any other moneys payable in respect of occupation and/or usage of any Property and every fixture and fitting therein and any and every fixture thereon for display or advertisement, on licence or otherwise;

(g) any profits awarded or agreed to be payable as a result of any proceedings taken or claim made for the same;

(h) any damages, compensation, settlement or expenses for or representing loss of rent or interest thereon awarded or agreed to be payable as a result of any proceedings taken or claim made for the same net of any costs, fees and expenses paid (and which have not been reimbursed to, and which are not recoverable by, the Borrower from any party) in furtherance of such proceedings so taken or claim so made;

(i) any moneys payable under any policy of insurance in respect of loss of rent or interest thereon;

(j) any sum payable or the value of any consideration to be given by or on behalf of a tenant for the surrender or variation of any Occupational Lease or occupancy agreement;

    (k) any sum payable by any guarantor of any occupational tenant under any Occupational Lease; and

    (l) any interest payable on any sum referred to above and any damages, compensation or settlement payable in respect of the same;

Purpose/Lender/Borrower: *used for the purposes of Clause 11 (*bank accounts*) and Clause 20 (*financial covenants*).*

'Repayment Date'	means [ ];
['Repayment Instalment'	means [ ];]
'Repeating Representations'	means each of the representations set out in Clauses 18.[ ], 18.[ ] and 18.[ ];

Purpose: *This definition is used principally in Clause 18.18 (Repetition) to identify which of the representations and warranties in that clause will be periodically repeated and which will apply only at the start of the loan. There is some room to negotiate the list, although in many cases it is clear which representations should be repeated and which should not. It is generally accepted that the legal representations (ie status, binding obligations, non-conflict, power and authority, validity and admissibility, and governing law and enforcement) should be repeated. Others are more open to debate.*

Lender: *The lender's natural instinct will be to argue that all of the representations and warranties should be repeated, although certain of them can readily be conceded. For example, representations relating to deduction of tax and stamp duty should be day-one representations only because the lender is protected from changes in withholding tax and stamp duty by gross-up and indemnity clauses. The representations and warranties relating to the accuracy of the factual information delivered as conditions precedent to the loan and the original financial statements of the borrower are also not really appropriate for repetition because they relate to the factual position of the borrower at the outset. There is generally a representation as to the preparation of future accounts delivered periodically and, in contrast, this clearly should be repeated.*

Borrower: *It is generally necessary for the borrower to concede that most of the representations and warranties need to be repeated. However, there are some open areas. For example, the representation that no proceedings are pending or threatened is acceptable as a day-one representation but ought to be repeated because going forward it is unfair to create a default from litigation which may never be adversely determined. Another debatable* *representation is the one to the effect that the borrower is not in breach of any other agreement to which it is a party. This is significant information for the lender at the outset, not least to ensure that it is not inducing the borrower's breach of contract, but going forward the lender should be relying on the cross-default clause (Clause 23.5 of this document) which focuses on default by the borrower of other financial indebtedness.*

'Reservations'	means [limitations to enforceability representation];
'Sale and Purchase Agreement'	means the sale and purchase agreement dated [ ] between [ ] and the Borrower in respect of the Property;
'Screen Rate'	means, in relation to LIBOR, the British Bankers' Association Interest Settlement Rate for Sterling for the relevant period displayed on the appropriate page of the [Telerate]/[Reuters] screen. If the agreed page is replaced or service ceases to be available, the Lender may specify another page or service displaying the appropriate rate after consultation with the Borrower;
'Security'	means a mortgage, charge, pledge, lien or other security interest securing any obligation of any person or any other agreement or arrangement having a similar effect;

Purpose: This definition describes what constitutes a security interest, ie interests giving creditors priority claim on specified assets for repayment of the debt owed to them. It does not include guarantees which, though often referred to by bankers as security, are in themselves merely unsecured promises to pay the obligations of a third party. This definition is important because it is referred to in the negative pledge, representations and warranties and cross-default clauses.

Lender: The lender should not permit any watering down of this definition. It is paramount to a lender to be able to control the creation of security on the assets to which it intends to have recourse on default. If the borrower has concerns with the width of the definition these can be accommodated within the definition of Permitted Security.

Borrower: The borrower needs to consider its business carefully to ascertain what activities (for example factoring, invoice discounting or retention of title issues) might fall within this definition. It then needs to ensure that appropriate carve-outs are included in the definition of Permitted Security.

'Selection Notice'	means a notice substantially in the form set out in Part II of Schedule 2 (*Requests*) given in accordance with Clause 9 (*Interest Periods*);
'Sterling' or **'£'**	means the lawful currency from time to time in the United Kingdom;
'Subordinated Creditor'	means [ ]

Purpose: It is often the case in the types of deal which would be documented by this agreement that the shareholders or directors of the borrower have made an investment in the borrower by way of loan rather than equity subscription. If this is the case the lender will want to ensure that the loans are subordinated to its own facility, ie may not be repaid or enforced without the lender's consent whilst the senior debt remains outstanding.

'Subordination Deed'	means the subordination deed executed or to be executed by the Borrower and the Subordinated Creditor in favour of the Lender, substantially in the agreed form;

Purpose: This is the document by which the subordination referred to above is effected. It will be a tripartite agreement between the lender, the subordinated creditor and the borrower.

'Subsidiary'	means a subsidiary within the meaning of section 736 of the Companies Act 1985;
'Tax'	means any tax, levy, impost, duty or other charge or withholding of a similar nature (including any penalty or interest payable in connection with any failure to pay or any delay in paying any of the same);
'Taxes Act'	means the Income and Corporation Taxes Act 1988;
'Termination Date'	means [ ];
'Transaction Document'	means any Finance Document or any Lease Document;
'Unpaid Sum'	means any sum due and payable but unpaid by the Borrower under the Finance Documents;
'Utilisation'	means a utilisation of the Facility;

'Utilisation Date'	means the date of a Utilisation, being the date on which the relevant Loan is to be made;
'Utilisation Request'	means a notice substantially in the form set out in Part I of Schedule 2 (*Requests*);
'Valuation'	means a valuation of the Property by the Valuer on the basis of the lower of open market value and estimated realisation price as those terms are defined in the then current Statements of Asset Valuation Practice and Guidance Notes issued by the Royal Institution of Chartered Surveyors;
'Valuer'	means [ ] or such other surveyor or valuer as may be appointed by the Lender;
'VAT'	means value added tax as provided for in the Value Added Tax Act 1994 and any other tax of a similar nature.

1.2   **Construction**

1.2.1   Unless a contrary indication appears, any reference in this Agreement to:

(a) the 'Lender', the 'Borrower' or any 'Party' shall be construed so as to include its successors in title, permitted assigns and permitted transferees;

(b) '**assets**' includes present and future properties, revenues and rights of every description;

(c) a '**Finance Document**' or any other agreement or instrument is a reference to that Finance Document or other agreement or instrument as amended or novated;

(d) '**indebtedness**' includes any obligation (whether incurred as principal or as surety) for the payment or repayment of money, whether present or future, actual or contingent;

(e) a '**person**' includes any person, firm, company, corporation, government, state or agency of a state or any association, trust or partnership (whether or not having separate legal personality) or two or more of the foregoing;

(f) a '**regulation**' includes any regulation, rule, official directive, request or guideline (whether or not having the force of law) of any governmental, intergovernmental or supranational body, agency, department or regulatory, self-regulatory or other authority or organisation;

(g) a provision of law is a reference to that provision as amended or re-enacted; and

(h) unless a contrary indication appears, a time of day is a reference to London time.

1.2.2 Section, Clause and Schedule headings are for ease of reference only.

1.2.3 Unless a contrary indication appears, a term used in any other Finance Document or in any notice given under or in connection with any Finance Document has the same meaning in that Finance Document or notice as in this Agreement.

1.2.4 A Default (other than an Event of Default) is '**continuing**' if it has not been remedied or waived and an Event of Default is '**continuing**' if it has not been [remedied or waived] [waived].

1.3 **Third Party Rights**

A person who is not a Party has no right under the Contracts (Rights of Third Parties) Act 1999 to enforce or enjoy the benefit of any term of this Agreement.

Purpose: This clause disapplies the Contracts (Rights of Third Parties) Act 1999. This legislation changes the common law principle of privity of contract by allowing persons who are not parties to a document to enforce provisions in the document which benefit it.

2 **The Facility**

Subject to the terms of this Agreement, the Lender makes available to the Borrower a secured term loan facility in an aggregate amount equal to the Facility Commitments.

Purpose: This clause describes the type of facility being provided. For more information on the characteristics of various facility types please refer to the glossary.

3 **Purpose**

3.1 **Purpose**

The Borrower shall apply all amounts borrowed by it under the Facility towards [   ].

Purpose: The purpose of this clause is to focus both the lender's and borrower's mind on why the money is needed and what it is going to be used for.

Lender: The lender needs to be sure that the loan is to be used for the purposes set out in its credit approval which may stipulate for example that the loan is an acquisition facility. The lender also needs to be sure that the loan will not be used to finance an unlawful transaction. If the purpose is unlawful the agreement may be unenforceable or voidable despite any severability clause. Furthermore, if the loan is used for a purpose other than the ones stipulated, the lender may be able to establish a tracing claim over the proceeds. Clause 3.2 provides that it is not the lender's obligation to ensure that the loan will be used for the designated purpose and therefore the lender is not fixed with notice if it is not so used.

Borrower: *The borrower must identify why it requires the funds and should give itself as much flexibility as possible. It is generally helpful to the borrower if the clause is very general such as 'for working capital purposes'.*

3.2   Monitoring

The Lender is not bound to monitor or verify the application of any amount borrowed pursuant to this Agreement.

4   Conditions of Utilisation

4.1   Initial conditions precedent

The Borrower may not deliver a Utilisation Request unless the Lender has received all of the documents and other evidence listed in Schedule 1 (*Conditions precedent*) in form and substance satisfactory to the Lender. The Lender shall notify the Borrower promptly upon being so satisfied.

Purpose: *The purpose of this clause is to suspend the lender's commitment to advance the funds until it is satisfied that it has received all the necessary finance documentation together with all company secretarial, transactional and due diligence documentation which it is prudent to get before making the loan. Conditions precedent will vary according to the particular circumstances and should be tailor-made for each individual transaction. For a real estate banking transaction, however, it will invariably be the case that the lender will require, for example, a valuation of the property, a report on or certificate of title and a charge over the property. If the property is held by a foreign-incorporated company, a legal opinion will be needed from lawyers qualified in the law of its jurisdiction of incorporation.*

Lender: *The lender needs to be satisfied that it has all appropriate documentation for the loan. Often its credit approval will stipulate that certain reports or confirmations need to be obtained before the loan can be made. The lender's lawyers should also suggest suitable documentation to achieve the lender's commercial objectives. The lender wants to be in a position to withdraw from the loan commitment if something is wrong or the documentation it has received is not to its satisfaction. The conditions precedent are included for the benefit of the lender and can therefore always be waived as if they were never included in the first place. It is common for internal management and audit purposes for a lender to* *require before releasing funds a letter from its solicitors confirming in detail how each condition precedent has been satisfied.*

Borrower: *The borrower needs to be certain that once the agreement has been signed the lender will advance the monies if the borrower satisfies the conditions precedent. The borrower must ensure that the conditions precedent are conditions to the loan advance and not to the agreement itself as it is only in the former case that the borrower will have a commitment from the lender from the outset. The list of conditions precedent must also be as objective and complete as possible. If it is not, the lender may use it as an excuse for not permitting drawdown and wording such as 'any other information as the lender may require' should be resisted. The lender must stipulate what it wants from the borrower at the outset or, at the very latest, before the loan agreement is signed. The borrower should also seek to have all condition precedent documents agreed before the agreement is signed (key documents such as security may be annexed to the agreement or 'initialled by the parties hereto for the purposes of identification'). Satisfaction of conditions precedent is always in the discretion of the lender ('in form and substance satisfactory to the lender'). Rather than attempting to water down this wording it is better to manage the process of satisfying the conditions by agreeing them with the lender's lawyers at the earliest opportunity. It is worth trying to limit the length of the list and ensuring that as many of the items as possible are within the borrower's control.*

4.2 **Further conditions precedent**

The Lender will only be obliged to fund a proposed Utilisation if on the date of the Utilisation Request and on the proposed Utilisation Date:

4.2.1 no Default is continuing or would result from the proposed Loan; and

4.2.2 the Repeating Representations to be made by the Borrower are true in all material respects.

Purpose: *this standard clause is designed to protect the lender from changes in circumstances which occur between the date of the agreement and the date of drawdown. If there is a Default (ie not only an Event of Default but also a 'potential event of default') then the lender need not lend the money. Note that the appropriate wording is that the Default is 'continuing'. If there was a Default outstanding which has since been remedied or waived and is therefore no longer continuing it is inappropriate for the lender to be in a position to refuse drawdown. There is some room to argue over the meaning of 'continuing' (see Clause 1.2.4). A lender might want to confine the meaning of 'continuing' to 'waived' in the context of an event of default (rather than a potential event of default) because 'remedied' is an imprecise and subjective term. It is arguable whether in Clause 4.2.2 the representations should be true in* *all material respects (which is the wording in the LMA documentation) or unqualified (which is sometimes seen in more leveraged transactions).*

4.3   Maximum number of Loans

4.3.1   The Borrower may not deliver a Utilisation Request if as a result of the proposed Utilisation [   ] or more Loans would be outstanding.

4.3.2   The Borrower may not request that a Loan be divided if, as a result of the proposed division, [   ] or more Loans would be outstanding.

5   Utilisation

5.1   Delivery of a Utilisation Request

The Borrower may utilise the Facility by delivery to the Lender of a duly completed Utilisation Request not later than 10.00 am two Business Days before the proposed Utilisation Date.

5.2   Completion of a Utilisation Request

5.2.1   Each Utilisation Request is irrevocable and will not be regarded as having been duly completed unless:

(a)   the proposed Utilisation Date is a Business Day within the Availability Period;

(b)   the amount of the Utilisation complies with Clause 5.3 (*Amount*); and

(c)   the proposed Interest Period complies with Clause 9 (*Interest Periods*).

5.2.2   Only one Loan may be requested in each Utilisation Request.

5.3   Amount

The amount of the proposed Loan must be a minimum of [   ] or, if less, the Available Facility.

Purpose: Clause 5 sets out the mechanics and conditions for notifying the lender of the amount of funds the borrower requires, the currency needed and the time and place for payment.

Lender: The lender needs to receive instructions as to where, when and in what currency the loan should be made and over what period for calculating interest. The lender needs sufficient time to obtain the funds (usually same day for a Sterling loan and two days for a foreign currency). The notice of drawdown must be irrevocable because the lender makes arrangements with third parties to fund the loan on the strength of the request. It is, however, doubtful whether a lender would be able to oblige a borrower to borrow money as compensation for breaking the funding arrangements would be an adequate remedy.

Borrower: *The borrower will want to minimise the notice period for drawing so that it can obtain the money when it needs it. If there is a long period (3 or 4 business days) then there can be complications with any interest rate swap which the parties may have agreed should be put in place. Many lenders have difficulty procedurally in obtaining a firm swap rate on the day the drawing request is served so the borrower will often be taking a risk that swap rates change significantly between submission of the request and the setting of the rate. The borrower should try to minimise the restrictions (if any) on the frequency of drawing notices so that it can draw as and when it needs to. Although all notices of drawdown have to be (from the lender's perspective) irrevocable, the borrower should try to argue that they become revocable if there has been a change in circumstances (although the borrower would then be liable for breach of funding costs). Most importantly, the borrower should check and ensure that the amounts available, currency and timing give it as much flexibility as it requires.*

6   Repayment

6.1   Repayment of Loans

[   ].

6.2   Reborrowing

The Borrower may not reborrow any part of the Facility which is repaid.

Purpose: *unless the loan is a revolving credit or similar facility available for drawing until the final repayment date it will not be permitted to reborrow amounts which are repaid (or prepaid or cancelled – see Clauses 7.7.3 and 7.7.5 on page 43). The lender is required to allocate capital to its loan commitments. This has a cost which in a revolving credit or other long-draw facility is compensated by a non-utilisation fee. In the absence of such a fee it will never be possible to redraw.*

7   Prepayment and Cancellation

7.1   Illegality

If it becomes unlawful in any applicable jurisdiction for the Lender to perform any of its obligations as contemplated by this Agreement or to fund or maintain its participation in any Loan:

7.1.1   that Lender shall promptly notify the Borrower upon becoming aware of that event;

7.1.2   upon the Lender notifying the Borrower, the Facility Commitment
            will be immediately cancelled; and

7.1.3   the Borrower shall repay the Loans on the last day of the Interest
            Period for each Loan occurring after the Lender has notified the
            Borrower or, if earlier, the date specified by the Lender in the notice
            delivered to the Borrower (being no earlier than the last day of any
            applicable grace period permitted by law).

> ***Purpose:*** *The purpose of this clause is to enable a lender to withdraw from
> the facility if it becomes illegal for it either to perform its obligations or to
> allow the loans to remain outstanding. It is a clause originating in the
> syndicated loan markets which has become standard in all loan
> documentation.*
>
> ***Lender:*** *The lender would like this clause to be drafted widely not only to
> include laws but also statements which do not have the force of law. The
> Financial Services Authority, for example, may make various stipulations
> that although do not have the force of law have a substantial degree of
> influence.*
>
> ***Borrower:*** *The events contemplated by this clause are essentially out of the
> control of the borrower and are therefore particularly onerous. The
> borrower should argue that in a domestic loan situation this type of clause
> is completely inappropriate and designed to cater for political upheaval
> such as a war between the country of the lender and the country of the
> borrower. Furthermore, the borrower should try to obtain a degree of
> objectivity in the clause so that the clause only applies to laws and
> regulations in force in England and Wales rather than any jurisdiction
> (this is the LMA wording which is really intended for international
> syndications – UK loans should be treated differently). The borrower
> should also try to get the lender to mitigate against this by transferring the
> loan to another of the lender's lending offices located in a jurisdiction in
> which the loan would not constitute an illegal/unlawful agreement. No
> penalty or premium should be payable on the repayment.*

7.2   Change of control

7.2.1   If [[   ] ceases to control the Borrower]/[any person or group of
            persons acting in concert gains control of the Borrower]:

            (a) the Borrower shall promptly notify the Lender upon becoming
                 aware of that event;
            (b) the Lender may, by not less than [   ] days' notice to the
                 Borrower, cancel the Facility and declare all outstanding
                 Loans, together with accrued interest, and all other amounts
                 accrued under the Finance Documents immediately due and
                 payable, whereupon the Facility will be cancelled and all such
                 outstanding amounts will become immediately due and
                 payable.

7.2.2   For the purpose of Clause 7.2.1 above '**control**' means [   ].

7.2.3   [For the purpose of Clause 7.2.1 above '**acting in concert**' means [   ].]

> *Purpose: In real estate banking and leveraged buyout transactions it is usual for the lender to agree to fund a special purpose vehicle backed by particular investors. Where the ownership of the borrower changes the lender commonly has the right to require prepayment of the loan.*
>
> *Lender: The lender's credit sanction will often be expressed as an offer to a vehicle backed by a particular individual or company. If that individual or company ceases to own the vehicle the lender will want to be able to reconsider its position. Another consideration is that lenders often set limits on their permitted exposure to particular customers in order to minimise the risk of catastrophic default. It is possible that those limits might be breached by one borrower's acquisition of another borrower.*
>
> *Borrower: The borrower will argue that the lender is backing the qualities of the site or business being financed rather than the qualities of the borrower and that change of control is therefore irrelevant. This argument seldom succeeds, notwithstanding that, in real estate banking, at least, it is probably true.*

7.3   Reduction of commitment

If, on or before any Utilisation Date, the Lender determines that the amount of the Loan to be drawn on that Utilisation Date when aggregated with the Loans then outstanding exceeds [   ] per cent of the aggregate of the estimated value of the Property as shown in the then latest Valuation the Lender may reduce the Loan to be advanced on that Utilisation Date so that when aggregated with the Loans then outstanding it is equal to [   ] per cent of the aggregate of the estimated value of the Property as shown in the then latest Valuation.

> *Purpose: this provision is in effect a day-one loan to value test (see Clause 20.1 at page 72). However, whereas the loan to value test is an ongoing control which if breached leads to a default this provision adjusts the amount lent so that the loan to value test can be met at the outset.*

7.4   Voluntary cancellation

The Borrower may, if it gives the Lender not less than [   ] Business Days' (or such shorter period as the Lender may agree) prior notice, cancel the whole or any part (being a minimum amount of [   ]) of the Available Facility.

7.5   **Voluntary prepayment of Loans**

7.5.1   The Borrower may, if it gives the Lender not less than [   ]
             Business Days' (or such shorter period as the Lender may agree)
             prior notice, prepay the whole or any part of any Loan (but, if in
             part, being an amount that reduces the Loan by a minimum amount
             of [   ]).

7.5.2   A Loan may only be prepaid after the last day of the Availability
             Period (or, if earlier, the day on which the Available Facility is zero).

7.5.3   Any prepayment under this Clause 7.5 shall satisfy the obligations
             under Clause 6.1 (*Repayment of Loans*) in [   ] order.

7.6   **Right of repayment and cancellation**

7.6.1   If:

             (a) any sum payable to the Lender by the Borrower is required to
                  be increased under Clause 13.2.3 (*Tax gross-up*);
             (b) the Lender claims indemnification from the Borrower under
                  Clause 13.3 (*Tax indemnity*) or Clause 14.1 (*Increased costs*); or
             (c) the Lender notifies the Borrower of its Additional Cost Rate
                  under paragraph 3 of Schedule 3 (*Mandatory Cost Formulae*),

             the Borrower may, whilst (in the case of paragraphs (a) and (b)
             above) the circumstance giving rise to the requirement or indemni-
             fication continues or (in the case of paragraph (c) above) that
             Additional Cost Rate is greater than zero, give the Lender notice of
             cancellation of the Facility Commitment and its intention to
             procure the repayment of the Loans.

7.6.2   On receipt of a notice referred to in Clause 7.6.1 above, the Facility
             Commitment of that Lender shall immediately be reduced to zero.

7.6.3   On the last day of each Interest Period which ends after the
             Borrower has given notice under Clause 7.6.1 above (or, if earlier,
             the date specified by the Borrower in that notice), the Borrower
             shall repay that Loan.

7.7   **Restrictions**

7.7.1   Any notice of cancellation or prepayment given by any Party under
             this Clause 7 shall be irrevocable and, unless a contrary indication
             appears in this Agreement, shall specify the date or dates upon
             which the relevant cancellation or prepayment is to be made and
             the amount of that cancellation or prepayment.

7.7.2   Any prepayment under this Agreement shall be made together with
             accrued interest on the amount prepaid and, subject to any Break
             Costs, without premium or penalty.

Purpose: It is sometimes the case that the terms agreed between lender and borrower provide for a prepayment fee to be paid on amounts prepaid (this compensates the lender for loss of income received if the loans had remained outstanding and earning interest for the originally agreed term). In this agreement there is no such fee but Clause 7.7.2 makes clear that notwithstanding the lack of premium or penalty there may be Break Costs payable. Break Costs are the costs to the lender of unwinding its funding of the loan in the interbank market (for more on this see the commentary on Clause 8.1). Note that if the loan is prepaid at the end of an interest period there will be no Break Costs because the lender will not have to break its funding of the loan.

7.7.3   The Borrower may not reborrow any part of the Facility which is prepaid.

7.7.4   The Borrower shall not repay or prepay all or any part of the Loans or cancel all or any part of the Facility Commitment except at the times and in the manner expressly provided for in this Agreement.

7.7.5   No amount of the Facility Commitment cancelled under this Agreement may be subsequently reinstated.

8   Interest

8.1   Calculation of interest

The rate of interest on each Loan for each Interest Period is the percentage rate per annum which is the aggregate of the applicable:

8.1.1   Margin;

8.1.2   LIBOR; and

8.1.3   Mandatory Cost, if any.

Purpose: This clause sets out the interest rate which the borrower will have to pay the lender for the loan. The interest rate is made up of three elements:

8.1.1 Margin
The margin is expressed as a percentage per annum and represents the return to the lender above its cost of funds (LIBOR) or its base rate if base rate is used. Sometimes the margin is referred to as the 'spread' over LIBOR and sometimes it is referred to in terms of 'basis points'. 100 basis points = 1%.

8.1.2 LIBOR
Most real estate banking deals use LIBOR (London Interbank Offered Rate) as the basis for interest rates. In traditional banking a lender would take deposits from customers and lend the deposits out in order to earn a return. In more modern times a lender will tend not to look to its retail depositors to fund the loan but will instead turn to other banks. The market in which banks fund each other is the London Interbank Market.

*Once the lender has borrowed on the interbank market it will then lend
that amount to the borrower.*

*The London Interbank Market was established in or around 1949 and is
predominantly a short-term market. Most deposits are made for one, three
or six months, although some are made for up to five years. These deposit
periods equate to interest periods of the loan (see Clause 9 below). Rates
are fixed mid-morning every day. The lender's funding in the interbank
market will match his loan to the borrower both in amount and in the
duration of individual interest periods. LIBOR funding is described as
being variable or floating rate funding because during the term of the
loan there will be different rates of interest applicable for different interest
periods. Nonetheless during each interest period the interest rate remains
fixed. The rate will depend largely on the market's view of likely changes
in the Bank of England interest rate during the interest period.*

*The definition of LIBOR provides first that a screen rate should be
obtained. This is a generic rate for the rate offered to leading banks (ie
banks which are considered a good risk). It is not the actual cost to the
lender of borrowing. This may be higher or lower depending on the
market's view of its creditworthiness and its actual sources of funds. If no
screen rate is available then specified reference banks are asked to give
quotes of the rates they would offer to leading banks. The borrower should
ensure that the reference banks' offices are specified as being their London
offices as this may have an impact on the cost of funds. Care should be
taken to pick three substantial and reputable institutions as reference
banks. Ideally they would be the borrower's usual relationship banks.*

8.1.3 Mandatory cost
*Mandatory costs are sometimes referred to as 'associated costs', 'reserve
assets costs', 'mandatory liquid asset costs' or simply 'MLA costs'.
Essentially, these are costs for a lender of complying with the liquidity or
other similar requirements imposed by the Financial Services Authority,
Bank of England or European Central Bank affecting all loans made by
a lender in the United Kingdom. The effect of these requirements is that
there will be an additional hidden cost to the lender when it makes a
Sterling loan in the United Kingdom which is passed on to the borrower.
The formula for calculating the cost is set out in Schedule 3. It is market
standard and not negotiable.*

8.2   **Payment of interest**

The Borrower shall pay accrued interest on each Loan on the last
day of each Interest Period (and, if the Interest Period is longer than
six Months, on the dates falling at six monthly intervals after the first
day of the Interest Period).

8.3 **Hedging**

8.3.1 On or before the first Utilisation Date, the Borrower shall ensure that it has entered into Hedging Arrangements with respect to the interest payable under this Agreement:

(a) which comply with Clause 8.3.2 below; and

(b) so that, at any time, the notional principal amount of such Hedging Arrangements is, or will be, not less than the aggregate Loans outstanding at that time.

8.3.2 The Hedging Arrangements referred to in Clause 8.3.1 above shall be:

(a) with [   ];

(b) for a term commencing on or before the first Utilisation Date and not ending before the Termination Date;

(c) in form and substance satisfactory to the Lender; and

(d) (if so required by the Lender) assigned to or otherwise secured in favour of the Lender in a manner acceptable to the Lender.

Purpose: In an investment property transaction the rental income of the site will be predictable assuming the credit of the tenant remains good. One of the principal risks that can cause a default is the risk that variable rates may increase to a point where they cannot be serviced out of the income from the property. Accordingly, it is likely to be in the interests of both parties to agree to swap the LIBOR-based interest payments under this agreement for a fixed rate that can be serviced comfortably out of the rental income.

Lender: The lender will want to retain maximum control over the terms of the hedging in order to ensure that its interest will be paid.

Borrower: The borrower will be keen to ensure that the rate is a mutually agreed rate and will want to avoid being stuck with an expensive swap which eats into its equity return, particularly if there is a likelihood that fixed rates will reduce in the foreseeable future. It is advantageous to get the flexibility to obtain a swap from a counterparty other than the lender since the lender may well quote a poor rate to a captive customer.

8.4 **Default interest**

8.4.1 If the Borrower fails to pay any amount payable by it under a Finance Document on its due date, interest shall accrue on the overdue amount from the due date up to the date of actual payment (both before and after judgment) at a rate [ ] per cent higher than the rate which would have been payable if the overdue amount had, during the period of non-payment, constituted a Loan in the currency of the overdue amount for successive Interest Periods, each of a duration selected by the Lender (acting reasonably). Any interest accruing under this Clause 8.4 shall be immediately payable by the Borrower on demand by the Lender.

8.4.2   Default interest (if unpaid) arising on an overdue amount will be compounded with the overdue amount at the end of each Interest Period applicable to that overdue amount but will remain immediately due and payable.

> **Purpose:** *This clause serves as an added incentive to the borrower to make all payments punctually on their due date. In the event that it does not it would be required to pay an additional sum. The non-payment of interest would also constitute an Event of Default. Default interest may amount to a contractual penalty if set too high.[1] The courts have considered and approved an additional margin of 1%.[2]*

> **Lender:** *It is highly unlikely for the lender to concede on this clause. The lender's rationale is that if the borrower fails to make a payment on the due date, the lender is out of pocket and should be reimbursed for this risk. It is important for the clause to state that the interest is paid both before and after judgment as judgment debts carry interest at specified rates which may well be lower than general market rates.*

> **Borrower:** *The borrower should try to negotiate a reduction of the default interest rate but is unlikely to be able to negotiate a further weakening of this clause. The borrower may also try to avoid compounding and try and negotiate some grace periods for itself which will prevent the immediate operation of the default interest provisions on the occurrence of an Event of Default.*

8.5   **Notification of rates of interest**

The Lender shall promptly notify the Borrower of the determination of a rate of interest under this Agreement.

9   **Interest Periods**

9.1   **Selection of Interest Periods**

9.1.1   The Borrower may select an Interest Period for a Loan in the Utilisation Request for that Loan or (if the Loan has already been borrowed) in a Selection Notice.

9.1.2   Each Selection Notice for a Loan is irrevocable and must be delivered to the Lender by the Borrower not later than 10.00 am two Business Days before the commencement of the Interest Period to which it relates.

---

1   *Dunlop Pneumatic Tyre Company Limited v New Garage and Motor Company Limited* [1915] AC 79, but distinguish para 2(b) of Sch 3 to the Unfair Terms in Consumer Contracts Regulations 1994 (SI 1994/3159).
2   *Lordsvale Finance Plc v Bank of Zambia* [1996] QB 752.

9.1.3   If the Borrower fails to deliver a Selection Notice to the Lender in accordance with paragraph 9.1.2 above, the relevant Interest Period will be [one] Month.

9.1.4   Subject to this Clause 9, the Borrower may select an Interest Period of [or   ] Months or any other period agreed between the Borrower and the Lender. [In addition the Borrower may select an Interest Period of a period of less than [one] Month, if necessary to ensure that there are Loans equal to or greater than the Repayment Instalment which have an Interest Period ending on a Repayment Date for the Borrower to make the Repayment Instalment due on that date].

9.1.5   An Interest Period for a Loan shall not extend beyond the Termination Date.

9.1.6   Each Interest Period for a Loan shall start on the Utilisation Date or (if already made) on the last day of its preceding Interest Period.

9.2   **Non-Business Days**

         If an Interest Period would otherwise end on a day which is not a Business Day, that Interest Period will instead end on the next Business Day in that calendar month (if there is one) or the preceding Business Day (if there is not).

9.3   **Consolidation and division of Loans**

9.3.1   Subject to Clause 9.3.2 below, if two or more Interest Periods:

         (a) relate to Loans in the same currency; and
         (b) end on the same date,

         those Loans will, unless the Borrower specifies to the contrary in the Selection Notice for the next Interest Period, be consolidated into, and treated as, a single Loan on the last day of the Interest Period.

9.3.2   Subject to Clause 4.3 (*Maximum number of Loans*) and Clause 5.3 (*Amount*), if the Borrower requests in a Selection Notice that a Loan be divided into two or more Loans, that Loan will, on the last day of its Interest Period, be so divided.

         Purpose: *This clause provides the borrower with the option of selecting different interest periods as a point of reference for calculating LIBOR and charging interest. Interest will be payable at the end of the designated interest period. LIBOR will vary depending on the prevailing view of interest rates when it is calculated and the borrower will obviously be seeking the lowest LIBOR. In some deals, particularly smaller ones, there will be no choice of interest period.*

         Lender: *The lender will usually retain the ability to choose an interest period if the borrower fails to do so by a certain date. The lender will want to be sure that the interest period selected by the borrower fits in with the* *cashflow of the borrower's business. Thus in real estate banking the borrower is likely to be receiving quarterly rents so interest periods should be of three months so that the rents can 'service' the interest payments.*

Borrower: *The option to select the interest period gives the borrower maximum flexibility and enables it to make an assessment as to where it sees interest rates moving. If interest rates are low but the borrower believes they are going to increase it would be advisable to select a six-month period and if interest rates are high but the borrower believes they are going to reduce it would be more sensible to select a one-month period. It is, however, necessary to bear in mind that sufficient principal should 'roll over' (ie come to the end of an interest period) on any scheduled principal repayment dates to avoid incurring break costs (see Clause 9.1.4 at page 47).*

Where the borrower has drawn down the loan in several advances, it can choose either to run separate interest periods for each drawing or it can have all the advances consolidated into one amount. The borrower's decision as to which is the preferred route will usually depend on its cashflow position. As drafted, Clause 9.3 provides for automatic consolidation unless the borrower gives notice to the contrary.

10   Changes to the Calculation of Interest

10.1   Absence of quotations

Subject to Clause 10.2 (*Market disruption*), if LIBOR is to be determined by reference to the Reference Banks but a Reference Bank does not supply a quotation by 10.00 am on the Quotation Day, the applicable LIBOR shall be determined on the basis of the quotations of the remaining Reference Banks.

10.2   Market disruption

10.2.1   If a Market Disruption Event occurs in relation to a Loan for any Interest Period, then the rate of interest on that Loan for the Interest Period shall be the rate per annum which is the sum of:

(a)   the Margin;
(b)   the rate which expresses as a percentage rate per annum the cost to the Lender of funding its participation in that Loan from whatever source it may reasonably select; and
(c)   the Mandatory Cost, if any, applicable to the Loan.

10.2.2   In this Agreement '**Market Disruption Event**' means:

(a)   at or about noon on the Quotation Day for the relevant Interest Period the Screen Rate is not available and none or only one of the Reference Banks supplies a rate to the Lender to determine LIBOR for the relevant currency and Interest Period; or

(b) before close of business in London on the Quotation Day for the relevant Interest Period, the Lender determines that the cost to it of obtaining matching deposits in the London Interbank Market would be in excess of LIBOR.

10.3   **Alternative basis of interest or funding**

If a Market Disruption Event occurs and the Lender or the Borrower so requires, the Lender and the Borrower shall enter into negotiations (for a period of not more than thirty days) with a view to agreeing a substitute basis for determining the rate of interest.

Purpose: If for some reason the lender is unable to establish its cost of funds in the interbank market, it needs to be able to find another basis for establishing its cost of funds. As the interbank market is substantial, this risk is highly unlikely.

Lender: The lender will want to be able to cancel any obligations to make further advances and either pass on its actual cost of funds or, alternatively (probably less attractively), have the outstanding amounts immediately repaid. Although the lender will be willing to consult with the borrower about the substitute cost of funds it is unlikely to give the borrower a veto over the rate since this could result in there being no interest rate applying to the loan.

Borrower: The borrower will want to ensure that it has some input in the setting of the alternative rate. Ultimately, however, the remedy for an unsatisfactory substitute rate is to prepay the facility.

10.4   **Break Costs**

10.4.1   The Borrower shall, within three Business Days of demand by the Lender, pay to the Lender its Break Costs attributable to all or any part of a Loan or Unpaid Sum being paid by the Borrower on a day other than the last day of an Interest Period for that Loan or Unpaid Sum.

10.4.2   The Lender shall, as soon as reasonably practicable after a demand by the Lender, provide a certificate confirming the amount of its Break Costs for any Interest Period in which they accrue.

11   **Bank Accounts**

11.1   **Designation of Accounts**

11.1.1   The Borrower shall maintain the following bank accounts:

(a) a current account in the name of the Borrower designated the **'General Account'** at the Account Bank; and

(b) a current account in the name of the Borrower designated the **'Rent Account'** at the Lender;

11.1.2   The Borrower shall not, without the prior consent of the Lender, maintain any bank account other than those specified in Clause 11.1.1 above.

Purpose: Clause 11 sets out a simple account structure for a real estate banking transaction. The income from the property is collected and paid into the rent account net of sums attributable to service charge, insurance rent, VAT and similar deductions. These deductions are not the property of the Borrower and the Lender should not therefore have recourse to them. The monies standing to the credit of the rent account are applied in repayment of loan obligations as they fall due. Any surplus is transferred to the general account for the borrower's use, unless a Default is outstanding.

11.2   **Rent Account**

11.2.1   The Lender shall have sole signing rights on the Rent Account.

11.2.2   The Borrower shall ensure that all Net Rental Income is, and any amounts payable to it under any Hedging Arrangements are, paid into the Rent Account.

11.2.3   If any tenant of any Property sends or makes one payment (whether by cheque or otherwise) in respect of Net Rental Income and amounts which should be paid into an Account other than the Rent Account:

(a) that payment must be paid into the Rent Account; and
(b) unless a Default is outstanding, the Lender shall, at the request of the Borrower and on receipt of evidence satisfactory to the Lender that the payment includes an amount that should be paid into another Account, pay that amount to that other Account.

11.2.4   On each Interest Payment Date, the Lender shall (and is irrevocably authorised by the Borrower to) withdraw from the Rent Account such amount as may be necessary on such date in or towards the following items (and, if the credit balance in the Rent Account is insufficient to pay all those items, in the following order):

(a) first, payment of any unpaid fees, costs and expenses of the Lender under the Finance Documents;
(b) secondly, payment of any amount due under the Hedging Arrangements;
(c) thirdly, payment to the Lender of any other amounts due but unpaid under the Finance Documents;

and any balance shall be transferred to the General Account provided that the Lender shall not be obliged to make any such transfer if:

(i) the Borrower is in breach of Clause 20.1 (*Ratio of rental income to debt service*); or

(ii) a Default is outstanding; or

(iii) any of the representations and warranties set out in Clause 18 (*Representations*) are not true on and as of the proposed date for making such withdrawal.

11.2.5 The Lender may authorise withdrawals at any time from the Rent Account to pay any amounts due but unpaid under the Finance Documents.

11.3 General Account

11.3.1 The Borrower shall, subject to Clause 11.3.4 below, have signing rights on the General Account.

11.3.2 The Borrower shall ensure that all amounts whatsoever recoverable or receivable by any of them when paid, other than those amounts required under this Agreement to be paid into any other Account, are paid into the General Account.

11.3.3 Unless a Default is outstanding, the Borrower may, subject to the restrictions in the Subordination Deed, make withdrawals from the General Account to pay any liability of the Borrower.

11.3.4 Whilst a Default is outstanding, the Lender may give notice to the Borrower that no amount may be withdrawn by the Borrower from the General Account without the consent of the Lender. If the Lender gives such notice, the Lender shall thereafter, to the exclusion of the Borrower (unless the Lender otherwise consents), be entitled (and is irrevocably authorised by the Borrower) to withdraw amounts from the General Account and to operate the General Account in or towards any of the purposes for which moneys in any Account may be applied.

11.4 Miscellaneous Accounts provisions

11.4.1 The Borrower shall ensure that none of the Accounts is overdrawn at any time.

11.4.2 The Lender may delegate its powers of withdrawal from any Account to any administrative receiver, receiver and/or manager.

11.4.3 If the Borrower receives or recovers any amount otherwise than by credit to the relevant Account, the Borrower shall pay the amount to the appropriate Account or to the Lender immediately after receipt or recovery and in like funds as received or recovered by the Borrower and shall in the meantime hold the same subject to the security created by the Finance Documents.

11.4.4 On the Termination Date or on the Loans becoming immediately due and payable under this Agreement, the monies standing to the credit of each Account may be applied by the Lender in or towards repayment of the Loans and all other amounts due to the Lender under the Finance Documents.

11.4.5   The Lender shall not be responsible to the Borrower for any non-payment of any liability of the Borrower which could be paid out of moneys standing to the credit of an Account. The Lender shall not be liable to the Borrower for any withdrawal wrongly made if made in good faith.

11.4.6   The Borrower shall provide the Lender within ten Business Days of any request by the Lender the following information in relation to any payment received in an Account:

(a) date of payment/receipt;
(b) payer; and
(c) purpose of/for payment/receipt.

11.5   **Change of Bank Accounts**

11.5.1   If the Lender so requests (acting reasonably), an Account may be moved to another bank.

11.5.2   A change of Account only becomes effective upon the proposed new bank agreeing with the Lender and the Borrower, in a manner satisfactory to the Lender, to fulfil the role of the bank holding that Account.

12   Fees

12.1   **Commitment fee**

12.1.1   The Borrower shall pay to the Lender a fee computed at the rate of [   ] per cent per annum on the Available Facility for the Availability Period.

12.1.2   The accrued commitment fee is payable on the last day of each successive period of three Months which ends during the Availability Period, on the last day of the Availability Period and, if cancelled in full, on the cancelled amount of the Facility Commitment at the time the cancellation is effective.

Purpose: The commitment fee compensates the Lender for having to allocate capital to the undrawn loan whilst earning no interest on it. It is typically set at about half the margin.

12.2   **Arrangement fee**

The Borrower shall pay to the Lender on the date of this Agreement an arrangement fee in the amount of £ [   ].

13   Tax Gross-up and Indemnities

13.1   Definitions

13.1.1   In this Clause 13:

'Qualifying Lender'   means a person which is beneficially entitled to interest payable to that person in respect of an advance under a Finance Document and:

(a) which is a bank (as defined for the purpose of section 349 of the Taxes Act) making an advance under a Finance Document or, in respect of an advance made under a Finance Document by a person, which was a bank (as defined for the purpose of section 349 of the Taxes Act) at the time that that advance was made, and in either case which is within the charge to United Kingdom corporation tax as respects any payments of interest made in respect of that advance; or
(i)   [which is:
(ii) a company resident in the United Kingdom for United Kingdom tax purposes;
(iii) a partnership each member of which is a company resident in the United Kingdom for United Kingdom tax purposes; or
(b) a company not so resident in the United Kingdom which carries on a trade in the United Kingdom through a branch or agency and which brings into account interest payable in respect of that advance in computing its chargeable profits (within the meaning given by section 11(2) of the Taxes Act); or]
(c) [which is a Treaty Lender];

'Tax Credit'   means a credit against, relief or remission for, or repayment of any Tax;

'Tax Deduction'	means a deduction or withholding for or on account of Tax from a payment under a Finance Document;
'Tax Payment'	means an increased payment made by the Borrower to the Lender under Clause 13.2 (*Tax gross-up*) or a payment under Clause 13.3 (*Tax indemnity*).
['Treaty Lender'	means a Lender which:

(a) is treated as a resident of a Treaty State for the purposes of the Treaty;
(b) does not carry on a business in the United Kingdom through a permanent establishment with which the Lender's participation in the Loan is effectively connected[; and
(c)   ];

'Treaty State'	means a jurisdiction having a double taxation agreement (a **'Treaty'**) with the United Kingdom which makes provision for full exemption from tax imposed by the United Kingdom on interest.]

13.1.2 Unless a contrary indication appears, in this Clause 13 a reference to **'determines'** or **'determined'** means a determination made in the absolute discretion of the person making the determination.

13.2 Tax gross-up

13.2.1 The Borrower shall make all payments to be made by it without any Tax Deduction, unless a Tax Deduction is required by law.

13.2.2 The Borrower or the Lender shall promptly upon becoming aware that the Borrower must make a Tax Deduction (or that there is any change in the rate or the basis of a Tax Deduction) notify the other accordingly.

13.2.3 If a Tax Deduction is required by law to be made by the Borrower, the amount of the payment due from the Borrower shall be increased to an amount which (after making any Tax Deduction) leaves an amount equal to the payment which would have been due if no Tax Deduction had been required.

13.2.4 The Borrower is not required to make an increased payment to the Lender under Clause 13.2.3 above for a Tax Deduction in respect of tax imposed by the United Kingdom from a payment of interest on a Loan, if on the date on which the payment falls due:

(a) the payment could have been made to the relevant Lender without a Tax Deduction if it was a Qualifying Lender, but on that date that Lender is not or has ceased to be a Qualifying Lender other than as a result of any change after the date it became a Lender under this Agreement in (or in the interpretation, administration, or application of) any law or Treaty, or any published practice or concession of any relevant taxing authority[; or

(b) the relevant Lender is a Treaty Lender and the Borrower is able to demonstrate that the payment could have been made to the Lender without the Tax Deduction had that Lender complied with its obligations under Clause 13.2.7 below].

13.2.5   If the Borrower is required to make a Tax Deduction, it shall make that Tax Deduction and any payment required in connection with that Tax Deduction within the time allowed and in the minimum amount required by law.

13.2.6   Within thirty days of making either a Tax Deduction or any payment required in connection with that Tax Deduction, the Borrower shall deliver to the Lender evidence reasonably satisfactory to the Lender that the Tax Deduction has been made or (as applicable) any appropriate payment paid to the relevant taxing authority.

13.2.7   If the Lender is a Treaty Lender the Lender and the Borrower shall co-operate in completing any procedural formalities necessary for the Lender to obtain authorisation to make a payment to which the Lender is entitled without a Tax Deduction.

Purpose: The purpose of Clause 13 is to ensure that a qualifying lender (defined in Clause 13.1) receives 100% of payments due to it irrespective of any obligation to deduct tax from the payment. At present, banks are entitled to receive payments of interest and principal without tax withholding and the clause is in essence a protection against a change of tax law. In brief, the clause provides that, if the borrower is obliged to make a tax withholding from payments to a qualifying lender, then the borrower must gross up the payment so that, after the deduction, the lender would receive an amount equivalent to the whole payment due. The logic for this is that the lender will have a funding arrangement in the London Interbank Market and will need to receive 100% of interest payments to meet its obligations to that counterparty.

The basic position in the United Kingdom is that, by virtue of s 349 of the Income and Corporation Taxes Act 1988 (ICTA 1988), a payer of annual interest is obliged to deduct income tax from that payment at the basic rate and to pay the tax direct to the Inland Revenue. Annual interest is essentially interest on a loan with a term of one year or more. The tax is the lender's income tax because the interest is the lender's income.

There are, however, a number of exceptions to the withholding obligation and their scope has been much widened by the Finance Act 2001. The position until April 2001 was that there was no obligation to deduct tax on payments of annual interest to a bank as defined in s 840A of ICTA 1988; and in some cases foreign-domiciled entities could take advantage of double tax treaties permitting them to receive interest gross provided the appropriate Inland Revenue forms were completed. This is the tax landscape reflected in Clause 13, in particular the definition of 'Qualifying Lender'. The Finance Act 2001 introduced additional categories of lender entitled to receive interest gross. These are set out in s 349B of ICTA 1988 and include, most importantly, companies resident in the United Kingdom and partnerships each member of which is a company resident in the United Kingdom.

At the time of writing, the market practice remains to give banks and double tax treaty lenders the benefit of qualifying lender status but not the new categories of lender that can be paid gross. This is likely to continue to be the case because these are entities which would generally be considered to be entitled to the protection against a change of law. The law is favourable to them now, but if it changes, then this should be their own risk and not that of the borrower. This is consistent with the way non-bank transferees of banks were treated before April 2001 (and still are). Both before and since the Finance Act 2001, if a bank (ie a qualifying lender) transfers its interest in a loan to, say, a UK corporate, the corporate is entitled to receive interest payments gross (ie without withholding) just as the transferor was. However, it does not have qualifying lender status and if the law were to change then the borrower would not have to gross up payments to the transferee.

Lender: *The lender will require the clause to be drafted as widely as possible (ie to apply to any tax imposed in any country whether it is the country of the borrower, the lender, the currency of the loan or the country where the repayments are to be made). It is important to the lender to receive 100% of the interest payment due to it because it will have a corresponding liability to pay its funding counterparty in the interbank market. If it does not receive 100% then it will need to find additional cash from another source to meet the shortfall which will have a cost attached to it.*

Borrower: *The borrower should strenuously resist a wide definition and should limit the application of this clause to a change in the tax regulations in the country where it carries on business and where it is resident. Otherwise the borrower would be exposed to risks which would be completely out of its control and unknown to it.*

If withholding is made and the grossing-up applies, the lender will still receive the same amount of money had no withholding been made but, in addition, the lender would be entitled to a credit for its own tax purposes which would be broadly equivalent to the income tax withheld. This tax credit should be repaid to the borrower and most lenders will agree to a tax

credit clause in the form of Clause 13.4. Thus it is often said that
gross-up creates a cashflow problem for the borrower, because he has to
fund the amount of the gross-up for a limited period until receiving the
benefit of the tax credit. This is not entirely accurate and there will be a
cost to the borrower if gross-up applies.

13.3 **Tax indemnity**

13.3.1 The Borrower shall (within three Business Days of demand by the Lender) pay to the Lender an amount equal to the loss, liability or cost which the Lender determines will be or has been (directly or indirectly) suffered for or on account of Tax by the Lender in respect of a Finance Document.

13.3.2 Clause 13.3.1 above shall not apply with respect to any Tax assessed on the Lender:

(i) under the law of the jurisdiction in which the Lender is incorporated or, if different, the jurisdiction (or jurisdictions) in which the Lender is treated as resident for tax purposes; or

(ii) under the law of the jurisdiction in which the Lender's Facility Office is located in respect of amounts received or receivable in that jurisdiction,

if that Tax is imposed on or calculated by reference to the net income received or receivable (but not any sum deemed to be received or receivable) by it; or

(iii) as a result of the Lender's not being a Qualifying Bank.

Purpose: This clause caters for the situation where the lender has incurred
a tax liability as a result of lending the money. This clause is seldom
negotiated. However, the borrower should make sure that it understands
what additional tax liabilities (if any) the lender has by virtue of making
the advance and if there are any, it should find another lender.

13.4 **Tax Credit**

If the Borrower makes a Tax Payment and the Lender determines that:

13.4.1 a Tax Credit is attributable to that Tax Payment; and

13.4.2 the Lender has obtained, utilised and retained that Tax Credit,

the Lender shall pay an amount to the Borrower which the Lender determines will leave it (after that payment) in the same after-Tax position as it would have been in had the Tax Payment not been made by the Borrower.

Purpose: This clause is intended to give the borrower the benefit of any tax
credit the lender receives following a withholding tax deduction. The
difficulty with these clauses is that there is no precisely predictable

relationship between the withholding and any tax credit and therefore it may not be possible to pass back the excess payment. It is likely that there will be some shortfall and the gross-up therefore becomes a significant additional cost rather than simply a cashflow issue. It is not possible to agree a tax credit clause that will return both borrower and lender to an entirely satisfactory position after a gross-up so the borrower needs to make sure that prepayment is possible in these circumstances.

13.5   **Stamp taxes**

The Borrower shall pay and, within three Business Days of demand, indemnify the Lender against any cost, loss or liability the Lender incurs in relation to all stamp duty, registration and other similar Taxes payable in respect of any Finance Document.

13.6   **Value added tax**

13.6.1   All consideration expressed to be payable under a Finance Document by the Borrower to the Lender shall be deemed to be exclusive of any VAT. If VAT is chargeable on any supply made by the Lender to the Borrower in connection with a Finance Document, the Borrower shall pay to the Lender (in addition to and at the same time as paying the consideration) an amount equal to the amount of the VAT.

13.6.2   Where a Finance Document requires the Borrower to reimburse the Lender for any costs or expenses, it shall also at the same time pay and indemnify the Lender against all VAT incurred by the Lender in respect of the costs or expenses save to the extent that the Lender reasonably determines that it is not entitled to credit or repayment of the VAT.

14   Increased Costs

14.1   **Increased Costs**

14.1.1   Subject to Clause 14.2 (*Exceptions*) the Borrower shall, within three Business Days of a demand by the Lender, pay for the account of the Lender the amount of any Increased Costs incurred by the Lender or any of its Affiliates as a result of (i) the introduction of or any change in (or in the interpretation, administration or application of) any law or regulation or (ii) compliance with any law or regulation made after the date of this Agreement.

14.1.2   In this Agreement '**Increased Costs**' means:

(a) a reduction in the rate of return from the Facility or on the Lender's (or its Affiliate's) overall capital;
(b) an additional or increased cost; or
(c) a reduction of any amount due and payable under any Finance Document,

which is incurred or suffered by the Lender or any of its Affiliates to the extent that it is attributable to the Lender having entered into its Commitment or funding or performing its obligations under any Finance Document.

14.1.3 The Lender shall, as soon as practicable after a demand by the Borrower, provide a certificate confirming the amount of its Increased Costs.

14.2 Exceptions

14.2.1 Clause 14.1 (*Increased Costs*) does not apply to the extent any Increased Cost is:

(a) attributable to a Tax Deduction required by law to be made by the Borrower;

(b) compensated for by Clause 13.3 (*Tax indemnity*) (or would have been compensated for under Clause 13.3 (*Tax indemnity*) but was not so compensated solely because one of the exclusions in Clause 13.3.2 (*Tax indemnity*) applied);

(c) compensated for by the payment of the Mandatory Cost; or

(d) attributable to the wilful breach by the Lender or its Affiliates of any law or regulation.

14.2.2 In this Clause 14.2, a reference to a '**Tax Deduction**' has the same meaning given to the term in Clause 13.1 (*Definitions*).

Purpose: This clause aims to protect the lender if its return is being diminished due to a change in the law, or capital adequacy, liquidity or reserve asset requirements. The clause is not really relevant where the loan has been made at a base rate of interest as by definition that rate will include the various reserves asset, liquidity and capital adequacy requirements. It is peculiar to LIBOR-related loans which are essentially pure cost of funding loans. The rationale therefore is that if the cost of funding is increased for regulatory reasons the borrower has to bear this cost.

Borrower: The borrower is potentially being asked to pay additional amounts where there might be a change in the taxation as well as a change in reserve assets/capital adequacy requirements. The borrower should seek to limit the change in regulation, to regulations occurring in the country where the loan is being advanced. It should also ensure that it does not have to pay for a change in the rate of taxation on a lender's profits as opposed to changing the basis of tax and should ensure that the lender has a duty to mitigate.

15   Other Indemnities

15.1   **Currency indemnity**

15.1.1   If any sum due from the Borrower under the Finance Documents (a '**Sum**'), or any order, judgment or award given or made in relation to a Sum, has to be converted from the currency (the '**First Currency**') in which that Sum is payable into another currency (the '**Second Currency**') for the purpose of:

(a) making or filing a claim or proof against the Borrower;

(b) obtaining or enforcing an order, judgment or award in relation to any litigation or arbitration proceedings,

the Borrower shall as an independent obligation, within three Business Days of demand, indemnify the Lender against any cost, loss or liability arising out of or as a result of the conversion including any discrepancy between (A) the rate of exchange used to convert that Sum from the First Currency into the Second Currency and (B) the rate or rates of exchange available to that person at the time of its receipt of that Sum.

15.1.2   The Borrower waives any right it may have in any jurisdiction to pay any amount under the Finance Documents in a currency or currency unit other than that in which it is expressed to be payable.

15.2   **Other indemnities**

The Borrower shall, within three Business Days of demand, indemnify the Lender against any cost, loss or liability incurred by the Lender as a result of:

15.2.1   the occurrence of any Event of Default;

15.2.2   funding, or making arrangements to fund, its participation in a Loan requested by the Borrower in a Utilisation Request but not made by reason of the operation of any one or more of the provisions of this Agreement (other than by reason of default or negligence by the Lender alone); or

15.2.3   a Loan (or part of a Loan) not being prepaid in accordance with a notice of prepayment given by the Borrower.

15.3   **Indemnity to the Lender**

The Borrower shall promptly indemnify the Lender against any cost, loss or liability incurred by the Lender (acting reasonably) as a result of:

15.3.1   investigating any event which it reasonably believes is a Default; or

15.3.2   acting or relying on any notice, request or instruction which it reasonably believes to be genuine, correct and appropriately authorised.

16   Mitigation by the Lender

16.1   Mitigation

16.1.1   The Lender shall, in consultation with the Borrower, take all reasonable steps to mitigate any circumstances which arise and which would result in any amount becoming payable under or pursuant to, or cancelled pursuant to, any of Clause 7.1 (*Illegality*), Clause 13 (*Tax gross-up and indemnities*), Clause 14 (*Increased Costs*) or paragraph 3 of Schedule 3 (*Mandatory Cost Formulae*) including (but not limited to) transferring its rights and obligations under the Finance Documents to another Affiliate or Facility Office.

16.1.2   Clause 16.1.1 above does not in any way limit the obligations of the Borrower under the Finance Documents.

16.2   Limitation of liability

16.2.1   The Borrower shall indemnify the Lender for all costs and expenses reasonably incurred by the Lender as a result of steps taken by it under Clause 16.1 (*Mitigation*).

16.2.2   The Lender is not obliged to take any steps under Clause 16.1 (*Mitigation*) if, in its opinion (acting reasonably), to do so might be prejudicial to it.

Purpose: The purpose of the clause is to oblige the lender to take reasonable steps to remove circumstances or mitigate the consequences to the borrower where there has been an increased cost, illegality or gross-up requirement. This is primarily a borrower's point and most lenders will agree to it.

Lender: Most lenders will agree to such a clause provided it is qualified along the lines set out in Clause 16.2. It is LMA standard and uncontroversial.

17   Costs and Expenses

17.1   Transaction expenses

The Borrower shall promptly on demand pay the Lender the amount of all costs and expenses (including legal fees) reasonably incurred by the Lender in connection with the negotiation, preparation, printing, and execution of:

17.1.1   this Agreement and any other documents referred to in this Agreement; and

17.1.2   any other Finance Documents executed after the date of this Agreement.

17.2   Amendment costs

If (a) the Borrower requests an amendment, waiver or consent or (b) an amendment is required pursuant to Clause 27.6 (*Change of currency*), the Borrower shall, within three Business Days of demand, reimburse the Lender for the amount of all costs and expenses (including legal fees) reasonably incurred by the Lender in responding to, evaluating, negotiating or complying with that request or requirement.

17.3   Enforcement costs

The Borrower shall, within three Business Days of demand, pay to the Lender the amount of all costs and expenses (including legal fees) incurred by the Lender in connection with the enforcement of, or the preservation of any rights under, any Finance Document.

Purpose: The above clause is relatively standard and is not the subject of major negotiation. The question of costs and fees is a commercial issue to be agreed between lender and borrower, although there is a market position in banking transactions which is almost invariably adhered to.

Lender: The obligation proposed by the borrower to ensure all costs are reasonably incurred is acceptable where costs are incurred at the outset of the transaction or in non-default situations. Reasonable and, to a lesser extent, proper are not appropriate qualifications where costs arise after an Event of Default or on enforcement by which stage the lender should have total discretion as to which rights it exercises and in which manner; and therefore should not have to demonstrate to a defaulting borrower that its costs are reasonable.

Borrower: The borrower should ensure that pre-enforcement the fees and costs should be reasonably incurred or reasonably and properly incurred. A borrower is invariably well-advised to obtain an estimate before commencing negotiation of the agreement. In some cases a cap can be agreed though this may result in the work being charged at a premium. The reasonable or reasonable and proper wording is likely to be accepted for all costs save for those arising after an Event of Default. Proper does not add a great deal to the qualification since unless the lender is acting in bad faith (and therefore unreasonably) the costs will be properly incurred.

18   Representations

The Borrower makes the representations and warranties set out in this Clause 18 to the Lender on the date of this Agreement.

Purpose: The fundamental principle in every form of lending is 'understand and know'. Representations and warranties are incorporated in loan and security agreements to ascertain the fundamental facts about the borrower, but are no substitute for due diligence in respect of the borrower and its assets. Representations and warranties set out the factual basis on which the lender makes the credit available. This purpose is, however, to be contrasted to the representations and warranties in a corporate sale and purchase agreement in which the principal aim is to elicit full disclosure and to found a financial claim from the vendor to the extent that hidden information comes to light. Banking agreement warranties are not disclosed against; they are framed in such a way that the borrower should be able to operate without breaching them. The intended consequences of breach are not a claim for financial compensation but, potentially, the acceleration of the loan and the insolvency of the borrower.

Generally, the representations and warranties in the loan agreement fall into two categories: (i) those giving assurances as to the legal validity of the obligations of the borrower; and (ii) those relating to the condition of the borrower. Warranties relating to the borrower's assets (and, in particular, those charged, mortgaged or assigned to the lender pursuant to the security documents) are generally set out in the security documents. Although there would be a remedy for misrepresentation or even, in some circumstances, rescission, in the event that the representations and warranties are inaccurate, the real teeth of the representations and warranties is in the fact that breach (usually material breach) constitutes an Event of Default.

In addition to creating an event of default, it will be a condition precedent to the initial advance and any further advances that the representations and warranties are true and correct as at the date of the intended further advance.

Finally, a breach of representation may in theory entitle the lender to rescind the contract. In practice, there are likely to be supervening third party rights preventing the return of the parties to their original position before the loan is made.

There are certain standard representations and warranties which will be incorporated into all loan agreements although the extent of the type of representations and warranties will depend on the type of transaction, the security available and the type of borrowing vehicle.

Lender: *The lender will seek to have representations and warranties which are as extensive as possible; first, to ascertain as much as it can about the borrower and, secondly, so that if the condition of the borrower changes, the lender will be able to call an event of default and trigger repayment of the loan.*

Borrower: *It is crucial from the borrower's perspective that it examines the representations and warranties in detail to make sure that they all are accurate. Usually, there is not much room for negotiating as it is more an exercise in providing factually accurate statements. The borrower will normally be able to include exceptions to the warranties which reflect the factual situation. With warranties relating to the actions or inactions of* *third parties, for example that 'no litigation is pending', the borrower should seek a caveat that the warranty is true 'so far as it is aware' or 'to the best of its knowledge and belief'. The borrower should resist giving unqualified representations and warranties that all of the information it has supplied is true and accurate and correct and should try and limit the scope of this representation to 'written' information.*

18.1   **Status**

18.1.1   It is a corporation, duly incorporated and validly existing under the law of its jurisdiction of incorporation.

18.1.2   It and each of its Subsidiaries has the power to own its assets and carry on its business as it is being conducted.

18.2   **Binding obligations**

The obligations expressed to be assumed by it in each Finance Document are, subject to the Reservations, legal, valid, binding and enforceable obligations.

Lender: The borrower may attempt to delete this where the lender is obtaining a formal opinion on the validity of the documents, but this (and the warranty regarding status) should be retained as the warranty gives the lender a cause of action for breach in damages and as an Event of Default, while an erroneous legal option simply gives for the lender to sue the lawyers who provided the opinion. The lender has chosen to lend on the credit of the borrower not the law firm giving the opinion.

Borrower: Where the lender is obtaining a legal opinion from the borrower's solicitors as part of the transaction, it is usual to argue for this clause to be deleted, as it and the warranty relating to status will be the substance of the legal opinion. The lender normally regards this warranty as fundamental and will usually never delete it. The borrower should, however, be successful in qualifying the reference to enforceability. This is truly the domain of the legal opinion. It is appropriate to refer to the usual enforceability qualifications, for example that the finance documents are subject to the laws affecting creditors' rights generally. In the sample document these qualifications are contained within the definition of Reservations.

18.3   **Non-conflict with other obligations**

The entry into and performance by it of, and the transactions contemplated by, the Finance Documents do not and will not conflict with:

18.3.1   any law or regulation applicable to it;

18.3.2   the constitutional documents of any member of the Group; or

18.3.3   any agreement or instrument binding upon it or any member of the Group or any of its or any member of the Group's assets.

18.4   **Power and authority**

It has the power to enter into, perform and deliver, and has taken all necessary action to authorise its entry into, performance and delivery of, the Finance Documents to which it is a party and the transactions contemplated by those Finance Documents.

18.5   **Validity and admissibility in evidence**

All Authorisations required or desirable:

18.5.1   to enable it lawfully to enter into, exercise its rights and comply with its obligations in the Finance Documents to which it is a party; and

18.5.2   to make the Finance Documents to which it is a party admissible in evidence in its jurisdiction of incorporation,

have been obtained or effected and are in full force and effect.

18.6   **Governing law and enforcement**

18.6.1   The choice of English law as the governing law of the Finance Documents will be recognised and enforced in its jurisdiction of incorporation.

18.6.2   Any judgment obtained in England in relation to a Finance Document will be recognised and enforced in its jurisdiction of incorporation.

18.7   **Deduction of Tax**

It is not required under the law of its jurisdiction of incorporation to make any deduction for or on account of Tax from any payment it may make under any Finance Document.

18.8   **No filing or stamp taxes**

Under the law of its jurisdiction of incorporation it is not necessary that the Finance Documents be filed, recorded or enrolled with any court or other authority in that jurisdiction or that any stamp, registration or similar tax be paid on or in relation to the Finance Documents or the transactions contemplated by the Finance Documents.

18.9   **No default**

18.9.1   No Event of Default is continuing or might reasonably be expected to result from the making of any Utilisation.

18.9.2   No other event or circumstance is outstanding which constitutes a default under any other agreement or instrument which is binding on it or any of its Subsidiaries or to which its (or its Subsidiaries') assets are subject which might have a Material Adverse Effect.

> **Borrower:** *The borrower should note that the event of default representation should not be permitted to extend to potential events of default (ie events which with the passage of time, giving of notice or fulfilment of any other condition would become an event of default. If a representation that there is no potential default is repeated when a potential event of default is outstanding then this would itself create an event of default even though the underlying circumstances do not.*

18.10   No misleading information

18.10.1   Any factual information provided by it pursuant to Clause 4 (*Conditions of Utilisation*) was true and accurate in all material respects as at the date it was provided or as at the date (if any) at which it is stated.

18.10.2   The financial projections delivered pursuant to Clause 4 (*Conditions of Utilisation*) have been prepared on the basis of recent historical information and on the basis of reasonable assumptions.

18.10.3   Nothing has occurred or been omitted from the information and projections referred to above and no information has been given or withheld that results in the information and projections referred to above being untrue or misleading in any material respect.

18.11   Financial statements

18.11.1   Its Original Financial Statements were prepared in accordance with GAAP consistently applied [unless expressly disclosed to the contrary].

18.11.2   Its Original Financial Statements fairly represent its financial condition and operations (consolidated if appropriate) during the relevant financial year [unless expressly disclosed to the contrary].

18.11.3   There has been no material adverse change in its business or financial condition (or the business or consolidated financial condition of the Group) since [   ].

18.12   No proceedings pending or threatened

No litigation, arbitration or administrative proceedings of or before any court, arbitral body or agency which, if adversely determined, might reasonably be expected to have a Material Adverse Effect have (to the best of its knowledge and belief) been started or threatened against it or any of its Subsidiaries.

18.13   **Pari passu ranking**

Its payment obligations under the Finance Documents rank at least pari passu with the claims of all its other unsecured and unsubordinated creditors, except for obligations mandatorily preferred by law applying to companies generally.

Purpose: This clause applies even in secured facilities notwithstanding that it refers to unsecured indebtedness. It is an assurance that the lender's rights will, if the security fails, rank pari passu with the rights of the borrower's own unsecured creditors. It should be noted that the clause applies to existing as well as future obligations. Its relevance comes if there is a shortfall in the security on enforcement or if the security is for any reason defective.

Lender: The lender's objective is to ensure that its loan is not subordinated to another lender on insolvency. Most lenders are aware that there will be certain priority rankings stipulated by law[3] and will not contest this. In addition, the clause serves as a means of flushing out the extent of the borrower's existing borrowings, although the lender should be making its own enquiries by, at the very least, carrying out a search of the borrower's charges register at Companies House (if it is a United Kingdom company).

Borrower: As mentioned above this clause is rarely contested. The borrower must make sure that it is factually correct and will want to ensure that the mandatory preference qualification is included.

18.14   **Ranking of security**

The security conferred by the Debenture constitutes a first priority security interest of the type therein described over the security assets therein referred to which are not subject to any prior or pari passu Security.

18.15   **Title to Properties**

The Borrower is the legal and beneficial owner of the Property and has good and marketable title to the Property free from Security (other than those permitted under the Finance Documents), restrictions and onerous covenants, and all deeds and documents necessary to show good and marketable title to those interests in the Property are in the possession of, or held at an appropriate Land Registry to the order of, the Lender.

---

3   Under the Insolvency Act 1986, s 386 certain creditors will be entitled to preferential payments which rank ahead of general unsecured creditors and floating charge holders. The categories of preferential creditor include Inland Revenue, HM Customs & Excise, pensions and employees.

18.16   **Registration requirements**

Except for due registration of the Debenture under s 395 of the Companies Act 1985 and under the Land Registration Acts 1925 to 1986, it is not necessary that any of the Finance Documents be filed, recorded or enrolled with ally authority or that any stamp, registration or similar tax be paid on or in respect thereof.

18.17   **Valuation**

18.17.1   To the best of its knowledge and belief (after due enquiry) all information provided by it or on its behalf to the Valuer for the purposes of each Valuation was true, complete and accurate in all material respects as at its date.

18.17.2   The information did not omit as at its date any information which, if disclosed, might materially and adversely affect the Valuation.

18.17.3   Nothing has occurred since the date the information was provided which, if it had occurred prior to that Valuation, might have materially and adversely affected that Valuation.

18.18   **Repetition**

The Repeating Representations are deemed to be made by the Borrower by reference to the facts and circumstances then existing on the date of each Utilisation Request and the first day of each Interest Period.

__Purpose:__ This clause extends the life of the representations and warranties so that they apply not only on the date the loan is executed but also periodically throughout the duration of the loan agreement. They are often referred to as 'evergreen' representations and warranties. Commentary on which representations should be repeated can be found under the definition of 'Repeating Representations' on page 31.

__Lender:__ Some lenders expect the representations and warranties to apply and to be repeated daily throughout the life of the loan agreement. Most lenders will, however, accept a repetition of representations and warranties on days when further amounts are drawn down (ie as a condition precedent to further drawing) and on interest payment dates.

__Borrower:__ The borrower would prefer the representations and warranties to apply on the date of execution and on the date of drawing of the first advance and in no other circumstances. The rationale is that the borrower has examined the accuracy of the statements as at that specific time and cannot know in the future whether the statements will be true and correct. Most lenders will not accept this argument because the risk of circumstances changing should be on the borrower. The borrower will usually be able to find some middle ground, namely to give the representations and warranties on the date of execution, each drawdown and on interest payment dates. In addition, to lessen the burden of this *clause, the borrower should try and have wording inserted stating that the representations and warranties should be examined with reference to the facts and circumstances existing as at the time that they are deemed to be repeated.*

The borrower might try to argue that if the lender is so concerned that these representations and warranties need to be repeated (to provide protection against change in circumstances) they should be inserted as events of default rather than as representations and warranties. Whilst this suggestion may make some sense, the net effect is similar to having them repeated; as if they are breached, there will be an Event of Default. The principal difference is that because the representations are repeated only, say, quarterly, they are less likely to be breached than an equivalent default.

19 Information Undertakings

The undertakings in this Clause 19 remain in force from the date of this Agreement for so long as any amount is outstanding under the Finance Documents or any part of the Facility Commitment is in force.

19.1 Financial statements

The Borrower shall supply to the Lender:

19.1.1   as soon as the same become available, but in any event within [   ] days after the end of each of its financial years its audited consolidated financial statements for that financial year; and

19.1.2   as soon as the same become available, but in any event within [   ] days after the end of each half of each of its financial years its consolidated financial statements for that financial half year.

19.2 Compliance certificate

19.2.1   The Borrower shall supply to the Lender, with each set of financial statements delivered pursuant to Clauses 19.1.1 and 19.1.2 (*Financial statements*), a compliance certificate setting out (in reasonable detail) computations as to compliance with Clause 20 (*Financial covenants*) as at the date as at which those financial statements were drawn up.

19.2.2   Each compliance certificate shall be signed by two directors of the Borrower and, if required to be delivered with the financial statements delivered pursuant to Clause 19.1.1 (*Financial statements*), [shall be reported on by the Borrower's auditors in the form agreed by the Borrower and the Lender before the date of this Agreement]/[by the Borrower's auditors].

19.3   **Requirements as to financial statements**

19.3.1   Each set of financial statements delivered by the Borrower pursuant
             to Clause 19.1 (*Financial statements*) shall be certified by a director of
             the relevant company as fairly representing its financial condition as
             at the date as at which those financial statements were drawn up.

19.3.2   The Borrower shall procure that each set of financial statements
             delivered pursuant to Clause 19.1 (*Financial statements*) is prepared
             using GAAP.

19.4   **Information: miscellaneous**

             The Borrower shall supply to the Lender:

19.4.1   all documents dispatched by the Borrower to its shareholders (or
             any class of them) or its creditors generally at the same time as they
             are dispatched;

19.4.2   promptly upon becoming aware of them, the details of any
             litigation, arbitration or administrative proceedings which are
             current, threatened or pending against the Borrower, and which
             might, if adversely determined, have a Material Adverse Effect; and

19.4.3   promptly, such further information regarding the financial con-
             dition, business and operations of the Borrower as the Lender may
             reasonably request.

19.5   **Notification of default**

19.5.1   The Borrower shall notify the Lender of any Default (and the steps,
             if any, being taken to remedy it) promptly upon becoming aware of
             its occurrence.

19.5.2   Promptly upon a request by the Lender, the Borrower shall supply
             to the Lender a certificate signed by two of its directors or senior
             officers on its behalf certifying that no Default is continuing (or if a
             Default is continuing, specifying the Default and the steps, if any,
             being taken to remedy it).

             Purpose: *Most agreements will contain covenants obliging the borrower to
             provide the lender with all types of information from accounts (audited
             and management) to information disclosed to shareholders. It is also
             common to require the borrower to submit compliance certificates
             confirming that the financial covenants are being met.*

             *The prime purpose is to ensure that the lender knows exactly what is going
             on so that it can monitor the loan throughout its duration. The borrower
             has to examine what it can and cannot realistically provide to the lender
             and a balance has to be reached between burdening the borrower too
             heavily with obligations to provide information and providing the lender
             with sufficient information to monitor the borrower's business.*

Where the loan agreement requires the borrower's auditors to certify compliance with financial covenants a dialogue will be needed with the auditors. Generally, they will be unwilling to certify without separately engaging with the lender. This will entail additional fees which the borrower will be expected to pay. Accordingly, as borrower you should seek to persuade the lender that auditors' certifications are unnecessary.

[19.6   **Use of websites**

19.6.1   The Borrower may satisfy its obligation under this Agreement to deliver any information to the Lender by posting this information onto an electronic website designated by the Borrower and the Lender (the **'Designated Website'**) if:

(a) the Lender expressly agrees that it will accept communication of the information by this method;

(b) both the Borrower and the Lender are aware of the address of and any relevant password specifications for the Designated Website; and

(c) the information is in a format previously agreed between the Borrower and the Lender.

19.6.2   The Borrower shall promptly upon becoming aware of its occurrence notify the Lender if:

(a) the Designated Website cannot be accessed due to technical failure;

(b) the password specifications for the Designated Website change;

(c) any new information which is required to be provided under this Agreement is posted onto the Designated Website;

(d) any existing information which has been provided under this Agreement and posted onto the Designated Website is amended; or

(e) the Borrower becomes aware that the Designated Website or any information posted onto the Designated Website is or has been infected by any electronic virus or similar software.

If the Borrower notifies the Lender under Clause 19.6.2(a) or Clause 19.6.2(e) above, all information to be provided by the Borrower under this Agreement after the date of that notice shall be supplied in paper form [unless and until the Lender is satisfied that the circumstances giving rise to the notification are no longer continuing].

19.6.3   The Lender may request one paper copy of any information required to be provided under this Agreement which is posted onto the Designated Website. The Borrower shall comply with any such request within ten Business Days.]

Purpose: This clause allows information to be delivered electronically which will be appropriate where there is a large quantity of information to convey. For larger syndicated facilities, electronic information dissemination is extremely helpful. However, for most bilateral facilities there should be no need unless, for example, the security assets are numerous and require intensive monitoring.

20   Financial Covenants

20.1   Ratio of rental income to debt service

20.1.1   The Borrower shall ensure that at all times projected annual rental is no less than 125 per cent of projected annual finance costs.

20.1.2   If at any time the Borrower is in breach of Clause 20.1.1, the Lender may prohibit the transfer to the General Account of surplus amounts standing to the credit of the Rent Account in accordance with Clause 11.2.4 (*Rent Account*) until such time as projected annual rental is equal to or greater than 125 per cent of semi-annual finance costs.

20.1.3   For the purposes of this Clause 20.1:

(a) '**projected annual rental**' means, an estimate by the Lender, at any time, of the aggregate of the net rental income from the Property paid into the Rent Account with respect to the immediately preceding 12 month period except that, to the extent that 12 month period covers a period (the '**shorter period**') prior to the establishment of the Rent Account, semi-annual rental will mean net rental income received by the Borrowers during that shorter period plus net rental income the Borrowers received during the balance of the 12 month period; and

(b) '**projected annual finance costs**' means on each date that the Lender calculates projected annual rental, the Lender's estimate of the aggregate amount (excluding principal) payable to the Lender under the Finance Documents with respect to the immediately succeeding 12 month period.

20.1.4   On request by the Borrower, the Lender shall notify the Borrower of any calculation the Lender makes of projected annual rental and projected annual finance costs. The Lender may notify the Borrower if as a result of any calculation, the Lender considers that the Borrowers are in breach of Clause 20.1.1 above or if the provisions of Clause 20.1.2 above are operative.

Purpose: Generally, the purpose of the covenants clauses is to monitor the financial condition of the borrower throughout the duration of the facility and to test it at regular intervals. If drafted effectively, these covenants will serve as alarm bells for the lender who can then either negotiate with the borrower to rectify the situation before it gets out of hand, or cancel the facility and trigger the security before it is too late. The examples given above are common in real estate banking transactions and focus on the income produced by the property relative to debt servicing costs and the value of the property relative to the principal amount outstanding.

The sample debt service cover test is a lock-up test which means that breach of the clause prevents the borrower accessing surplus income; it does not create an Event of Default. In contrast, breach of the loan to value test does result in an Event of Default. This is for illustrative purposes only and it would generally be the case that any covenant would be an event of default.

Lender: *The financial covenants should define the financial parameters within which the borrower's business can operate and with which the lender feels comfortable. A balance must be established and the lender must be practical. Financial covenants which are too stringent will not be effective as they will result in premature breaches by the borrower. The lender should seek to obtain a degree of control and a reasonable level of comfort, so that it can take pre-emptive action if necessary when things start to go wrong.*

Borrower: *If the financial covenants are too onerous and stringent, the borrower will be unable to conduct its business effectively. Where the financial covenants go beyond the examples given above and are concerned more with the financial health of the company than the value of assets (which would be the case for a leveraged buyout loan, for example), it is crucial that its finance director (and possibly external accountant) plays an active role in the discussion and negotiation of the clauses as he will usually have a more thorough understanding of the borrower's finances than a lawyer or commercial director would and will know what covenants can and cannot be complied with. If the financial covenants are impractical from the borrower's perspective, their breach may give lenders additional opportunities for renegotiating terms and increasing fees.*

As a borrower, it is often worth arguing for a remedy arrangement for breach of financial covenant, particularly in the context of real estate finance. If there is a breach of income cover or asset cover then there is little that the lender can do about it in the short term and he may well be better off giving the borrower a reasonable period (for example 30 days) in which to prepay sufficient of the loan to remedy the breach or put up additional cash collateral or security properties. This kind of approach is much less appropriate in corporate facilities where the covenants measure the financial health of the borrower and asset cover is not good. In such cases, it is vital that the lender should be able to take quick action, especially since covenants of that nature are inevitably measured on the basis of historic information.

The covenants shown above are standard in real estate banking transactions. In corporate lending there will be many others. Some examples of other financial covenants are as follows:

Minimum net worth: This is a number reflecting the book value of the borrower's assets net of liabilities. Net worth is normally defined as comprising paid-up share capital and revenue reserves less intangible assets such as goodwill. The value of the net assets of the borrower (the right-hand side of the balance sheet) is therefore defined by reference to the amount of its share capital and reserves (the left-hand side of the balance sheet).

Gearing covenant: This is the ratio of net worth to liabilities and it indicates the amount of assets available to meet liabilities.

Interest cover ratio: This is the ratio of profit before interest and tax (PBIT) to interest payable and it is useful to monitor whether the borrower is able to service the interest on the loan. This is particularly important when interest rates are rising.

Total borrowings (financial indebtedness): This provides that the total borrowing or financial indebtedness of the borrower should not exceed a certain figure.

Current ratio: This is the ratio of current assets to current liabilities and provides an indication of the strength of the borrower's cash flow.

21   General Undertakings

The undertakings in this Clause 21 remain in force from the date of this Agreement for so long as any amount is outstanding under the Finance Documents or any Commitment is in force.

21.1   Authorisations

The Borrower shall promptly:

21.1.1   obtain, comply with and do all that is necessary to maintain in full force and effect; and

21.1.2   supply certified copies to the Lender of,

any Authorisation required under any law or regulation of its jurisdiction of incorporation to enable it to perform its obligations under the Finance Documents and to ensure the legality, validity, enforceability or admissibility in evidence in its jurisdiction of incorporation of any Finance Document.

21.2   Compliance with laws

The Borrower shall comply in all respects with all laws to which it may be subject, if failure so to comply would materially impair its ability to perform its obligations under the Finance Documents.

21.3   Negative pledge

21.3.1   The Borrower shall not create or permit to subsist any Security over any of its assets other than Permitted Security.

21.3.2   The Borrower shall not:

(a) sell, transfer or otherwise dispose of any of its assets on terms whereby they are or may be leased to or re-acquired by the Borrower;

(b) sell, transfer or otherwise dispose of any of its receivables on recourse terms;

(c) enter into any arrangement under which money or the benefit of a bank or other account may be applied, set-off or made subject to a combination of accounts; or

(d) enter into any other preferential arrangement having a similar effect,

in circumstances where the arrangement or transaction is entered into primarily as a method of raising Financial Indebtedness or of financing the acquisition of an asset other than Permitted Financial Indebtedness.

Purpose: This is a fundamental clause in both secured and unsecured financing. In unsecured financing it protects the lender from being subordinated to subsequent secured creditors and in secured financing it assists the lender in maintaining its priority position and avoids potential conflicts with subsequent security holders. The negative pledge prevents the borrower from raising secured finance thus giving the lender a degree of control over the borrower. However, it is important to be aware that the negative pledge operates in contract and security created in breach of it may be valid.

Lender: Lenders are aware that in certain circumstances the borrower will need to grant some form of security and exemptions are often permitted thus ensuring that the borrower is able to conduct its business effectively. It is common as in the sample agreement to include these within a defined term such as Permitted Security. A lender is more likely to insist on a restrictive negative pledge where the borrower is a special purpose vehicle.

Many negative pledge clauses in unsecured facilities contain provisions providing that, if the borrower creates a security interest (in breach of the negative pledge clause), then the obligations of the borrower will automatically and immediately be secured upon the same assets. This is the equal and rateable clause. The precise effect and meaning of this clause (and whether it gives the lender an equitable interest in the asset) has been the subject of much academic debate;[4] but even if the clause is ineffective in that regard, it does trigger an Event of Default if breached.

There has also been discussion as to whether the existence alone of the negative pledge in a loan agreement is sufficient to impute constructive notice on any purported subsequent chargee where there has been a breach

---

4   See, for example, RM Goode *Legal Problems of Credit and Security* (Sweet & Maxwell, 1988), pp 17–23 and Penn and Haynes *Law and Practice of International Banking* 2nd edn (Sweet & Maxwell).

of this clause.[5] *As the law stands, constructive notice of a negative pledge could be imputed to a person who has failed to make such enquiries as in all the circumstances he ought reasonably to have made. Professionally advised persons might reasonably be expected to check the records at Companies House, for example.*

In secured loans the lender should prevent further security being granted to another lender, although such further security would normally rank behind the first lender's security in terms of priority, it may still prejudice the first lender's rights. For example, the second creditor will have independent rights of enforcement which it could exercise in a manner which is inconvenient for the first lender. Normally, the lender will grant permission to create a second security provided that a deed of priority or intercreditor agreement is entered into specifying when the second lender can enforce its rights. There may also be serious implications where the lender is not under an obligation to make further advances to the borrower.

Borrower: *The sensible borrower realises that this clause is vitally important to all lenders and that it is therefore impossible to remove in its entirety. However, it is crucial that the borrower is able to conduct its business and therefore the borrower should strenuously argue for the following (obviously depending on its peculiar circumstances):*

- *the negative pledge should apply to the borrowing entity only and not to its subsidiaries or parent. Obviously, where there is a group facility the lender will want all the relative companies tied in;*
- *security of 'de minimis' value should be permitted. This would allow the creation of security for indebtedness not to exceed a certain amount which the lender deems insignificant;*
- *security interests which arise during the normal course of business such as the pledging of bills of lading and other documents of title, any liens arising by operation of law in the normal course of business, any security created in favour of the lender and possibly also retention of title claims, rights of set-off and assets required whilst encumbered with existing security interests. There are various liens which arise by operation of law such as a common law lien entitling someone who has done work for another to retain goods in his possession, for example banker, lawyer, repairer, equitable lien, possessory lien and statutory lien;*
- *the borrower should be permitted to create security with the consent of the lender (sometimes though rarely such consent not to be unreasonably withheld or delayed); and*
- *the negative pledge should only restrict the creation of security interests which rank in priority to or pari passu with the lender's security (ie the borrower should be able to create subordinated debt) – though generally a lender would expect any subsequent creditor to*

---

5   See Lingard *Banking Security Documents* 3rd edn (Butterworths, 1993), paras 1.6 et seq.

*enter into a subordination deed regulating its enforcement and
repayment.*

*The most commonly-conceded carve outs appear in the definition of
Permitted Security.*

21.4   **No Financial Indebtedness**

The Borrower shall not incur Financial Indebtedness other than
Permitted Financial Indebtedness.

21.5   **Disposals**

The Borrower shall not enter into a single transaction or a series of
transactions (whether related or not) and whether voluntary or
involuntary to sell, lease, transfer or otherwise dispose of any asset
other than Permitted Disposals.

***Purpose:** This clause seeks to prevent the borrower from selling any of its
assets and thereby diminishing the value of the security granted to the
lender. This clause will almost certainly be contained in the security
documents as well. The clause must operate in conjunction with the
negative pledge (ie restriction against creating further security) and the
pari passu clause, as it would generally be inconsistent to allow the
borrower to dispose of its assets on the one hand and not allow it to grant
security on the other.*

***Lender:** This clause, like the negative pledge clause, provides the lender
with a certain degree of control. With unsecured lending, the value of the
borrower's assets and the fact that these should be maintained is crucial.
The clause is widely drafted and covers disposals which might be
individually small but collectively substantial.*

***Borrower:** The borrower must ensure that it can conduct its business
effectively and, in addition to negotiating 'carve outs' analogous to those
in the negative pledge clause (see the definition of Permitted Disposals),
the borrower should try to negotiate:*

- *a 'de minimis' figure (ie that the borrower should be entitled to sell
  assets provided that they do not exceed a certain amount in value);*
- *that the borrower should be entitled to dispose of assets in the
  ordinary course of its trade (generally lenders will find ordinary
  course of business to be too wide since this arguably extends to every
  type of activity the borrower's memorandum of association permits);*
- *that the borrower should be able to replace obsolete assets with
  equivalent or better assets; and*
- *that the borrower should be able to dispose of assets within its group
  (ie to its parent company or subsidiaries).*

21.6   **Merger**

The Borrower shall not enter into any amalgamation, demerger, merger or corporate reconstruction.

21.7   **Change of business**

The Borrower shall procure that no substantial change is made to the general nature of its business from that carried on at the date of this Agreement.

22   Property Undertakings

22.1   **Duration**

The undertakings in this Clause 22 (*Property undertakings*) remain in force from the date of this Agreement for so long as any amount is or may be outstanding under this Agreement or any part of the Facility Commitment is in force.

22.2   **Occupational Leases**

22.2.1 The Borrower shall not without the consent of the Lender (such consent not to be unreasonably withheld or delayed where, under the terms of any Lease Document, the consent of the Borrower cannot be unreasonably withheld or delayed):

(a) enter into any Agreement for Lease;
(b) grant or agree to grant any new Occupational Lease;
(c) agree to any amendment or waiver or surrender in respect of any Agreement for Lease or Occupational Lease;
(d) commence any forfeiture proceedings in respect of any Occupational Lease;
(e) grant any new contractual licence or right to occupy any part of any Property after the date of this Agreement;
(f) consent to any assignment of any tenant's interest under any Agreement for Lease or Occupational Lease;
(g) agree to any rent reviews in respect of any Occupational Lease; or
(h) serve any notice on any former tenant under any Occupational Lease under s 17(2) of the Landlord and Tenant (Covenants) Act 1995 or on any guarantor of any such former tenant under s 17(3) of that Act.

22.2.2 The Borrower shall use its reasonable endeavours to find tenants for any vacant lettable space in the Property with a view to granting Agreements for Lease or Occupational Leases of that space.

22.2.3 The Borrower shall not grant or agree to grant any new Occupational Lease without including in the alienation covenant a provision for the proposed assignor on any assignment to guarantee the obligations of the proposed assignee until that assignor is released as tenant under the terms of the Landlord and Tenant (Covenants) Act 1995.

22.3   **Monitoring of Property**

22.3.1   The Borrower shall provide to the Lender, on the last day of each successive quarterly period, the first of which shall commence on the date of this Agreement, the following information (in form and substance satisfactory to the Lender in respect of that quarterly period):

(a) a schedule of the existing occupational tenants of the Property showing for each tenant the rent, service charge, value added tax and any other payments payable (and, separately, paid) in that period by each of those tenants;

(b) copies of any management accounts and management cash-flows produced by or for the Borrower;

(c) details of any arrears of rent or service charges under any Occupational Lease and any steps being taken to recover them;

(d) details of any rent reviews with respect to any Occupational Lease in progress or agreed;

(e) details of any Occupational Lease which has expired or been determined or surrendered and any new lettings proposed;

(f) copies of all material correspondence with insurance brokers handling the insurance of the Property;

(g) details of any proposed capital expenditure with respect to the Property;

(h) details of any material repairs required to the Property; and

(i) details of situations where it has become entitled to serve any notice on any former tenant of any Occupational Lease under s 17(2) of the Landlord and Tenant (Covenants) Act 1995 or on any guarantor of any such former tenant under s 17(3) of that Act.

22.3.2   The Borrower will notify the Lender of:

(a) any potential occupational tenant of the Property or any part of it;

(b) each meeting at which the marketing of the Property or any part of it will be discussed and the minutes of such meeting; and

(c) any potential buyer of the Property or any part of it (including terms of reference).

22.4   **Managing agents**

22.4.1   The Borrower shall not appoint any managing agent of the Property without the prior written consent of, and on terms approved by, the Lender.

22.4.2   The Borrower shall procure that each managing agent of any Property enters a duty of care agreement with the Lender in form and substance satisfactory to the Lender and acknowledges to the Lender that it has notice of the Security Interests created by the Finance Documents and that it agrees to pay all Net Rental Income received by it into the Rent Account without withholding, set-off, or counterclaim.

22.4.3   If the managing agent is in default in its obligations under the management agreement to an extent entitling the Borrower to rescind or terminate that contract, then if the Lender so requires the Borrower will promptly terminate that contract and appoint a new managing agent approved, as to identity and terms of appointment, by the Lender.

22.5   **Insurances**

22.5.1   The Borrower shall effect or procure to be effected:

   (a) insurance of the Property and the plant and machinery on the Property including fixtures and improvements on a full reinstatement basis, including, without limitation, site clearance, professional fees, value added tax, subsidence and riot and less than three years' loss of rent on all occupational tenancies of the Property;
   (b) third party liability insurances;
   (c) insurance against acts of terrorism; and
   (d) such insurance as a prudent company in the same business as the Borrower would effect,

all such insurances to be in amount and in form and with an insurance company or underwriters acceptable to the Lender (acting reasonably).

22.5.2   The Borrower will procure that the Lender is named as co-insured on all insurance policies required under paragraph (a) above. Every such policy shall contain:

   (a) a standard mortgagee clause whereby such insurance shall not be vitiated or avoided as against the Lender in the event or as a result of any misrepresentation, act or neglect or failure to make disclosure on the part of any insured party or any circumstances beyond the control of an insured party; and
   (b) terms providing that it shall not be invalidated so far as the Agent is concerned for failure to pay any premium due without the insurer first giving to the Agent not less than 14 days' written notice.

22.5.3   The Borrower will use its best endeavours to procure that there be given to the Agent such information in connection with the insurances and copies of the policies as the Lender may reasonably require and will notify the Lender of renewals made and variations or cancellations of policies made or, to its knowledge, threatened or pending.

22.5.4 The Borrower shall not do or permit anything to be done which may make void or voidable any insurance policy in connection with any part of the Property.

22.5.5 The Borrower shall procure prompt payment all premiums and all other things necessary to keep all of the insurances policies in force.

22.5.6 If the Borrower fails to comply with any of the provisions of this Clause 22.5 (*Insurances*), the Lender shall immediately be entitled to effect the insurances concerned at the expense of the Borrower.

22.5.7 Subject to paragraph 22.5.8 below, the Borrower shall apply all moneys received or receivable under any insurance in respect of the Property towards replacing, restoring or reinstating the Property or towards compensating the applicable third party, as appropriate.

22.5.8 To the extent that the relevant insurance policy and the Agreements for Lease and the Occupational Leases do not restrict the proceeds of insurance being used to prepay the Loans, the proceeds of insurance shall be used, at the option of the Lender, to prepay the Loans.

23   Events of Default

Each of the events or circumstances set out in Clause 23 is an Event of Default.

Purpose: This is a centrally important clause in the loan agreement. It is this clause which gives teeth to the covenants, representations and warranties and other clauses. It is the platform for the enforcement of the security. Without this clause the lender is unable to terminate the facility, prevent further advances or accelerate existing outstanding amounts.

Events of Default will vary for each type of transaction and, unfortunately from the borrower's perspective, are rather extensive. Within transaction types there is a degree of commonality and the defaults given in this sample agreement are typical for a real estate banking transaction.

23.1   **Non-payment**

The Borrower does not pay on the due date any amount payable pursuant to a Finance Document at the place at and in the currency in which it is expressed to be payable unless:

23.1.1 its failure to pay is caused by administrative or technical error; and

23.1.2 payment is made within two Business Days of its due date.

Lender: This is probably the most fundamental clause to the lender (ie that it receives payment of interest and any other amount payable under the loan agreement on the due date). Most lenders will never negotiate this clause because of its importance.

Borrower: The borrower may try to distinguish between interest payments and principal payments and may be able in some circumstances to obtain a longer grace period for interest payments before the lender may enforce. Occasionally, the borrower may obtain a grace period even where there has not been a technical or administrative error.

23.2   **Financial covenants**

Any requirement of Clause 20 (*Financial covenants*) is not satisfied.

It is unusual to include a grace period for the breach of financial covenant default because the financial covenants should themselves contain grace periods for remedy to the extent that it is appropriate.

23.3   **Other obligations**

23.3.1   The Borrower does not comply with any provision of the Finance Documents (other than those referred to in Clause 23.1 (*Non-payment*) and Clause 23.2 (*Financial covenants*)).

23.3.2   No Event of Default under Clause 23.3.1 above (except in relation to Clauses 21 (*General undertakings*), 22.2 (*Occupational Leases*) and 22.5 (*Insurances*)) will occur if the failure to comply is capable of remedy and is remedied within:

(a)   (in relation to [   ]) [   ] Business Days; or
(b)   (in relation to [   ]) [   ] Business Days

of the earlier of the Lender giving notice to the Borrower or the Borrower becoming aware of the failure to comply.

Lender: This clause focuses on the defaults other than non-payment including breaches of covenant, undertaking and other terms of the facility. This clause gives teeth to the provisions of the loan agreement by giving the lender the ability to call a default on breach.

Borrower: The borrower should try to obtain a grace period in order to give it the opportunity to rectify the situation. Lenders do usually agree a grace period for most breaches and the sample clause assumes that different grace periods may be available for different breaches. It is likely that the lender will grant grace periods for most breaches whilst carving out some for instant default. This may be because the breach is particularly serious, for example breach of negative pledge, or because the covenant as drafted already contains a remedy period.

Although you might try to limit the breach to material breaches, thus avoiding the triggering of an Event of Default when an insignificant breach occurs, it is more likely that a lender would accept a materiality qualification to the covenant itself rather than the default.

23.4   **Misrepresentation**

Any representation or statement made or deemed to be made by the Borrower in the Finance Documents or any other document delivered by or on behalf of the Borrower under or in connection with any Finance Document is or proves to have been incorrect or misleading in any material respect when made or deemed to be made.

***Lender:** The lender will want this to apply to representations made at the outset of the loan as well as to those repeated during the continuance of the loan. As in the sample text it is usual to include in this Event of Default any representation or warranty which was made not just in the loan agreement but in any other documents; less common is inclusion of verbal discussions in connection with the loan agreement.*

***Borrower:** The borrower should ensure that the clause is limited to written statements made by the borrower. The borrower should also try to include a concept of materiality (so that only those statements which have a material effect should trigger the Event of Default). This is very commonly done as shown in the clause above.*

It is occasionally possible to obtain a grace period in respect of statements which have to be repeated. Generally, however, the lender will resist this, pointing out that the representations are (as a rule) repeated on interest payment dates only which itself operates as a kind of grace period.

23.5   **Cross-default**

23.5.1   Any Financial Indebtedness of the Borrower is not paid when due nor within any originally applicable grace period.

23.5.2   Any Financial Indebtedness of the Borrower is declared to be or otherwise becomes due and payable prior to its specified maturity as a result of an event of default (however described).

23.5.3   Any commitment for any Financial Indebtedness of the Borrower is cancelled or suspended by a creditor of the Borrower as a result of an event of default (however described).

23.5.4   Any creditor of the Borrower becomes entitled to declare any Financial Indebtedness of the Borrower due and payable prior to its specified maturity as a result of an event of default (however described).

23.5.5   No Event of Default will occur under this Clause 23.5 if the aggregate amount of Financial Indebtedness or commitment for Financial Indebtedness falling within Clauses 23.5.1 to 23.5.4 above is less than [   ] (or its equivalent in any other currency or currencies).

Purpose: *This clause creates an event of default under the loan agreement when the borrower (or other obligors or group companies) defaults under another financial facility. This is so even if there is no breach of the loan agreement.*

Lender: *This clause is extremely contentious because of the potential implications it has for the borrower's other facilities. The lender's concern is that, although its own loan may be performing, the borrower has defaulted under another loan and the lender is prevented from taking any pre-emptive action until there is an actual breach under its own facility. The cross default is the classic anticipatory Event of Default which gives the lender a seat at the negotiating table notwithstanding that its loan may not be in default per se.*

At the outset, the lender may want the clause to be drafted as widely as possible. However, it should be tempered with the fact that a clause drafted too extensively will prohibit the borrower from conducting business efficiently and trigger premature Events of Default. Where the borrower has granted a floating charge to the lender, this may crystallise that charge and the effect that this has on the borrower's ability to run its own business may be undesirable for both borrower and lender.

This clause is generally tied into the definition of financial indebtedness, which will usually be widely defined, so that any non-payment by the borrower of any monies will trigger the event.

In addition, the clause will be triggered if an Event of Default under another facility is capable of being called but has not actually been called. The clause will apply whether a loan has been accelerated or is capable of being accelerated. The advantage of the 'capable of' wording is that it gives the lender the benefit of all the other loan agreement covenants that the borrower has entered into.

Borrower: *In view of the serious consequences of the occurrence such a clause (ie the domino effect of all the borrower's loan facilities being triggered), it is crucial that the borrower mitigates and obtains some exemptions from its provisions. The borrower may be able to negotiate the following dilutions (most likely first):*

- *it should include a threshold amount thus allowing for default in respect of insignificant amounts such as those on the monthly bill for the corporate credit card or, in the case of larger credits, even smaller loan facilities;*
- *it may be possible to limit the triggering of the event to 'cross-acceleration events' (ie events which have actually led to the acceleration of the other plan) rather than events which are capable of being, but have not yet been, accelerated;*

- *rather than financial indebtedness it may be possible to limit the clause to borrowed monies or at least excluding monies which may be owing in the ordinary course of trade; and*
- *sometimes the lender may be persuaded that the clause should only apply in respect of non-payment defaults under other facilities and should therefore exclude breaches of representations, warranties and undertakings in other facilities.*

23.6   **Insolvency**

23.6.1   The Borrower is unable or admits inability to pay its debts as they fall due, suspends making payments on any of its debts or, by reason of actual or anticipated financial difficulties, commences negotiations with one or more of its creditors with a view to rescheduling any of its indebtedness.

23.6.2   The value of the assets of the Borrower is less than its liabilities (taking into account contingent and prospective liabilities).

23.6.3   A moratorium is declared in respect of any indebtedness of the Borrower.

23.7   **Insolvency proceedings**

Any corporate action, legal proceedings or other procedure or step is taken in relation to:

23.7.1   the suspension of payments, a moratorium of any indebtedness, winding-up, dissolution, administration or reorganisation (by way of voluntary arrangement, scheme of arrangement or otherwise) of the Borrower;

23.7.2   a composition, assignment or arrangement with any creditor of any member of the Group;

23.7.3   the appointment of a liquidator, receiver, administrator, administrative receiver, compulsory manager or other similar officer in respect of the Borrower or any of its assets; or

23.7.4   enforcement of any Security over any assets of the Borrower,

or any analogous procedure or step is taken in any jurisdiction.

23.8   **Creditors' process**

Any expropriation, attachment, sequestration, distress or execution affects any asset or assets of the Borrower and is not discharged within [   ] days.

Purpose: *These clauses are usually very widely drafted to catch every step in a potential insolvency process.*

Lender: *The petitioning for the appointment of an administrator must always be included as an Event of Default so that on the occurrence of* *such event the secured debt becomes immediately due and payable which thereby entitles the lender to appoint an administrative receiver to block the appointment of an administrator.*

Borrower: *It is very difficult to negotiate these clauses and yet lenders will often accept the following type of 'carve outs':*

- *the 'step' taken against the borrower (usually a petition) should be bona fide (good faith) and not vexatious;*
- *the borrower should be given a grace period within which to discharge petitions or creditors' processes; and*
- *petitions and creditors' processes which are being contested in good faith should be excluded.*

23.9   **Unlawfulness**

It is or becomes unlawful for the Borrower to perform any of its obligations under the Finance Documents.

23.10   **Repudiation**

The Borrower repudiates a Finance Document or evidences an intention to repudiate a Finance Document.

23.11   **Compulsory purchase**

All or any part of the Property is compulsorily purchased or the applicable local authority makes an order for the compulsory purchase of the same where such purchase might have a material adverse effect on the business or financial condition of the Borrower or on the ability of the Borrower to perform its obligations under the Transaction Documents to which it is or will become a party.

23.12   **Major damage**

All or any part of the Property is destroyed or is damaged to an extent such that, taking into account the proceeds of insurance effected under Clause 22.5 (*Insurances*) and the timing of receipt of those proceeds, in the opinion of the Lender that destruction or damage will have a material and adverse effect on the financial condition of the Borrower or on the ability of the Borrower to comply with its obligations under the Transaction Documents.

23.13   **Forfeiture**

Any action is taken, or any proceedings are commenced, to forfeit any Headlease.

23.14   **Material adverse change**

Any circumstances arise which in the opinion of the Lender give grounds for belief that the Borrower may not (or may be unable to) perform, or comply with, its obligations under any Finance Document to which it is a party.

Lender: This is a difficult Event of Default for the lender to negotiate as it is a 'sweep up' provision designed to catch any event which has not been properly or adequately dealt with by the other Events of Default. The attraction of this clause to the lender is that it allows acceleration of the loan when a specific Event of Default has not actually occurred but the lender believes that the condition of the borrower is deteriorating.

Borrower: This clause is usually very unpopular with borrowers as it leaves them rather exposed and unable to define at the outset what situations might trigger the event. The subjectivity of the clause also gives rise to concern. If there is no actual default then the lender should remain committed. What are the financial covenants for?!

The borrower should try to mitigate the harshness of this clause either by trying to delete it completely or by insisting that the lender should act reasonably in the exercise of this clause. The borrower should also argue that the material and adverse change cited should have a direct effect on the ability of the borrower to comply with its financial obligations under the loan rather than merely a material change in the borrower's business as, arguably, in some instances this may have no effect on the borrower's ability to perform its financial obligations under the loan facility. In addition, the borrower may want to limit the application of this clause to the borrowing entity only and not to its subsidiaries or other members of the group.

23.15   **Acceleration**

On and at any time after the occurrence of an Event of Default which is continuing the Lender may by notice to the Borrower:

23.15.1   cancel the Facility Commitment whereupon it shall immediately be cancelled;

23.15.2   declare that all or part of the Loans, together with accrued interest, and all other amounts accrued or outstanding under the Finance Documents be immediately due and payable, whereupon they shall become immediately due and payable; and/or

23.15.3   declare that all or part of the Loans be payable on demand, whereupon they shall immediately become payable on demand by the Lender.

Purpose: This clause gives the lender the opportunity to terminate its obligation to provide any further advances (only relevant in a revolving facility or where the loan has not been fully drawn down), to call for

repayment of the principal of and interest on the loan and to suspend further advances. In contrast with, for example, the ISDA standard documentation governing swaps transactions there are no events which lead to an automatic acceleration or termination.

This is not a contentious clause and is seldom negotiated. Obviously, calling in the loan is a last resort which will trigger Events of Default in other facilities if there are any (by means of cross-default) and may lead to insolvency proceedings.

24   Changes to the Lenders

24.1   Assignments by the Lenders

Subject to this Clause 24, a Lender (the '**Existing Lender**') may assign any of its rights to another bank or financial institution [or to a trust, fund or other entity which is regularly engaged in or established for the purpose of making, purchasing or investing in loans, securities or other financial assets] (the '**New Lender**').

24.2   Conditions of assignment

24.2.1   The consent of the Borrower is required for an assignment by the Lender, unless the assignment or transfer is to an Affiliate of the Lender.

24.2.2   The consent of the Borrower to an assignment or transfer must not be unreasonably withheld or delayed. The Borrower will be deemed to have given its consent five Business Days after the Lender has requested it unless consent is expressly refused by the Borrower within that time.

24.2.3   The consent of the Borrower to an assignment or transfer must not be withheld solely because the assignment or transfer may result in an increase to the Mandatory Cost.

24.2.4   If:

(a) the Lender assigns any of its rights or obligations under the Finance Documents or changes its Facility Office; and

(b) as a result of circumstances existing at the date the assignment or change occurs, the Borrower would be obliged to make a payment to the New Lender or the Lender acting through its new Facility Office under Clause 13 (*Tax Gross-up and Indemnities*) or Clause 14 (*Increased Costs*),

then the New Lender or the Lender acting through its new Facility Office is only entitled to receive payment under those Clauses to the same extent as the Existing Lender or the Lender acting through its previous Facility Office would have been if the assignment or change had not occurred.

24.3   **Disclosure of information**

The Lender may disclose to any of its Affiliates and any other person:

24.3.1   to (or through) whom the Lender assigns (or may potentially assign) all or any of its rights under this Agreement;

24.3.2   with (or through) whom the Lender enters into (or may potentially enter into) any sub-participation in relation to, or any other transaction under which payments are to be made by reference to, this Agreement or the Borrower; or

24.3.3   to whom, and to the extent that, information is required to be disclosed by any applicable law or regulation,

any information about the Borrower, the Group and the Finance Documents as that Lender shall consider appropriate.

25   **Changes to the Borrower**

The Borrower may not assign any of its rights or transfer any of its rights or obligations under the Finance Documents.

Purpose: Clauses 24 and 25 should always be read together. A distinction must be drawn between rights and benefits on the one hand and obligations on the other. Under English law, it is not possible to assign obligations and thus a lender would not be able to assign its obligations (such as that to make further advances under a revolving credit facility) without the consent of the borrower as well as the acceptance of the obligations by the new lender (transferee/assignee). Such an agreement is a tripartite agreement called a novation. By contrast, rights and benefits can be assigned but it is common in most loan agreements for the lender to seek to exercise this right without requiring the borrower's consent.

A further distinction has to be drawn between assignments and sub-participations. The assignment will give the new lender (assignee) a direct contractual right against the borrower whereas a sub-participation will not. A sub-participation is a back-to-back contract between the lender and the sub-participant under which the existing lender maintains its right of recourse against the borrower and sub-participates to a third party who will only have a remedy/right of recourse against the existing lender and no direct link against the borrower. The sub-participant therefore has a double exposure (ie to both lender and borrower).

Lender: It is crucial that the borrower is not able to assign its rights and benefits under the loan agreement as it is with respect to this borrower that the lender has carried out all of its due diligence and its financial calculations. It is highly unlikely that any lender will agree to the borrower assigning to a third party without its prior written consent.

The lender must be able to assign its rights and benefits in order to manage its balance sheet effectively. It may, for example, wish to syndicate the facility and thus share part of its exposure. Alternatively, it may wish to securitise or sell a loan book. It is also usual for banks to maintain exposure limits to certain sectors and groups and as circumstances change over time it will want to be able to sell its interests in loans which no longer meet its criteria.

In June 2001, the LMA issued guidelines on loan transfers in the light of changes in the market which they believe will reduce liquidity. The paper contemplates larger syndicated facilities but the principles are of general application. The purpose of the recommendations in the guidelines is to reduce the number of impediments to transfers. The recommendations include the removal of the requirement for borrower consent in the following circumstances:

- *for event-driven financing, for example large acquisition facilities;*
- *for term loans once they have been fully drawn, ie where the creditworthiness of the lenders is no longer a significant issue for the borrower;*
- *after the borrower defaults;*
- *transfers to existing lenders and their affiliates (this is already a feature of the LMA primary documents).*

It seems likely that the LMA standard documents will be amended soon to incorporate these features and a number of the other guidelines.

Borrower: *The assignment clause should be considered carefully. The borrower is entering into a loan agreement with a lender whom it knows and with whom it has a relationship. The borrower should also review the assignment clause in the context of both when the loan is performing and when it is not. While in good times the relationship is less important, it is in the bad times when things may be going wrong that it is crucial for the borrower to be able to rely on its relationship with its existing lenders. The reliance on one lender with whom it has a relationship may be more important than various banks, hedge funds and other institutions holding a piece of the borrower's debt. In such situations, unanimity may be difficult to achieve.*

In the case of a syndicated loan there may well be a host of different lenders with whom the borrower has no direct relationship. It becomes correspondingly more difficult for the borrower to negotiate terms, especially where the lenders are in different jurisdictions and/or have different cultural approaches to difficult times.

The borrower will want to be sure that an assignment will not increase its cost under the loan agreement and therefore a provision should be inserted that the lender is entitled to assign, provided that there is no increased tax liability, increased cost of funding, or anything which will increase the borrower's exposure under the facility. The borrower may well be concerned that the loan should only be assigned to a reputable institution and not to some institution which does not have the resources the borrower requires or which is not well disposed to the borrower.

While lenders appreciate the concerns of the borrower and will go some way to accommodate them, they do require some form of discretion as to their ability to assign.

Historically, many loan agreements contain provisions which require the lender to obtain the borrower's consent unless the transfer is, for example, to a similar institution and/or certain designated/specified institutions which have a net worth of £[ ] or institutions which are Qualifying Lenders. These qualifications are all aimed to one extent or another at ensuring that the assignee is a reputable institution. At the very least they tend to have the restrictions on assignment set out in Clause 24.2 above. At the time of writing, it remains to be seen whether the market will shift to the position suggested in the LMA liquidity paper referred to above.

26   Conduct of Business by the Lender

No provision of this Agreement will:

26.1   interfere with the right of the Lender to arrange its affairs (tax or otherwise) in whatever manner it thinks fit;

26.2   oblige the Lender to investigate or claim any credit, relief, remission or repayment available to it or the extent, order and manner of any claim; or

26.3   oblige the Lender to disclose any information relating to its affairs (tax or otherwise) or any computations in respect of Tax.

27   Payment Mechanics

27.1   **Payments**

On each date on which the Borrower is required to make a payment under a Finance Document, the Borrower shall make the same available to the Lender for value on the due date at the time and in such funds specified by the Lender as being customary at the time for settlement of transactions in Sterling in the place of payment.

Purpose: This clause stipulates that the borrower must pay the lender unconditionally so that the lender is entitled to the full and free use of the funds immediately on transfer. This clause is not usually negotiated. From a practical point of view, the borrower should be advised to which account it is required to pay into. Where the transaction has an international flavour there may be some conflict of law implications regarding place of performance.

27.2   **Partial payments**

27.2.1   If the Lender receives a payment that is insufficient to discharge all the amounts then due and payable by the Borrower under the Finance Documents, the Lender shall apply that payment towards the obligations of the Borrower under the Finance Documents in the order determined by the Lender in its absolute discretion.

27.2.2   Clause 27.2.1 above will override any appropriation made by the Borrower.

27.3   **No set-off by Borrower**

All payments to be made by the Borrower under the Finance Documents shall be calculated and be made without (and free and clear of any deduction for) set-off or counterclaim.

27.4   **Business Days**

27.4.1   Any payment which is due to be made on a day that is not a Business Day shall be made on the next Business Day in the same calendar month (if there is one) or the preceding Business Day (if there is not).

27.4.2   During any extension of the due date for payment of any principal or an Unpaid Sum under this Agreement interest is payable on the principal at the rate payable on the original due date.

27.5   **Currency of account**

27.5.1   Sterling is the currency of account and payment for any sum due from the Borrower under any Finance Document.

27.6   **Change of currency**

27.6.1   Unless otherwise prohibited by law, if more than one currency or currency unit are at the same time recognised by the central bank of any country as the lawful currency of that country, then:

(a)   any reference in the Finance Documents to, and any obligations arising under the Finance Documents in, the currency of that country shall be translated into, or paid in, the currency or currency unit designated by the Lender (after consultation with the Borrower); and

(b)   any translation from one currency or currency unit to another shall be at the official rate of exchange recognised by the central bank for the conversion of that currency or currency unit into the other, rounded up or down by the Lender (acting reasonably).

27.6.2   If a change in any currency of a country occurs, this Agreement will, to the extent the Lender (acting reasonably and after consultation with the Borrower) specifies to be necessary, be amended to comply with any generally accepted conventions and market practice in the London Interbank Market and otherwise to reflect the change in currency.

Purpose: This clause is included to take account of the possibility that the United Kingdom may adopt the euro as its currency in place of Sterling. It is deliberately vague to give flexibility for adjustments in market practice going beyond simple mechanical matters.

28 Set-off

The Lender may set off any matured obligation due from the Borrower under the Finance Documents against any matured obligation owed by the Lender to the Borrower, regardless of the place of payment, booking branch or currency of either obligation. If the obligations are in different currencies, the Lender may convert either obligation at a market rate of exchange in its usual course of business for the purpose of the set-off.

Purpose: This clause supplements the lender's existing contractual and statutory rights by consolidating and reconciling the obligations and rights of both parties against each other.

Lender: This is a valuable clause to the lender for the rights of set-off arising before and after an Event of Default enable the lender to reduce the borrower's liability without triggering a formal Event of Default. Combination of accounts involves aggregating debit balances while set-off broadly involves the application against each other of mutual obligations between lender and borrower. It is, however, an extremely complex area.[6] Combination is arguably only relevant to banks holding accounts, while the 'account' in set-off can be any ledger entry held by any entity. Contractual rights of set-off do not survive a liquidation.[7]

Borrower: These are market standard extensions of the lender's implied rights. The key point is to ensure that it is only matured obligations that can be set off. If the lender is able to set off obligations which are not yet due this has the effect of making the facility on-demand to the extent of the set-off available.

29 Notices

29.1 Communications in writing

Any communication to be made under or in connection with the Finance Documents shall be made in writing and, unless otherwise stated, may be made by fax, letter or telex.

---

6 Wood *The Law and Practice of International Finance* (Sweet & Maxwell, 1980).
7 Rule 4.90 (Mutual Credit and Set-off) of the Insolvency Rules 1986 provides for mandatory set-off of mutual debits and credits, but excludes sums due from the borrower to the lender if the lender had notice that a meeting of creditors had been called or a petition for the winding up of the borrower was pending at the time the sums became due.

29.2 **Addresses**

The address, fax number and telex number (and the department or officer, if any, for whose attention the communication is to be made) of each Party for any communication or document to be made or delivered under or in connection with the Finance Documents is that identified with its name below or any substitute address, fax number, telex number or department or officer as the Party may notify to the other party by not less than five Business Days' notice.

29.3 **Delivery**

29.3.1 Any communication or document made or delivered by one person to another under or in connection with the Finance Documents will only be effective:

(a) if by way of fax, when received in legible form; or

(b) if by way of letter, when it has been left at the relevant address or [five] Business Days after being deposited in the post postage prepaid in an envelope addressed to it at that address; or

(c) if by way of telex, when despatched, but only if, at the time of transmission, the correct answerback appears at the start and at the end of the sender's copy of the notice;

and, if a particular department or officer is specified as part of its address details provided under Clause 29.2 (*Addresses*), if addressed to that department or officer.

29.3.2 Any communication or document to be made or delivered to the Lender will be effective only when actually received by the Lender and then only if it is expressly marked for the attention of the department or officer identified with the Lender's signature below (or any substitute department or officer as the Lender shall specify for this purpose).

Purpose: *The notice clause is particularly important in the context of ascertaining the date a demand or a notice of a default requiring remedy is served, for it enables both parties to determine clearly the date upon which default interest and the grace period, respectively, starts running. Notice by telex is somewhat out of date and is used less and less, although it is still used in some international trade and shipping finance.*

Borrower: *You may want to run the argument that Clause 29.3.2 is unfair and that you should also have the benefit of it. The lender will counter that it is in fact reasonable. This is because (i) the lender may well be a huge institution and if the letter is not properly addressed then it will not be actioned properly, and (ii) there is a risk that a desperate borrower will claim to have sent communications which in fact it has not.*

Irrespective of the merits of these arguments, it is standard to have this one-sided clause, at least where the lender is a financial institution.

29.4   **English language**

29.4.1   Any notice given under or in connection with any Finance Document must be in English.

29.4.2   All other documents provided under or in connection with any Finance Document must be:

(a) in English; or
(b) if not in English, and if so required by the Lender, accompanied by a certified English translation and, in this case, the English translation will prevail unless the document is a constitutional, statutory or other official document.

30   **Calculations and Certificates**

30.1   **Accounts**

In any litigation or arbitration proceedings arising out of or in connection with a Finance Document, the entries made in the accounts maintained by the Lender are *prima facie* evidence of the matters to which they relate.

30.2   **Certificates and determinations**

Any certification or determination by the Lender of a rate or amount under any Finance Document is, in the absence of manifest error, conclusive evidence of the matters to which it relates.

Purpose: *Clauses 30.1 and 30.2 assist the lender in a situation where it is suing for amounts outstanding. It makes it simpler for the lender to prove the amount outstanding. From the borrower's perspective, clauses of this kind are acceptable in favour of a financial institution though it is sometimes possible to have the lender agree to provide a calculation of sums certified under Clause 30.2.*

30.3   **Day count convention**

Any interest, commission or fee accruing under a Finance Document will accrue from day to day and is calculated on the basis of the actual number of days elapsed and a year of 365 days or, in any case where the practice in the London Interbank Market differs, in accordance with that market practice.

Purpose: *Interest on Sterling denominated loans is calculated on the basis of a 365-day year (ie the actual number of days elapsed), while under a US dollar or Euro denominated facility the interest is calculated on the basis of a 360-day year (ie 12 months of 30 days each). The reference to* *market practice is included principally to take account of the possible replacement of Sterling with the Euro.*

31   Partial Invalidity

If, at any time, any provision of the Finance Documents is or becomes illegal, invalid or unenforceable in any respect under any law of any jurisdiction, neither the legality, validity or enforceability of the remaining provisions nor the legality, validity or enforceability of such provision under the law of any other jurisdiction will in any way be affected or impaired.

Purpose: When interpreting agreements, the courts can apply the 'blue pencil test' and strike out provisions which are for any reason invalid or illegal without changing the rest of the agreement. This clause preserves the clauses which are valid and ensures that they will not be tainted by clauses which are illegal or invalid. It is for similar reasons that a clause or clauses are repeated in all Facility Documents – in the event that any one of them is judged invalid. This may not be effective where a clause is deemed 'unfair' under the Unfair Terms in Consumer Contracts Regulations 1994 (SI 1994/3159).

32   Remedies and Waivers

No failure to exercise, nor any delay in exercising, on the part of the Lender, any right or remedy under the Finance Documents shall operate as a waiver, nor shall any single or partial exercise of any right or remedy prevent any further or other exercise or the exercise of any other right or remedy. The rights and remedies provided in this Agreement are cumulative and not exclusive of any rights or remedies provided by law.

Purpose: This is a standard 'boiler-plate' clause allowing the lender discretion as to whether to take or omit to take any action without its rights being prejudiced.

Lender: Notwithstanding this clause, if the lender is requested to provide a letter of waiver in respect of a particular Event of Default, it should be very wary of the principle of estoppel and ensure that the letter clearly reserves all the lender's future rights.

33   Counterparts

Each Finance Document may be executed in any number of counterparts, and this has the same effect as if the signatures on the counterparts were on a single copy of the Finance Document.

34   Governing Law

This Agreement is governed by English law.

35 Enforcement

35.1 Jurisdiction of English courts

35.1.1 The courts of England have exclusive jurisdiction to settle any dispute arising out of or in connection with this Agreement (including a dispute regarding the existence, validity or termination of this Agreement) (a '**Dispute**').

35.1.2 The Parties agree that the courts of England are the most appropriate and convenient courts to settle Disputes and accordingly no Party will argue to the contrary.

35.1.3 This Clause 35.1 is for the benefit of the Lender only. As a result, the Lender shall not be prevented from taking proceedings relating to a Dispute in any other courts with jurisdiction. To the extent allowed by law, the Lender may take concurrent proceedings in any number of jurisdictions.

35.2 Service of process

[Without prejudice to any other mode of service allowed under any relevant law, the Borrower:

35.2.1 irrevocably appoints [   ] as its agent for service of process in relation to any proceedings before the English courts in connection with any Finance Document; and

35.2.2 agrees that failure by a process agent to notify the Borrower of the process will not invalidate the proceedings concerned.]

The Borrower expressly agrees and consents to the provisions of this Clause 35.

Purpose: Clause 35 is appropriate where the borrower is domiciled outside England and Wales. Otherwise it can safely be omitted.

This Agreement has been entered into on the date stated at the beginning of this Agreement.

SCHEDULE 1

Conditions Precedent

1   Borrower

1.1   A copy of the constitutional documents of the Borrower.

1.2   A copy of a resolution of the board of directors of the Borrower:

(a) approving the terms of, and the transactions contemplated by, the Finance Documents to which it is a party and resolving that it execute the Finance Documents to which it is a party;

(b) authorising a specified person or persons to execute the Finance Documents to which it is a party on its behalf; and

(c) authorising a specified person or persons, on its behalf, to sign and/or despatch all documents and notices (including, if relevant, any Utilisation Request and Selection Notice) to be signed and/or despatched by it under or in connection with the Finance Documents to which it is a party.

(d) A specimen of the signature of each person authorised by the resolution referred to in paragraph (b) above.

(e) A certificate of the Borrower (signed by a director) confirming that borrowing the Facility Commitment would not cause any borrowing or similar limit binding on the Borrower to be exceeded.

(f) A certificate of an authorised signatory of the Borrower certifying that each copy document relating to it specified in this Schedule is correct, complete and in full force and effect as at a date no earlier than the date of this Agreement.

2   Valuation and Survey

2.1   A copy of the Valuation with respect to each Property including but not limited to:

(a) a Valuation of that Property in its current state with detailed planning permission;

(b) a detailed 'macro' and 'micro' market analysis of the letting and investment markets for that Property (including, without limitation, details of comparables, market trends and any other information requested by the Lender); and

(c) a commentary on environmental and ground condition issues for that Property.

2.2   Reports from appropriate professional advisers with respect to each Property addressing archaeological, party wall/adjoining owners (if applicable) and rights of light issues, addressed to the Lender.

3   Insurance

3.1   Evidence that the Borrower has complied with its obligations under Clause 22.5 (*Insurances*).

4   Property

4.1   All title documents relating to the Borrower's interests in each Property.

4.2   Copies of all Lease Documents in respect of each Property.

4.3   The results of HM Land Registry searches in favour of the Agent on the appropriate forms against all of the registered titles comprising the Borrower's interests in the Property giving not less than ten Business Days' priority beyond the date of the Debenture and showing no adverse entries.

4.4   A report on the title to each Property prepared by the Borrower's solicitors with an overview report by the Lender's solicitors.

4.5   An effective discharge of all mortgages, charges and liens affecting the Borrower's interests in each Property.

4.6   Appropriate Land Registry application forms duly completed accompanied by all necessary Land Registry fees.

5   Security

5.1   The Debenture.

5.2   The Subordination Deed.

5.3   Completed form 395 in respect of the Debenture.

5.4   Notices to the Account Bank of the charging or assignment of the Borrower's interests therein, together with a confirmation from the Account Bank that it will acknowledge those notices (if applicable) in the relevant forms set out in the Debenture.

5.5   Notices to parties to Development Documents of the charging or assignment of the Borrower's interests thereunder (if applicable) in the relevant form set out in the Debenture.

5.6   Notices to parties to the Hedging Arrangements of the charging or assignment of the Borrower's interests thereunder in the relevant form (if applicable) set out in the Debenture.

6   Tax

6.1   Evidence that the Borrower has duly elected to waive exemption in relation to the Property and that proper notification of that election was received by HM Customs & Excise prior to the date of this Agreement.

6.2   [Stamp duty]

7   Legal opinions

7.1   If the Borrower is incorporated in a jurisdiction other than England and Wales, a legal opinion of the legal advisers to the Lender in the relevant jurisdiction.

8   Other documents and evidence

8.1   Evidence that any process agent referred to in Clause 35.2 (*Service of process*), has accepted its appointment.

8.2   A copy of any other Authorisation or other document, opinion or assurance which the Agent considers to be necessary or desirable (if it has notified the Borrower accordingly) in connection with the entry into and performance of the transactions contemplated by any Finance Document or for the validity and enforceability of any Finance Document.

8.3   The Original Financial Statements.

8.4   Evidence that the Subordinated Creditor has provided the Borrower with at least £[   ] by way of paid up ordinary shares or unsecured loans subject to the Subordination Deed.

8.5   [A copy of the letting strategy for the Property.]

8.6   Evidence that the fees, costs and expenses then due from the Borrower pursuant to Clause 12 (*Fees*) and Clause 17 (*Costs and expenses*) have been paid or will be paid by the first Utilisation Date.

SCHEDULE 2

Requests

Part 1

Utilisation Request

From: [*Borrower*]

To: [*Agent*]

Dated:

Dear Sirs

[Borrower] – [   ] Facility Agreement

dated [   ] (the 'Facility Agreement')

1.   We refer to the Agreement. This is a Utilisation Request. Terms defined in the Agreement have the same meaning in this Utilisation Request unless given a different meaning in this Utilisation Request.

2.   We wish to borrow a Loan on the following terms:
     Proposed Utilisation Date: [   ] (or, if that is not a Business Day, the next Business Day)
     Currency of Loan: [   ]
     Amount: [   ] or, if less, the Available Facility
     Interest Period: [   ]

3.   We confirm that each condition specified in Clause 4.2 (*Further conditions precedent*) is satisfied on the date of this Utilisation Request.

4.   The proceeds of this Loan should be credited to [*account*].

This Utilisation Request is irrevocable.

Yours faithfully

....
authorised signatory for
[*name of Borrower*]

Part 2

Selection Notice

From: [*Borrower*]

To: [*Agent*]

Dated:

Dear Sirs

[Borrower] – [   ] Facility Agreement

dated [   ] (the 'Facility Agreement')

1. We refer to the Agreement. This is a Selection Notice. Terms defined in the Agreement have the same meaning in this Selection Notice unless given a different meaning in this Selection Notice.

2. We refer to the following Loan[s] in [*identify currency*] with an Interest Period ending on [   ].[8]

3. [We request that the above Loan[s] be divided into [   ] Loans with the following Interest Periods:][9]

    or

    [We request that the next Interest Period for the above Loan[s] is [   ]].[10]

4. We request that the above Loan[s] [is]/[are] [denominated in the same currency for the next Interest Period]/[denominated in the following currencies: [   ]. As this results in a change of currency we confirm that each condition specified in Clause 4.2 (*Further conditions precedent*) is satisfied on the date of this Selection Notice. The proceeds of any change in currency should be credited to [*account*].] .

5. This Selection Notice is irrevocable.

Yours faithfully

....

authorised signatory for
[*name of Borrower*]

---

8   Insert details of all Loans in the same currency which have an Interest Period ending on the same date.

9   Use this option if division of Loans is requested.

10   Use this option if sub-division is not required.

SCHEDULE 3

Mandatory Cost Formulae

1   The Mandatory Cost is an addition to the interest rate to compensate Lender for the cost of compliance with (a) the requirements of the Bank of England and/or the Financial Services Authority (or, in either case, any other authority which replaces all or any of its functions) or (b) the requirements of the European Central Bank.

2   On the first day of each Interest Period (or as soon as possible thereafter) the Lender shall calculate, as a percentage rate, a rate (the **'Additional Cost Rate'**) for the Lender, in accordance with the paragraphs set out below. The Mandatory Cost will be the Lender's Additional Cost Rates and will be expressed as a percentage rate per annum.

3   The Additional Cost Rate for the Lender if lending from a Facility Office in a Participating Member State will be the percentage notified by the Lender. This percentage will be certified by the Lender to be its reasonable determination of the cost (expressed as a percentage of all the Loans made from that Facility Office) complying with the minimum reserve requirements of the European Central Bank in respect of Loans made from that Facility Office.

4   The Additional Cost Rate for the Lender if lending from a Facility Office in the United Kingdom will be calculated by the Lender as follows:

(a)   in relation to a Sterling Loan:

$$\left.\frac{AB + C(B - D) + E \times 0.01}{100 - (A + C)}\right| \text{ per cent per annum}$$

(b)   in relation to a Loan in any currency other than Sterling:

$$\left.\frac{E \times 0.01}{300}\right| \text{ per cent per annum}$$

Where:

A is the percentage of Eligible Liabilities (assuming these to be in excess of any stated minimum) which the Lender is from time to time required to maintain as an interest free cash ratio deposit with the Bank of England to comply with cash ratio requirements.

B is the percentage rate of interest (excluding the Margin and the Mandatory Cost) payable for the relevant Interest Period on the Loan.

C is the percentage (if any) of Eligible Liabilities which the Lender is required from time to time to maintain as interest bearing Special Deposits with the Bank of England.

D is the percentage rate per annum payable by the Bank of England to the Lender on interest bearing Special Deposits.

E is the rate of charge payable by the Lender to the Financial Services Authority pursuant to the Fees Regulations (but, for this purpose, ignoring any minimum fee required pursuant to the Fees Regulations) and expressed in pounds per £1,000,000 of the Fee Base of the Lender.

5   For the purposes of this Schedule:

5.1   '**Eligible Liabilities**' and '**Special Deposits**' have the meanings given to them from time to time under or pursuant to the Bank of England Act 1998 or (as may be appropriate) by the Bank of England;

5.2   '**Fees Regulations**' means the Banking Supervision (Fees) Regulations 1999 or such other law or regulation as may be in force from time to time in respect of the payment of fees for banking supervision; and

5.3   '**Fee Base**' has the meaning given to it, and will be calculated in accordance with, the Fees Regulations.

6   In application of the above formulae, A, B, C and D will be included in the formulae as percentages (ie 5 per cent will be included in the formula as 5 and not as 0.05). A negative result obtained by subtracting D from B shall be taken as zero. The resulting figures shall be rounded to four decimal places.

7   The Lender shall have no liability to any person if such determination results in an Additional Cost Rate which over or under compensates the Lender.

8   Any determination by the Lender pursuant to this Schedule in relation to a formula, the Mandatory Cost, the Additional Cost Rate or any amount payable to the Lender shall, in the absence of manifest error, be conclusive and binding on the Borrower.

9   The Lender may from time to time, after consultation with the Borrower, determine and notify to the Borrower any amendments which are required to be made to this Schedule in order to comply with any change in law, regulation or any requirements from time to time imposed by the Bank of England, the Financial Services Authority or the European Central Bank (or, in any case, any other authority which replaces all or any of its functions) and any such determination shall, in the absence of manifest error, be conclusive and binding on the Borrower.

DOCUMENT 2: THE DEBENTURE

CONTENTS

1	Definitions and Interpretation	107
2	Covenant to Pay	117
3	Interest	118
4	Security	118
5	Negative Pledge	125
6	Conversion of Floating Charge	125
7	Further Assurance	126
8	Intellectual Property	127
9	Deposit of Documents and Title Deeds	128
10	The Book Debts Account	129
11	The Rental Account	131
12	Dividends, Voting Rights and Nominees	134
13	Representations and Warranties	135
14	Undertakings	136
15	Costs Indemnity	139
16	Enforcement	140
17	Statutory Power of Sale	140
18	Receiver	141
19	Protection of Third Parties	146
20	No Liability as Mortgagee in Possession	146
21	Release and Reassignment	147
22	Power of Attorney	147
23	Cumulative and Continuing Security	148
24	Avoidance of Payments	148
25	Prior Charges	150
26	Opening a New Account	150
27	Suspense Account	151
28	Payments and Withholding Taxes	151
29	Set-off	152
30	Assignment	152
31	Waivers	152
32	Severability	153
33	HM Land Registry	153
34	Notices	153
35	Governing Law and Jurisdiction	154
Schedule 1	Scheduled Property	156
Schedule 2	Form of Notice to Tenant	157
Schedule 3	Part 1: Notice to Bank	159
	Part 2: Acknowledgement from Bank	160

DOCUMENT 2: THE DEBENTURE

Debenture

DATE

PARTIES

(1)   [   ] (the **'Borrower'**); and

(2)   [   ] (the **'Lender'**).

It is agreed as follows:

1   **Definitions and Interpretation**

1.1   **Definitions**

In this Debenture the following expressions have the following meanings, unless the context otherwise requires:

Purpose: See equivalent clause in Document 1 at page 21.

'Assigned Intellectual Property'	means such of the Intellectual Property as is assigned to the Lender under this Debenture;
'Book Debts'	means:
	(a) all book and other debts in existence from time to time (including, without limitation, any sums whatsoever owed by banks or similar institutions), both present and future, due, owing to or which may become due, owing to or purchased or otherwise acquired by the Borrower; and

(b) the benefit of all rights whatsoever relating to the debts referred to above including, without limitation, any related agreements, documents, rights and remedies (including, without limitation, negotiable or non-negotiable instruments, guarantees, indemnities, legal and equitable charges, reservation of proprietary rights, rights of tracing, unpaid vendor's liens and all similar connected or related rights and assets);

'Book Debts Account' means such separate and denominated account or accounts with the Lender or any bank which the Lender may from time to time specify in writing for the purpose of receiving payments of the proceeds of realisation and collection of Book Debts;

Purpose: This definition is used to establish the lender's security over book debts. There may be any number of different accounts, and they may be foreign currency accounts set up to receive debts not denominated in Sterling.

Lender: Where security over book debts is an integral part of the lender's security package (which is more likely to be the case for corporate lending than for real estate banking), this account should be opened at the date of the debenture and £1 paid into it so as to confirm the existence of both the account and the deposit of monies in the account. The definition can therefore be amended to include the bank name, the account name, the account number and the sort code relating to the account. The mandates for the account should be obtained before completion and arrangements made for transferring any direct debit or standing order payments if these would not be permitted under the terms of the security (which would generally be the case if the charge is to be fixed rather than floating).

'Charged Property' means the whole or any part of the property, assets, income and undertaking of the Borrower from time to time mortgaged, charged or assigned to the Lender under this Debenture;

'Costs'	means all costs, charges or expenses of any kind including, without limitation, costs and damages in connection with litigation, professional fees, disbursements and any value added tax to be charged on those costs, charges, expenses and disbursements;
'Environment'	means all of the air, water and land including air within buildings and other natural or man-made structures above or below ground;
'Environmental Authorisations'	means all permits, licences, consents or other authorisations or approvals required at any time under any Environmental Legislation for the occupation or use of the Property by any person;
'Environmental Claim'	means any notice or other order requiring compliance with the terms of any Environmental Authorisation or Environmental Legislation or any other claim, notice, prosecution, action, official warning or other demand relating to:

    (a) the generation, disposal, treatment, storage, transportation or handling of any waste (as defined by the Environmental Protection Act 1990) or of any other substance which is toxic, hazardous, flammable, radioactive, highly reactive or explosive or otherwise capable of causing harm to human health or welfare or harm to any living organism or damage to the Environment;

    (b) any other act, default or phenomenon which is allegedly causing harm to human health or welfare or harm to any living organism or damage to the Environment;

'Environmental Legislation'	means all applicable statutes, statutory instruments, treaties, regulations, directives, codes of conduct and similar measures imposed by any relevant authority to which the Borrower or the Property is or has been or may be or may have been subject which relate to the pollution or protection of the Environment or the protection of the health of any living organism or the protection of public health or welfare;
'Finance Documents'	means any document containing provisions relating to the payment of any of the Secured Liabilities and each of the Security Documents;
'Intellectual Property'	means all subsisting patents and subsisting rights of a similar nature held in any part of the world, applications for patents and such rights, divisions and continuations of such applications for patents, domain name registrations, registered and unregistered trade marks, registered and unregistered service marks, registered designs, utility models (in each case for their full period and all extensions and renewals of them), applications for any of them and the right to apply for any of them in any part of the world, inventions, confidential information, know-how, business names, trade names, brand names, copyright and rights in the nature of copyright, design rights and get-up and any similar rights existing in any country (including rights in computer software); all the body of knowledge, technical experience, expertise and skills, technical processes, secret processes, formulae and technical information held by the Borrower and relating to its business, which is not in the public domain; and the benefit (subject to the burden) of any and all agreements, arrangements and licences in connection with any of the foregoing;

Lender: This is a broad definition, but for a company with extensive intellectual property it would be advisable to list the key intellectual property rights to get the best possible security over them. In particular, it is wise to include the registered numbers of registered patents.

'Occupational Leases' means all leasehold interests and other occupational rights whatsoever (including, without limitation, all licences and agreements for leases) in existence from time to time relating to the whole or any part of the Property, the immediate reversion to which is vested in the Borrower;

'Permitted Security Interest' means the security constituted by this Debenture and liens arising by operation of law in the ordinary course of business;

'Planning Acts' means the Town and Country Planning Act 1990, the Planning (Listed Buildings and Conservation Areas) Act 1990, the Planning (Hazardous Substances) Act 1990, the Planning and Compensation Act 1991, the Local Government Planning and Land Act 1980 and the Ancient Monuments and Archaeological Areas Act 1979;

'Plant and Machinery' means all plant and machinery, equipment, fittings, installations and apparatus, tools, motor vehicles and all other moveable assets (other than fixtures) of any kind and in any place which are the property of the Borrower at the date of this Debenture or which become the property of the Borrower after the date of this Debenture;

'Property' means all estates and other interests in any freehold, leasehold or other immovable property (including, without limitation, all fixtures (other than tenant's fixtures) on such property) which are the property of the Borrower at the date of this Debenture or which become the property of the Borrower after the date of this Debenture, all proceeds of sale derived from that property and the benefit of all covenants to which the Borrower is entitled in respect of that property (including the Scheduled Property);

| **'Receiver'** | means any receiver, administrative receiver or receiver and manager appointed pursuant to this Debenture; |

Purpose: This general definition serves to incorporate administrative receivers, receivers and managers and receivers appointed pursuant to the Law of Property Act 1925.

| **'Rental Account'** | means the account of the Borrower with [   ] account number [   ] sort code [   ], as that account may be renumbered or redesignated from time to time; |

| **'Rental Income'** | means all amounts payable to or for the benefit of the Borrower (including, for the avoidance of doubt, any amount actually received by the Borrower by way of apportionment upon completion of the acquisition of the Property) in connection with the letting of the Property or any part thereof, including (without duplication or limiting the generality of the foregoing) each of the following: |

(a) rent (and any amount equivalent thereto) payable whether it is variable or not and however or whenever it is described, reserved or made payable;

(b) any increase of rent payable by virtue of an offer falling within the proviso of s 3(1) of the Landlord and Tenant Act 1927;

(c) any rent payable by virtue of a determination made by the Court under s 24(A) of the Landlord and Tenant Act 1954;

(d) interest on or any sums released from any deposit held as security for performance of any tenant's obligations;

(e) any other moneys payable in respect of occupation and/or usage of the Property and every fixture and fitting therein and any and every fixture thereon for display or advertisement, on licence, lease or otherwise;

(f) any profits awarded or agreed to be payable as a result of any proceedings taken or claim made for the same;

(g) any damages, compensation, settlement or expenses for or representing loss of rent or interest thereon awarded or agreed to be payable as a result of any proceedings taken or claim made for the same net of any costs, fees and expenses paid (and which have not been reimbursed to, and which are not recoverable by, the Borrower from any party) in furtherance of such proceedings so taken or claim so made;

(h) any moneys payable under any policy of insurance in respect of loss of rent or interest thereon;

(i) any sum payable or the value of any consideration to be given by or on behalf of a tenant for the surrender or variation of any Occupational Lease or occupancy agreement;

(j) any other monies payable in respect of any dilapidations claim during or following the expiry of the term of any Occupational Lease;

(k) sums received from any guarantor of any occupational tenancy under any Occupational Lease; and

(l) any interest payable on any sum referred to above and any damages, compensation or settlement payable in respect of the same,

but after deducting the following amounts to the extent included in (a) to (l) above:

(x) those amounts (if any) (together with any value added or similar taxes charged thereon) due to the Borrower from any tenants under an Occupational Lease or other occupiers by way of contribution to insurance premiums and the cost of insurance valuations or by way of service charges in respect of costs incurred or to be incurred by the Borrower under any repairing or similar obligations or in providing services to such tenant or tenants of such building;

(y) any contribution to a sinking fund paid by any tenant or other occupier; and

(z) any value added tax or similar taxes payable on any of the items listed in paragraphs lettered (a) to (k) above and in respect of which the relevant Borrower is liable to account to HM Commissioners of Customs & Excise;

Purpose: Specific security over rental income is rarely taken under most standard form debentures, but some form of rental assignment is practically assured where a lender is taking security over land and the rental is required to cover interest payments under the underlying loan. These definitions are appropriate for a legal assignment of rent – the lender becomes the legal owner of the assigned rights so service charges, etc are excluded. If the assignment is merely equitable, it is sometimes the case that service charges would not be excluded from the definition.

'Rent Proceeds'   means all sums from time to time standing to the credit of the Rental Account, all interest on such sums and all other amounts of whatsoever nature deriving directly or indirectly from such sums;

'Rights'   means all the Borrower's rights, title and interest from time to time in any lease, licence or occupational right (or an agreement for any of them) together with all the Borrower's rights, title and interest from time to time in any renewal of, replacement of or variation to any lease, licence or occupational right (or an agreement for any of them);

'Scheduled Property'   means the property details of which are set out at Schedule 1;

'Secured Liabilities'   means all monies, debts and liabilities from time to time due, owing or incurred by the Borrower to the Lender on any current or other account whatsoever [pursuant to the Facility Documents];

Purpose: This is the fundamental definition of what is secured by the Debenture, sometimes appearing as 'Debt', 'Indebtedness' or 'Liabilities'. It is either 'all monies' or it is capped to monies owing under a specific loan, guarantee or debt instrument and its negotiation often rests on the commercial agreement between the parties. If the latter, a specific reference to those documents would be required.

Lender: *If the security is intended to cover a general lending relationship with the borrower such as a long-term overdraft facility, it is appropriate to retain this broad definition. It is helpful for the lender to do so, even when there is no such relationship. However, if the borrower subsequently creates security ranking behind that of the lender of which the lender has notice, it is important for the lender to be aware that its priority may not be assured for the future advances made after the date of that second ranking security.*

Borrower: *It is helpful to keep this as narrow as possible so that the borrower is free to re-finance with a clean slate once any particular debt has been paid off. The borrower should consider narrowing the definition of Secured Liabilities and ask if it is absolutely necessary that the definition covers 'all monies'. If it does, the Debenture will stay in place for as long as the borrower has even the smallest amount outstanding to the lender, even, for example, lender's charges of £1. On the other hand, it is not unusual for security to be 'all monies' and the borrower can take comfort that it is in control of the amount it borrows from the lender.*

'Security Documents'	means any document entered into by any person from time to time creating any Security Interest, directly or indirectly, for the Secured Liabilities including, without limitation, this Debenture;
'Security Interest'	means any mortgage, charge, assignment, pledge, lien, right of set-off, hypothecation, encumbrance, priority or other security interest (whether fixed or floating) including, without limitation, any 'hold-back' or 'flawed asset' arrangement together with any preferential right, retention of title, deferred purchase, leasing, sale or purchase, sale and leaseback arrangement, trust agreement, declaration of trust, trust arising by operation of law, any option or agreement for any of the same or any arrangement which has substantially the same commercial or substantive effect as the creation of security;

'Shares'	means all stocks, shares and other securities for the time being owned or held by the Borrower and all rights, dividends, interest and other property (whether of a capital or income nature) accruing, offered, issued or deriving at any time by way of dividend, bonus, redemption, exchange, purpose, substitution, conversion, consolidation, subdivision, preference, option or otherwise attributable to any of the Shares previously described;
'Subsidiary'	means a subsidiary within the meaning of s 736 of the Companies Act 1985.

1.2   **Interpretation**

1.2.1   In this Debenture:

(a) the contents page and clause headings are included for convenience only and do not affect the construction of this Debenture;

(b) words denoting the singular include the plural and vice versa;

(c) words denoting one gender include each gender and all genders.

1.2.2   In this Debenture, unless the context otherwise requires, references to:

(a) persons include references to natural persons, firms, partnerships, companies, corporations, associations, organisations and trusts (in each case whether or not having a separate legal personality);

(b) document, instruments and agreements (including, without limitation, this Debenture and any document referred to in this Debenture) are references to such documents, instruments and agreements as modified, amended, varied, supplemented or novated from time to time;

(c) receivers are references to receivers of whatsoever nature including, without limitation, receivers and managers and administrative receivers;

(d) the terms the **'Lender'** and the **'Receiver'** include, where the context so admits, references to any delegate of any such person;

(e) a party to this Debenture includes references to its successors, transferees and assignees;

(f) Recitals and Clauses are references to recitals to this Debenture and clauses of this Debenture;

(g) statutory provisions (where the context so admits and unless otherwise expressly provided) are construed as references to those provisions as respectively amended, consolidated, extended or re-enacted from time to time, and to any orders, regulations, instruments or other subordinate legislation made under the relevant statute; and

(h) a time of day is a reference to London time.

1.3   **Execution**

The parties intend that this Debenture takes effect as a deed notwithstanding the fact that the Lender may only execute this Debenture under hand or not at all.

2   **Covenant to Pay**

The Borrower shall on demand pay to the Lender or discharge, as the case may be, all the Secured Liabilities when the Secured Liabilities become due.

Purpose: A demand served by the lender is notice to the borrower and evidence to a third party that the Secured Liabilities have become due. The lender's power of sale and power to appoint a receiver only arise once due.[1] It also extends the start of the limitation period; instead of commencing on the date of the document, it will commence on the date of demand.

Lender: Where the mortgagor is not the borrower, it is appropriate that the mortgagor is responsible for the secured liabilities. If there is no guarantee from the mortgagor, then the covenant to pay provides the link between the parties under which a demand can legitimately be served for the secured liabilities (unless the security is 'limited recourse', ie the lender is not able to recover more from the mortgagor than the amount realised on some of the charged property). Deletion of the words 'on demand' is not acceptable as the service of a demand is an important part of the enforcement process demonstrating when the debt is formally due. The lender often accepts the addition of 'when the Secured Liabilities have become due', at the end of the clause to clarify that the words 'on demand' do not render the facility repayable on demand.

Borrower: The words 'on demand' do not mean the loan has become repayable literally on demand and so do not prejudice the borrower or override the terms of the loan agreement.[2] In any event, this matter is put beyond doubt because of the inclusion of the words 'when the Secured Liabilities become due' at the end of the clause.

---

1   Sections 101(1) and 109 of the Law of Property Act 1925.
2   *Cryne v Barclays Bank Plc* [1987] BCLC 548, CA.

3   Interest

The Borrower shall pay to the Lender interest ('**default interest**')
on the Secured Liabilities from the date of demand (or, in the case
of Costs, from the date they are incurred), after as well as before any
judgment obtained or the liquidation or administration of the
Borrower, at the highest rate from time to time agreed in any
Finance Document to be payable by the Lender on unpaid sums or
in the absence of agreement at 4 per cent per annum over the base
rate of the Lender from time to time on whatever days the Lender
may from time to time select. The Lender may compound default
interest if it is not paid when due. In the absence of other agreement
any compounding of unpaid default interest will take effect on a
quarterly basis in accordance with the usual practice of the Lender
from time to time.

*Purpose: This clause reiterates the obligation to pay interest at a higher
rate once a default has been made and/or demand served – 'default
interest'.*

*Lender: This clause should not be deleted for, although it repeats words of
the loan agreement, it is useful to retain it in a separate document,
particularly if the security is to be 'all monies' and is to survive the term of
a specific loan agreement. It is highly unlikely that the lender will concede
on this clause. Its rationale here is that if the lender is looking to this
clause, the borrower has clearly defaulted in some way. Accordingly, the
lender is out of pocket and should be reimbursed for this risk. It is
important for the clause to state that the interest is paid 'after as well as
before any judgment' as judgment debts carry interest at specified rates
which may well be lower than general market rates.*

*Borrower: The borrower is unlikely to obtain any amendment except
possibly the insertion of a specific default rate or a reduction in any
specific rate.*

4   Security

4.1   Fixed and floating charges

By way of continuing security in favour of the Lender for the
payment and discharge of the Secured Liabilities, the Borrower with
full title guarantee hereby charges to the Lender the property set
out below in the manner set out below:

*Purpose: This clause creates the security for the debt and could constitute
a security document all on its own. Indeed, the form of charge by way of
legal mortgage prescribed by HM Land Registry contains barely more than
this clause with a covenant to pay.*[3]

---

3   Section 117 of and Sch 5 to the Law of Property Act 1925.

Lender: The phrase 'charges as beneficial owner' has now been superseded by 'with full title guarantee';[4] which implies certain covenants by the mortgagor into the Debenture. The amendment to 'limited title guarantee' is not acceptable and any carve-outs to the borrower's title should be made in the representations and warranties.

The borrower may try to circumscribe the extent of the security, for example by asking the lender to identify exactly what assets it values in terms of its security. The lender should consider carefully the level of security it requires, for certain types of security may involve it in more day-to-day administration than that for which it is prepared. At the same time, the lender must be certain that its security is fully effective against at least those assets forming the core part of the borrower's business.

Borrower: The borrower should consider giving a 'limited title guarantee' rather than a 'full title guarantee'. This amendment will only affect the covenants implied by law. The express title covenants will also need to be removed if this amendment is to have any effect.

It is possible to negotiate this clause by 'scaling down' the level of security by using the full range available: legal mortgage, equitable charge and legal and equitable assignment,[5] and by asking the lender to identify where it sees the value in the Debenture. If, for example, the borrower has no intellectual property, it makes sense to delete all reference to it. The lender can then rely on the further assurance clause if the borrower ever acquires any intellectual property.

4.1.1   by way of first fixed charge by way of legal mortgage, the Scheduled Property and all Rights relating to the Scheduled Property in existence of the date hereof;

Purpose: Referring to the charge as 'first' is not definitive, for priority is not determined by how the security is described, but by the date it is registered or the provisions of any priority agreement. A description of security as 'first' or 'second', however, is often used for clarity and to focus the lender's mind to ensure it is obtaining the priority it is seeking.

4.1.2   by way of fixed charge, the Property and all Rights relating to it not effectively mortgaged in the Lender's favour as security for the Secured Liabilities;

Purpose: Particularly where the lender has an obligation to make further advances to the borrower and its exposure is likely to increase over time, it is important that its 'all-embracing' security covers all forms of asset which the borrower has at the date of the first advance and any which it may

---

4   Section 1 of the Law of Property (Miscellaneous Provisions) Act 1994.
5   For a summary of the alternatives, see Fisher and Lightwood *Law of Mortgage* 10th edn (Butterworths, 1995), at ch 1.

acquire subsequently – both tangible (physical assets) and intangible (rights, or 'choses in action').

4.1.3   by way of first fixed charge, all the Borrower's rights, title, interest and benefit in and to the Rental Account;

Purpose: *This clause creates a fixed charge over the Rental Account. For a number of years after the Charge Card case[6] there was a doubt as to whether it was conceptually possible for a bank to take security over an account if it was also the account bank. A 1997 House of Lords' decision[7] overruled Charge Card and this doubt can now be ignored. The case which settled the conceptual possibility point has, however, created some debate about the manner of enforcement of an account charge. This is a very theoretical debate and most lawyers take the view that the existing charge mechanisms are adequate to achieve the commercial objective of an account charge.*

4.1.4   by way of fixed charge, the Book Debts;

Lender: *As the law currently stands, it is difficult to create a fixed charge over book debts and there is a strong likelihood that most purported fixed charges would be construed as floating charges. In determining whether the security is to take effect as a fixed or as a floating charge, the key provision is Clause 10, which governs the collection and recovery of book debts. The lender should retain the words 'fixed charge' (even if the control element is lacking), in the hope rather than the expectation that this may assure the lender of security over book debts ranking ahead of preferential creditors, rather than behind them which would be the case if a floating charge had been created. These issues are discussed further in Clause 10 at p 129.*

Borrower: *Clause 10 (the book debts account clause) is the important clause to negotiate relating to book debts, as the law currently stands. Attempts to change the description of the charge to an express floating charge over book debts usually fail as the lender wishes to attempt, at least, to take a fixed charge. This is acceptable provided that the Borrower is not also required to represent that a valid fixed charge is created.*

4.1.5   by way of fixed charge, all the Intellectual Property owned, possessed or controlled by the Borrower which is not assigned to the Lender;

Lender: *If intellectual property is a significant part of the borrower's assets, the lender should seriously consider taking specific intellectual property security which would encumber the form of intellectual property in the appropriate manner (eg charge, assignment or mortgage) and include*

---

6   *Re Charge Card Services Limited* [1986] 3 All ER 289, [1987] Ch 150.
7   *Re Bank of Credit and Commerce International SA (No 8)* [1998] AC 214, HL.

specific covenants and representations and warranties. Most debentures are not very detailed on the subject.

Borrower: *The borrower should consider negotiating the definition of intellectual property to reduce the scope of the security and the restrictions imposed upon and the representations given in respect of the intellectual property. The borrower should also consider whether there are any restrictions against giving this security in any licence agreements or other documents relating to the borrower's intellectual property as certain forms of security may be regarded as tantamount to a disposal and therefore would constitute a breach of such agreements.*

4.1.6   by way of first fixed charge, the Plant and Machinery;

Lender: *In order to effectively charge any chattel, such as plant and machinery, it is advisable that the charged assets should be identified with a sticker or some other mark identifying the asset as charged to the lender. Practically, this will assist the lender when it enforces its security.*

4.1.7   by way of fixed charge, the Shares;

Lender: *The equitable charge is 'softer' than the legal mortgage of shares in terms of the rights it gives the lender and the rights it enables the borrower to retain before enforcement of the charge. The broad distinction is that with an equitable charge there is a transfer of shares into the lender's name only after an Event of Default, whereas the transfer takes place at the outset under a legal mortgage. Both forms typically entitle the borrower to receive dividends and to exercise voting rights before an Event of Default, although the mechanics are slightly different. It is unusual for a lender to wish to retain dividends and extremely unlikely it would wish to vote owing to possible tax and shadow directorship issues. There is an ability to protect an equitable charge over shares held in an English company with the stop notice procedure, by which notice of the charge is given to the secretary of the company the shares of which are charged requesting that the chargee be notified of any proposed transfer by the chargor of the charged shares. The lender may also be forced by the borrower to consider whether a simple deposit of share certificates pursuant to a memorandum of deposit would suffice.*

Borrower: *The borrower should try to dilute the share security to an equitable charge or even a memorandum of deposit, and should negotiate this clause in conjunction with Clause 9.*

4.1.8   by way of fixed charge, all the goodwill and uncalled capital for the time being of the Borrower;

Purpose: *Where the lender is taking security over all the undertaking and assets of the borrower, it is important that the encumbered assets include the goodwill of the business, for this will facilitate the sale of the borrower's business as a going concern by any administrative receiver appointed by* *the lender pursuant to its floating charge. For a business with few tangible assets, goodwill could be the most valuable asset.*

4.1.9   by way of floating charge, all the undertaking and assets of the Borrower whatsoever, wherever situate, whether movable, immovable, present or future (including, without limitation, its uncalled capital for the time being and all the undertaking and assets of the Borrower referred to above which are, for any reason, for the time being subject to a valid mortgage, assignment or fixed charge in favour of the Lender not under this Debenture or any other Security Document).

> **Purpose:** *At present, it is market practice to include a residual floating charge over the sundry assets of the borrower which are not specifically charged. Generally, the lender does not expect the floating charge to confer valuable security (because of the nature of the assets charged and the fact that floating charges rank after preferential creditors). Instead, the main purpose of the floating charge is to give the lender the ability to appoint an administrative receiver. In order to do this the lender must have the benefit of security including a floating charge over the whole or substantially the whole of the borrower's property.[8] If an administrative receiver has been appointed over a company's assets then it is not possible to obtain an administration order without the consent of the person who has appointed the administrative receiver.[9] Lenders dislike administration orders because they are unable to enforce their security during an administration.[10]*
>
> *However, there are developments on the horizon which challenge the rationale for taking a residual floating charge. First, the Insolvency Act 2000 introduced a moratorium concept for small companies[11] which cannot be overridden by floating charge holders (although as at July 2001 this provision has yet to be brought into force). A company will be a small company if it meets two of the following criteria: (i) turnover of under £2.8m; (ii) net assets of under £1.4m; and (iii) under 50 employees. There are concerns about the scope of the moratorium provisions, particularly in the context of securitisations where, notwithstanding that the transactions tend to have a value of at least £100m, the vehicles through which they are conducted may technically be small companies.*
>
> *The second development on the horizon is a move by the Government to reform insolvency law more widely.[12] In order to foster a 'rescue culture' in the United Kingdom, the Government is keen to dilute the control exercised currently by floating charge holders on insolvency. They are also considering removing the preferential status of the Inland Revenue and*

---

8   Section 29(2) of the Insolvency Act 1986.
9   Section 9(3) of the Insolvency Act 1986.
10   Section 11 of the Insolvency Act 1986.
11   Section 1 of and Sch 1 to the Insolvency Act 2000.
12   Consultation Paper 18 June 2001 and subsequent White Paper *Insolvency – A Second Chance* July 2001, Cm 5234.

HM Customs & Excise because companies are often brought down by the tax authorities in the knowledge that they will receive payment out of the assets of the company ahead of the general creditors. A White Paper was published on this issue in Summer 2001.

For the time being, lenders will continue to want residual floating charges, although it would seem that the time may soon come when it is no longer imperative that they do so.

Lender: *A floating charge over any less than the whole or substantially the whole of the borrower's assets will not entitle the lender to appoint an administrative receiver. It is therefore unusual for a lender to accept dilution of the clause to cover just a class of assets where the lender is seeking 'all-embracing' security. Nevertheless, it is technically possible to take a 'floating charge' over classes of assets such as book debts, stock or securities held in the lender's custody. Indeed, a floating charge may be the only alternative where the borrower needs freedom to dispose of the assets to be charged on a regular basis, such as in the case of stock.*

Borrower: *The borrower may be able to challenge whether the lender needs the all-encompassing floating charge and should in any event negotiate Clauses 8 to 12 generally as to the degree of lender's control.*

4.2 Assignments

By way of continuing security in favour of the Lender for the payment and discharge of the Secured Liabilities, the Borrower with full title guarantee hereby assigns absolutely (save for 4.2.7 which shall be by equitable assignment) to the Lender the property set out below:

4.2.1 all the Borrower's interest in any contract in respect of the whole or any part of the Property and in any collateral warranties with trade contractors or professionals relating to the Property;

Lender: Security may be taken over contracts by means of either a legal or equitable assignment. This assignment is legal, for by serving notice on the third party to the contract at the date of the Debenture, the assignment is perfected.[13] Legal title to all the benefits under that contract then vests in the lender, but the obligations under the contract are not transferred. In so far as and for so long as no notice is served, the assignment is therefore equitable. As with assignments of rent, it is more a question of when notice of the assignment is served than if, and it is market practice for an equitable assignment to provide for notice to be served following an Event of Default. Amending this clause to take effect as an equitable assignment is acceptable if the lender does not require day-to-day technical 'control' of the contracts which it would otherwise have pursuant to a legal assignment. Of course, the lender could still notify the third party to the

---

13   Section 136 of the Law of Property Act 1925.

contract clarifying that such notice is not a notice for the purposes of the statute; but requesting that the lender be notified of any default under any contract. This would give the lender some involvement and control pending formal notice being served and the assignment being perfected. This would effectively act as an 'upgrade' from a basic equitable assignment.

Aside from day-to-day control, the lender should also consider the question of priority when considering whether to take a legal or an equitable assignment. Assignments are proprietary rights, rather than pure security interests. That is, title in an asset which has been assigned may be transferred to the assignee, whereas under a security interest, the asset is merely appropriated to the chargee/mortgagee to repay the debt while title to the asset stays with the chargor/mortgagor. As a consequence, the question of the priority of various assignments as against various security interests should not arise. As soon as notice of an assignment is served, the assigned asset is technically no longer an asset of the assignor and thus cannot be included as such for the division of assets between creditors holding various security interests. Assignments over the same asset rank inter se, however, according to the date of the notice of the assignment.[14] A legal assignment will therefore rank ahead of an equitable assignment which is not perfected by notice, and a lender may choose to take a legal assignment on that basis. A lender may consider, however, that the risk of an assignor creating a legal assignment after and ranking ahead of, its own earlier equitable assignment of the same asset, is fairly slim. This may be the case particularly where (as in most assignments, mortgages, charges and debentures), there is a prohibition on the borrower assigning its assets. A diligent prospective assignee could, possibly, be imputed with some form of notice of that prohibition which may affect the validity of the second assignment.

Borrower: *A third party contracted to the borrower may be commercially sensitive to the existence of a lender on the scene and it may be preferable to serve a notice of assignment upon them only as a final resort, such as following an Event of Default. Indeed, the service of any notice before then could prove awkward in terms of the commercial relationship between borrower and customer. The borrower should negotiate for an equitable assignment with no notice being served at all if it wishes to keep control of the contract until a default. It is worth noting that some contracts (particularly those relating to the provision of consultancy or other personal services) may contain restrictions against assignment, and consent will need to be obtained before this clause can be agreed regardless of whether it is an equitable or a legal assignment. A counter-argument to the lender seeking a legal assignment for 'priority purposes' is that the borrower has covenanted not to dispose of its assets to any third party. A legal assignment to a third party would therefore be in breach of that*

---

14   *Dearle v Hall* [1824–1834] All ER Rep 28.

covenant and is clearly something the borrower would never do. The
lender should therefore be 'relaxed' and rely on an equitable assignment.

4.2.2 all the Borrower's present and future copyright, rights in the nature of copyright, design rights and get-up and similar rights existing in any country; and all the body of knowledge, technical experience, expertise and skills, technical processes, secret processes, formulae and technical information held by the Borrower which in each case relates to the software and content used in the operation of its websites and e-commerce activities;

4.2.3 the Borrower's registrations of domain names with InterNIC, Nominet UK and other bodies responsible for the registration of top and second level domain names throughout the world;

4.2.4 the Borrower's licences of software and content used in the operation of its websites and e-commerce activities;

4.2.5 the Borrower's present and future copyright in the object code and source code of any software and content used in the operation of its websites and e-commerce activities and the benefit of any escrow agreements relating to that code;

4.2.6 all the Borrower's rights, title, interest and benefit in and to the Rental Income; and

4.2.7 by way of equitable assignment the benefit of any security in favour of the Borrower over any rent deposits in respect of the Occupational Leases.

5 Negative Pledge

The Borrower shall not:

5.1 create, purport to create or allow to subsist, any Security Interest over the whole or any part of the Charged Property except for any Permitted Security Interest; or

5.2 convey, assign, transfer, or agree to convey, assign or transfer the whole or any part of the Charged Property except in the ordinary course of its trade in respect of that part of the Charged Property which is subject only to an uncrystallised floating charge in favour of the Lender.

Purpose/Lender/Borrower: *See Clauses 21.3 and 21.5 in Document 1.*

6 Conversion of Floating Charge

6.1 **Conversion by notice**

The Lender may by notice to the Borrower convert the floating charge contained in this Debenture into a fixed charge as regards such Charged Property as the Lender may specify (whether generally or specifically) in that notice (i) if it considers that it would be desirable to do so in order to protect, preserve or supplement the charges over the Charged Property or the priority of those charges; or (ii) on, or at any time after, this Debenture has become enforceable, or both.

Purpose: *This clause is essential for a lender with a floating charge as it identifies the time when that charge ceases to 'hover' over a class of assets and fixes to or crystallises upon specific assets, effectively preventing the borrower from disposing of them and trading normally. It extends the position implied by law. The difference between Clauses 6.1 and 6.2 is the service of notice on the borrower which is necessary where the borrower may not be aware of the occurrence of certain events (such as when the lender's subjective opinion renders it desirable that the floating charge be crystallised to preserve its priority).*

Lender: *Clause 6.1 is drafted as widely as possible to extend the implied law position. Upon crystallisation, a floating charge becomes fixed for priority purposes ranking ahead of 'younger' floating charges but behind preferential creditors and subsequent fixed charges.[15] By fixing on the borrower's assets, it serves to preserve the lender's priority. This is because crystallisation realistically freezes the borrower's business. This, however, may not be desirable for a lender seeking to work out of a situation.*

Borrower: *To avoid the consequences of crystallisation (ie the freezing of the business), the borrower should limit the events triggering crystallisation as much as possible, even deleting automatic crystallisation if at all acceptable, but certainly deleting 'desirable' in Clause 6.1 and replacing with 'necessary'.*

6.2   **Automatic conversion**

If, without the prior written consent of the Lender, the Borrower breaches or takes any step with a view to breaching any provision of the Clause headed 'Negative Pledge' in respect of any of the Charged Property which is subject to an uncrystallised floating charge under this Debenture, or if any person levies or attempts to levy any distress, attachment, execution or other legal process against any of that Charged Property, the floating charge created by this Debenture over the Charged Property to which the breach or step relates will automatically, without notice, be converted into a fixed charge as soon as that breach occurs or that step is taken.

7   **Further Assurance**

The Borrower shall forthwith, at any time if so required by the Lender, at its own expense execute and deliver to the Lender such

15   *Griffiths and Another v Yorkshire Bank and Others* [1994] 1 WLR 1427. See also *Re Benjamin Cope & Sons Ltd (Marshall v Benjamin Cope & Sons Ltd)* [1914] 1 Ch 800.

further legal or other mortgages, charges, assignments, securities, authorities, notices and documents as the Lender may in its discretion require of the whole or a specified part of the Charged Property, in whatever form the Lender may in its discretion require, to secure the payment or discharge of the Secured Liabilities, including, without limitation, in order to vest the whole or part of the Charged Property in the Lender, the nominee of the Lender or in any purchaser from the Lender or the Receiver.

Purpose: For whatever reason (and frequently because the financial condition of the borrower has deteriorated), it may be necessary to execute more documents and this clause clarifies the purpose of those documents, at whose cost they are executed and at whose request.

Lender: The lender should ensure this clause remains as wide as possible so as to catch any supplemental documentation it may require both before loan maturity (to enhance or perfect its security) and on enforcement (to realise its security). It may be that a vital clause was omitted from the signature copy of the final document, or that in order to sell some securities, the borrower needs to execute a stock transfer form.

Borrower: The borrower should negotiate for this clause to be limited, ideally to documents necessary to enforce security and to delete 'as the Lender may in its discretion require' and replace with 'as is necessary'. The lender should not have the ability to perfect its security after execution. The popular argument is that the lender (and its lawyers) should get it right first time! Usually, however, the clause is left unamended.

8   Intellectual Property

8.1   The Lender grants a licence to the Borrower of the Assigned Intellectual Property to use and develop the Assigned Intellectual Property for the purpose of the operation of its website and its e-commerce activities. The licence granted by this Clause is not assignable. The Borrower may not sub-license the Assigned Intellectual Property to any party without the prior written consent of the Lender.

8.2   The Borrower represents and warrants to the Lender on each day on which any of the Secured Liabilities remains outstanding that:

8.2.1   the Intellectual Property owned, possessed or controlled by it is all of the Intellectual Property required by it in order for it to carry on its business in all material respects and it does not, in carrying on its business, infringe in any material respect any Intellectual Property of any third party; and

8.2.2   to the best of its knowledge and belief, no Intellectual Property owned, possessed or controlled by it is being infringed, nor to the best of its knowledge is there any threatened infringement of any such Intellectual Property.

8.3   The Borrower shall:

8.3.1   make such registrations and pay such fees, registration taxes and similar amounts as are necessary to keep any Intellectual Property owned, possessed or controlled by it in existence;

8.3.2   take such steps as are necessary (including the institution of legal proceedings) to prevent third parties infringing any Intellectual Property owned, possessed or controlled by it and (without prejudice to its other obligations under this Debenture) take all such steps as are necessary to maintain and preserve its interest in them; and

8.3.3   except with the prior consent of the Lender, not permit any Intellectual Property owned, possessed or controlled by it to be abandoned or cancelled, to lapse or to be liable to any claim of abandonment for non-use or otherwise.

8.4   The Borrower shall on demand pay to the Lender or the Receiver, as the case may be, and discharge all Costs incurred by the Lender in connection with the assignments of the Assigned Intellectual Property in this Debenture and the title in the Assigned Intellectual Property which is thereby conferred on the Lender on a full and unlimited indemnity basis, together with interest at the rate specified in and calculated in accordance with Clause 3 (*Interest*) from the date the relevant Cost was expended, incurred or suffered (whichever is the earlier) by the Lender or the Receiver, as the case may be, until full discharge of such Cost.

9   Deposit of Documents and Title Deeds

9.1   The Borrower shall deposit with the Lender (and the Lender during the continuance of this security may hold and retain):

9.1.1   all deeds and documents of title relating to the Property including, without limitation, all Occupational Leases;

9.1.2   all stock or share certificates or other documents of title to or representing the Shares together with such duly executed transfers or assignments with the name of the transferees, date and consideration left blank as the Lender may require;

9.1.3   all such deeds and documents of title (if any) relating to the Book Debts as the Lender may from time to time specify; and

9.1.4   copies of all the contracts and collateral warranties assigned absolutely to the Lender under this Debenture certified to be true copies by one director of or a solicitor acting for the Borrower.

9.2   The Borrower shall:

9.2.1   whilst this Debenture is enforceable procure the registration of the transfer of the Shares to the Lender (or its nominees as the Lender may require), the entry of the Lender (or its nominees as the Lender may require) in the register of members of the relevant company as the holder or holders of the Shares, and the issue of new share certificates in respect of the Shares to the Lender (or its nominees as the Lender may require); and

9.2.2   upon the accrual, issue or receipt of any additional Shares deliver or pay to the Lender or procure the delivery or payment to the Lender of all such additional Shares or the stock or share certificates or other documents of title to or representing them together with such duly executed transfers or assignments with the name of the transferee, date and consideration left blank as the Lender may require.

> ***Purpose:*** *By taking all title deeds at the outset, the lender retains the documentation necessary to perfect a sale of the assets upon enforcement of the security. The lender cannot always guarantee it will still have the borrower's co-operation after a default.*

> ***Borrower:*** *This clause is a mechanical, rather than commercial clause which is only negotiable in conjunction with Clause 4. The mechanics are those which usually accompany equitable charges over shares, and if the borrower is unhappy with them it is possibly best to readdress the nature of the security over shares in the first place in commercial negotiation with the lender.*

10   The Book Debts Account

10.1   Until all the security constituted by this Debenture is discharged the Borrower shall collect and realise all Book Debts in the ordinary course of its business. The Borrower shall hold the proceeds of collection and realisation of the Book Debts upon trust for the Lender pending payment of those proceeds into its trading account for the time being.

10.2   If the Lender so requires, the Borrower shall pay the proceeds of the collection and realisation of its Book Debts into the Book Debts Account. It shall not except with the prior written consent of the Lender withdraw from the Book Debts Account all or any monies standing to the credit of the Book Debts Account.

10.3   The Borrower shall not release, exchange, compound, set off, grant time or indulgence in respect of, or in any other manner deal with, all or any of the Book Debts except as expressly provided in this Debenture.

Purpose: *This clause is intended to give the borrower sufficient flexibility to use the cash realised from its book debts to be used in its business whilst giving the lender sufficient control to create a fixed charge over the book debts rather than a floating charge. In practice, this is difficult to achieve. A charge will only be a fixed charge if the chargee has the requisite degree of control over the book debts. Until 1994, it was generally thought that it was impossible to create a fixed charge over book debts if the chargor had the right to use the proceeds of realisation of the book debts in its business. The ability to use the proceeds of realisation freely in the ordinary course of business was a characteristic of a floating charge.*[16] *The exception to this was if the book debts account was with the chargee, in which case the account terms would effectively permit the chargee to prevent withdrawal from the account at any time which therefore gave the requisite degree of control.*[17] *Then in 1994, the decision in New Bullas*[18] *overturned that orthodoxy by treating book debts and the proceeds of their realisation as separate assets. The unrealised book debts can be the subject of a fixed charge and the proceeds the subject of a floating charge. Accordingly, at the moment of enforcement of the charge the lender will have a priority problem as regards any cash standing to the credit of the book debts account, but will have a fixed charge over the unrealised book debts. This decision was repeatedly criticised by commentators and in the 2001 Privy Council decision of Brumark*[19] *was effectively overruled. The Privy Council held that it was not possible to distinguish the unrealised debts and the proceeds of realisation and that permitting the chargor free use of the proceeds of realisation in the ordinary course of business indicated a floating charge. At the time of writing, therefore, it appears that we have returned to the pre-New Bullas era in which only lenders which are also the account bank can obtain fixed charges of book debts and then only to the extent that they have effective control over withdrawals.*

Lender: *It is rarely appropriate to take a fixed charge over Book Debts given the rigidity it imposes on the borrower by restricting its access to cash. Allowing the flexibility in Clause 10.2 is therefore generally acceptable in most transactions and any limit upon the situation(s) in which a lender may require payment of the debts into a specified account, or call for a legal assignment of the debts, is usually resisted. That the lender can upgrade the security in this way on an event occurring which might with time or the happening of some other event, become an Event of Default (a 'potential' Event of Default) is however, a common concession.*

Borrower: *This is drafted to be acceptable for most lenders, for whom the flexibility in Clause 10.2 is sufficient control in most transactions. If the lender has the flexibility to upgrade the security from floating to fixed, and*

---

16   *Re Yorkshire Woolcombers' Association* [1903] 2 Ch 284.
17   *Siebe Gorman & Co Ltd v Barclays Bank Ltd* [1979] 2 Lloyd's Rep 142; *Re Brightlife Ltd* [1986] Ch 200, [1987] 2 WLR 197, [1986] 3 All ER 673.
18   *Re New Bullas Trading Ltd* [1994] BCC 36, [1994] 1 BCLC 485.
19   *Re Brumark Investments Ltd* [2001] 3 WLR 454.

from a charge to an assignment 'at the drop of a hat', the borrower has no assurance (other than the general good faith of the lender) that the lender is not going to apply Clause 10.2 until an Event of Default has occurred. It is unlikely that the clause could be watered down, however, save for perhaps Clause 10.2 only taking effect after an Event of Default or potential Event of Default. The flexibility permitted in this clause is not incompatible with the general restriction against dealing with all the borrower's Book Debts in aggregate in Clause 5 which is protecting the lender's security. Clause 10 effectively controls the lender's security (although here it is controlled to a lesser extent).

11 The Rental Account

11.1 The Rental Account

11.1.1 The Borrower shall open and maintain the Rental Account, [immediately on execution hereof] [after an Event of Default] give a notice to the bank of which the Rental Account is held in the form of Schedule 3 (Part 1) and procure that such bank promptly acknowledges such notice in the form of Schedule 3 (Part II).

> ***Purpose/Lender:*** *As the lender has no direct legal relationship with the tenant, he needs to monitor the flow of rent and ensure it is used to pay off interest on the loan (where that is part of the commercial arrangement). The lender therefore obliges the borrower to set up an account into which the rent is paid, to engage a managing agent to manage the Property and the collection of rents and payment of service charges on his behalf, and to procure that the managing agent gives the lender direct undertakings with respect to the rent. This clause therefore gives the lender 'belt and braces' security over the rent at every stage – that is, as it is paid by the tenants (assignment), as it is received by the borrower and paid into the Rental Account (charge), and as it 'sits' in the Rental Account (blocked account and rights of set-off). It is worth pointing out that not all security over rent is as thorough as that in this clause, and many documents may take only an equitable assignment of rent and a charge over the Rental Account.*
>
> *In contrast to an equitable assignment, pursuant to a legal assignment, notice of the assignment is served on the tenant at the outset and the legal entitlement to the rent then vests in the lender. There is no need for the lender to take additional security over the rent as he can sue the tenant directly for non-payment and can collect the rent himself.*
>
> *The wording in Clause 11 'tops up' the charge over the Rental Account and ensures the borrower cannot gain access to the rental payments save as permitted under the Debenture and in accordance with the loan arrangements as to the payment of interest. Where the Rental Account is not held by the lender (and not all lenders will be entitled to accept deposits), the lender may consider serving notice on the bank in question*

seeking an acknowledgement from it that it will not permit any
withdrawals (save for certain listed types), but this is rather unusual.

Borrower: *Given that an equitable assignment over rent is a 'lesser' form*
of rental security giving the borrower the continuing right to collect rents,
it is unlikely that a lender will accept any amendments to the security
clause. The important clause for the borrower to negotiate is Clause 11
(The Rental Account) which sets out how and when withdrawals from the
account may be made.

11.1.2   The Borrower shall forthwith [after an Event of Default] give to
           each person occupying the whole or any part of the Property under
           any Occupational Lease an irrevocable notice of assignment in the
           form set out in Schedule 2 (*Form of notice to tenant*) or such other
           form as the Lender may in its discretion require.

           Purpose/Lender: *Service of notice on the tenant will perfect the*
           assignment into a legal assignment vesting all the rent in the lender. If
           the notice can only be served after an Event of Default (in contrast to
           notice in a legal assignment which is served at the outset), the lender
           cannot be assured of the borrower's co-operation at that time. It is therefore
           necessary to empower the lender to serve the notice on the borrower's behalf.

           Borrower: *If the lender has placed a heavy reliance on rent servicing the*
           loan, the lender may insist on a legal rent assignment from the outset,
           thereby transferring the right to receive rent to the lender and enabling the
           lender to sue tenants directly for rent not received. A lender may argue for
           this to provide notice to be served on a 'potential' Event of Default (being
           an event which might with time become a 'proper' Event of Default). This
           is unacceptable as the lender should only be able to effectively seize the rent
           once a default has actually occurred as it is only then that it is faced with
           the very real prospect of incurring a loss.

11.1.3   The Borrower shall forthwith procure that at all times during the
           subsistence of the security constituted by this Debenture each
           person occupying the whole or any part of the Property under any
           Occupational Lease shall pay all Rental Income due to the Borrower
           by such person into the Rental Account on, or as soon as practicable
           after, the due date for payment of such Rental Income, without any
           set-off, counterclaim, restriction or condition and free and clear of,
           and without deduction or withholding for, or on account of, any
           Taxes.

           Purpose/Lender/Borrower: *This clause effects the flow of rent from*
           tenants to the Rent Account.

11.1.4   The Borrower shall hold any Rental Income it receives on trust for
           the Lender until it pays such Rental Income into the Rental
           Account.

Purpose/Lender/Borrower: *In that (short) time between when the borrower receives the rent (generally in error as it should be collected and received by the managing agents) and when it passes it on to the managing agents or to the Rental Account, it is important that the lender maintains an interest in the rent to minimise the lenders unprotected exposure, particularly if the borrower is wound up or made bankrupt in that time. By declaring the rent to be held 'on trust' for the lender, it is deemed separate from the borrower's other assets and should not then be distributed among the borrower's general creditors on a liquidation or bankruptcy.*

11.1.5   Unless an Event of Default has occurred, the Lender shall pay and apply the Rent Proceeds in or towards satisfaction of the Secured Liabilities as and when the Secured Liabilities become due and release any balance in the Rental Account to the Borrower. If an Event of Default has occurred, the Lender may deal with the Rent Proceeds in such manner as it in its discretion thinks fit.

Purpose/Lender/Borrower: *This clause effects the application of rent towards the debt. A more detailed provision is usually found in the loan agreement and, because of the application, it is usual to 'tie in' the dates interest is payable with the dates upon which rent is received (in cleared funds).*

11.2   **Rights of the Lender**

For the avoidance of doubt the Borrower agrees that:

11.2.1   the Lender is not obliged:

(a)   to make any enquiry as to the nature or the efficacy of any payment received by the Lender pursuant to the assignment contained in this Debenture; or

(b)   to make any claim or take any other action in order to collect any monies or in order to enforce any rights and benefits assigned by this Debenture to the Lender or to which the Lender may at any time be entitled under this Debenture;

Purpose/Lender/Borrower: *This is protective wording for the lender which actually rarely appears in a rental assignment but which would, nevertheless, be good practice to include. A borrower should ensure the lender is liable for its negligence and wilful default in all circumstances.*

11.2.2   the Lender may:

(a)   sue for, and exercise every power to recover, the whole or any part of the Rental Income; and

(b)   give an effective discharge or receipt for the Rental Income in its own name or in the name of the Borrower, as the Lender in its discretion thinks fit.

12   Dividends, Voting Rights and Nominees

12.1   **Dividends and voting rights**

Until this Debenture has become enforceable, the Borrower may:

12.1.1   receive and retain all dividends, interest and other income deriving from and received by it in respect of the Shares; and

12.1.2   exercise all voting and other rights and powers attached to the Shares if doing so does not adversely affect the Shares and is not otherwise inconsistent with the Debenture.

> ***Purpose:*** *Given that this document comprises an equitable charge over shares (and not a legal mortgage), the shares are not transferred into the lender's name until the occurrence of an Event of Default. The voting rights and dividend entitlements therefore continue to flow to the borrower. This clause, however, purports to instil some control over how those rights are exercised.*

> ***Lender:*** *This may need upgrading if, for example, the borrower is a holding company, and even if an equitable charge is retained, the control of the lender in respect of the charged shares until enforcement of the charge could be further tightened. For example, dividends could be paid into a blocked bank account and votes could only be exercised if the resulting resolution did not diminish the value of the lender's security.*

> ***Borrower:*** *Very tight control by the lender over the borrower's exercise of voting rights and dividends is incongruous with an equitable charge. A legal mortgage would evidence a lender's need to have superior security over the shares with more all round control, principally obtained by having the shares registered in its own name. Very tight control with an equitable charge should therefore be resisted by the borrower on the basis that if an equitable charge has been agreed commercially, the control provisions of a legal mortgage are inappropriate to the transaction.*

12.2   **Trustee powers**

The Lender may at its discretion (in the name of the Borrower or otherwise) whilst this Debenture is enforceable, and without any consent or authority on the part of the Borrower exercise all the powers given to trustees by s 10(3) and (4) of the Trustee Act 1925 (as amended by s 9 of the Trustee Investments Act 1961) in respect of those Shares subject to a trust.

12.3   **Lender's powers of enforcement over Shares**

12.3.1   Whilst this Debenture is enforceable, all dividends, interest and other income forming part of the Shares shall, unless otherwise agreed between the Lender and the Borrower, be paid without any set-off or deduction whatsoever to an interest bearing suspense account in the name of the Lender and shall be retained by the Lender until applied as hereinafter provided as part of the Shares and any such monies which may be received by the Borrower shall, pending such payment, be held in trust for the Lender.

12.3.2   The Lender shall not have any duty as to any Shares and shall incur no liability for:

(a) ascertaining or taking action in respect of any calls, instalments, conversions, exchanges, maturities, tenders or other matters in relation to any Shares or the nature or sufficiency of any payment whether or not the Lender has or is deemed to have knowledge of such matters; or

(b) taking any necessary steps to preserve rights against prior parties or any other rights pertaining to any Shares; or

(c) for any failure to present any interest, coupon or any bond or stock drawn for repayment or for any failure to pay any call or instalment or to accept any offer or to notify the Borrower of any such matter or for any failure to ensure that the correct amounts (if any) are paid or received in respect of the Shares.

12.4   **Custody**

The Lender shall be entitled to provide for the safe custody by third parties of all stock and share certificates and documents of title deposited with the Lender or its nominees at the expense of the Borrower and shall not be responsible for any loss of or damage to those certificates and documents.

13   Representations and Warranties

13.1   The Borrower represents and warrants to the Lender that:

13.1.1   *Ownership of the Charged Property*
it is absolutely, solely and beneficially entitled to all the Charged Property as from the date it or any part of it falls to be charged under this Debenture and the rights of the Borrower in respect of the Charged Property are free from any Security Interest of any kind other than a Permitted Security Interest; and

13.1.2   *No disposal*
it has not sold or agreed to sell or otherwise disposed of, or agreed to dispose of, the benefit of all or any of the Borrower's right, title and interest in and to the Charged Property.

13.2   The representations and warranties set forth in this Clause are given and made on and as of the date of this Debenture, shall survive the execution of this Debenture and are continuing representations and warranties which are deemed to be repeated during the continuance of the security constituted by this Debenture.

Purpose/Lender/Borrower: See Clause 18 in Document 1.

Lender: It is vital that the assets charged to the lender belong to the borrower. In some instances it may be necessary to include a third party (such as a nominee or a tenant-in-common or other joint owner) in the security document in order for the lender's intended security to be perfected. A limited title guarantee should be accepted in very limited situations, such as where assets are held on bare trust or by nominees, in which case the beneficial owner should also execute the security document. Particular types of asset may also suggest additional warranties: there has been no breach of any environmental laws (with respect to security over ships or land), and no breach of the laws on financial assistance (with respect to security over shares) for example.

14 Undertakings

14.1 Duration

The undertakings in this Clause shall remain in force during the continuance of the security constituted by this Debenture.

Purpose/Lender/Borrower: It is advisable to ensure that the undertakings in the debenture cover only the matters which are not covered by the undertakings in the loan agreement.

14.2 To comply with statutes

The Borrower shall comply with all obligations under any statute and all byelaws and regulations relating to the whole or any part of the Charged Property.

14.3 To provide information

The Borrower shall promptly provide to the Lender whatever information, documents or papers relating to the Charged Property as the Lender may from time to time request.

14.4 Insurance

The Borrower shall:

14.4.1 insure and keep insured all of its undertaking and assets with reputable and responsible insurers previously approved by the Lender in such manner and to such extent as is reasonable and customary for an enterprise engaged in the same or a similar business and in the same or similar localities such risks and contingencies as the Lender shall from time to time request;

14.4.2 procure that the interest of the Lender is noted on all its policies of insurance in such manner as the Lender may in its absolute discretion require;

14.4.3   duly and punctually pay all premiums and any other monies necessary for maintaining its insurance in full force and effect;

Lender: Rather than merely noting the lender's name on the insurance policies, it is preferable to have the policy reissued into the joint names of lender and borrower giving the lender an automatic entitlement to proceeds and information at the same time as the borrower. This would enable the lender to receive the proceeds of any insurance claim directly, rather than relying on the borrower holding them on trust for the lender, at the risk of the borrower absconding or becoming insolvent while holding the funds.

Borrower: An upgrade by the lender requiring the insurance to be taken out in joint names should be resisted, particularly where the borrower has a block policy for its insurance. If the borrower receives proceeds of any claim, it can hold them on trust for the lender thus holding them separately from the borrower's other assets on a liquidation for example, and rendering them the beneficial property of the lender at the time of the liquidation. However, joint names insurance is generally unavoidable where the lender is taking security over a single specified property or asset.

14.4.4   ensure that every one of its policies of insurance contains a first loss payee clause and a standard mortgagee clause, whereby such insurance will not be invalidated, vitiated or avoided as against a mortgagee in the event of any misrepresentation, act, neglect or failure to disclose on the part of the insured;

14.4.5   produce to the Lender on request copies of all policies and all receipts for the current premiums with respect to its insurance; and

14.4.6   immediately give notice to the Lender of any occurrence which gives rise, or might give rise, to a claim under any of its policies of insurance and, except with the prior written consent of the Lender, the Borrower shall not agree to settlement of any such claim.

14.5   **Insurance monies**

The Borrower shall apply all monies received by virtue of any insurance of the whole or any part of the Charged Property in making good, or in recouping expenditure incurred in making good, any loss or damage or, if the Lender in its discretion so requires, towards discharge of the Secured Liabilities. The Borrower shall ensure that all such monies which are not paid directly by the insurers to the Lender shall be held by the recipient upon trust for the Lender and be applied by the Borrower in accordance with this Clause.

Lender: It is often argued that if the assets charged to the lender are destroyed to any extent whatsoever, the lender should have the option of walking away from the transaction with the debt paid off. This is a very

strong argument where the sole asset charged has been completely destroyed and would otherwise take a number of months to reinstate.

Borrower: *The argument against the lender having the ability to apply insurance proceeds to pay off the debt, is that the risk of the assets charged to the lender being destroyed is simply one the lender has to take. The asset is insured and the proceeds of the insurance policy are probably charged to the lender too. It is never intended that the lender should be able to walk away from the transaction and pay off the debt before the end of the term unless the borrower is in default, and yet this provision effectively enables the lender to do so. At the very worst, the lender should have the discretion to pay off the Secured Liabilities if the assets are completely destroyed or if assets to the value of, say, 75 per cent of the amount of the Secured Liabilities are destroyed. A borrower with tenants or a chartered ship should note that it may be obliged under the terms of the lease/charterparty to reinstate a destroyed building/ship and thus the application by a lender of insurance proceeds to pay off the loan would result in the borrower breaching the terms of its lease/charterparty.*

14.6 **To repair**

The Borrower shall:

14.6.1 at all times keep in good and substantial repair and condition all the Charged Property including, without limitation, all buildings, erections and structures on and in the Property;

14.6.2 keep all Plant and Machinery in good repair, working order and condition and fit for its purpose; and

14.6.3 where it is uneconomic to repair any part of the Charged Property, replace such part by another similar asset of equal or greater quality and value.

Lender: *An acceptable amendment by the borrower could be to repair only to the extent that failure to repair might/could/would have a material adverse effect on the value of the lender's security. If the facility is asset driven, rather than income driven, and there is a low loan to value ratio in relation to the charged asset, this obligation should be as onerous as possible.*

Borrower: *The borrower should not be under any greater obligation here than it is under any lease, hire-purchase agreement or prior ranking security documents, and a carve-out could be added along the lines of 'provided that the borrower shall be under no greater obligations under this clause than under the lease dated [   ] between the borrower (1) and [   ] (2)'. The borrower should challenge the lender to dilute these obligations if the assets referred to are not an integral part of the lender's security.*

14.7   **Environment**

The Borrower shall:

14.7.1   and shall procure that any occupier of the Property shall, obtain and maintain in full force and effect all Environmental Authorisations and ensure that the Property, the Borrower and any such occupier complies with all Environmental Legislation; and

14.7.2   promptly on becoming aware of it inform the Lender of any Environmental Claim which has been made or threatened against the Borrower or any of its officers or any occupier of the Property or any requirement of any relevant authority, Environmental Authorisation or applicable Environmental Legislation to make any investment or expenditure or take or desist from taking any action which might, if substantial, have a material adverse effect on the financial condition of the Borrower, the ability of the Borrower to perform its obligations under the Finance Documents or the value or marketability of the Property.

Purpose: With a range of domestic environmental legislation in existence secured lenders are faced with the prospect of strict liability for environmental damage in certain situations, and increasingly documents are becoming 'environmentally focused'.

Lender: This drafting is actually very minimalist in terms of environmental provisions, and if the secured asset were to be a landfill site for example, the lender should think about more detailed environmental provisions including perhaps an obligation to undergo an environmental audit at regular intervals throughout the term of the loan.

Borrower: Clearly, environmental provisions are not relevant to a document merely charging shares and even for property-backed loans it is hard to see their relevance for an office block in, say, the city of London. In that case, the lender should be restricted to the very weakest of this type of restriction.

General: Additional covenants will be required when the lender is placing heavy reliance on a charge over a particular asset, for example if an important asset is an office block there will be undertakings in relation to any head lease and in respect of sub-leases.

15   **Costs Indemnity**

The Borrower shall on demand pay to the Lender or the Receiver, as the case may be, and discharge all Costs incurred by the Lender in connection with this Debenture (including Costs incurred by the Lender in performing covenants which the Borrower has failed to perform in accordance with the terms of this Debenture) on a full and unlimited indemnity basis, together with interest at the rate specified in and calculated in accordance with Clause 3 (*Interest*) from the date the relevant Cost was expended, incurred or suffered (whichever is the earlier) by the Lender or the Receiver, as the case may be, until full discharge of such Cost.

16   Enforcement

This Debenture will become enforceable when (i) any of the Secured Liabilities is not paid and/or discharged in accordance with the terms of this Debenture; or (ii) the Borrower requests the Lender to appoint a receiver over the whole or any part of its undertaking or assets.

Purpose: Before the lender can sell the charged assets, a number of steps (probably simultaneous), need to have occurred:[20]

(a)   the power of sale has to have become exercisable;

(b)   the power of sale has to have arisen;

(c)   the Secured Liabilities have to have become due;

(d)   demand has to have been served on the mortgagor; and

(e)   the security has to have become enforceable.

This clause sets the whole wheel in motion.

Lender/Borrower: This clause heralds the beginning of the less-negotiated boilerplate provisions which, although more or less standard in the market regardless of the type of security document, can, for the lender, include a number of potentially irrelevant provisions in the standard form which could well be deleted, and which can for the borrower throw up a few additional and sweeping powers for the lender.

17   Statutory Power of Sale

17.1   For the purposes of all powers implied by statute, and in particular the power of sale under s 101 of the Law of Property Act 1925 (Powers incident to estate or interest in a mortgage), the Secured Liabilities will be deemed to have become due when the security created by this Debenture becomes enforceable and s 103 of the Law of Property Act 1925 (Regulation of exercise of power of sale) and s 93 of the Law of Property Act 1925 (Restriction on consolidation of mortgages) will not apply.

17.2   The statutory powers of leasing conferred on the Lender are extended so as to authorise the Lender to lease, make arrangements for leases, accept surrender of leases and grant options on such terms and conditions as the Lender may in its discretion think fit. The Lender is not obliged to comply with any of the provisions of s 99 (Leasing powers of mortgagor and mortgagee in possession)

---

20   Section 101 of the Law of Property Act 1925.

and s 100 (Powers of mortgagor and mortgagee in possession to accept surrenders of leases) of the Law of Property Act 1925.

17.3 Each of the Lender and the Receiver may exercise their respective statutory powers of sale in respect of the whole or any part of the Property.

18   Receiver

18.1   Appointment of Receiver

18.1.1 At any time after the security constituted by this Debenture has become enforceable, whether or not the Lender has entered into or taken possession of the whole or any part of the Charged Property pursuant to this Debenture:

(a) the Lender may, by writing under the hand of any authorised officer of the Lender, appoint any person to be a receiver of the Charged Property and that person shall, with effect from the date of such appointment, be a **'Receiver'**;

(b) the Lender may, from time to time, in similar manner, remove the Receiver and appoint another in his place;

(c) the Lender may, either at the time of appointment or at any time thereafter, fix the remuneration of the Receiver;

(d) the Lender and any nominee wheresoever situate may, without further notice and without the restrictions contained in s 103 of the Law of Property Act 1925 (Regulation of exercise of power of sale), exercise in respect of all or any part of the Shares all the powers and rights exerciseable by the registered holder of the Shares and all other powers conferred on mortgagees by the Law of Property Act 1925 as varied or extended by this Debenture; and

(e) the Lender and any nominee wheresoever situate may apply any dividends, interest or other payments received or receivable by the Lender or by any nominee in respect of the Shares as if they were proceeds of sale.

None of the restrictions imposed by the Law of Property Act 1925 in relation to the appointment of receivers, the giving of notice or otherwise shall apply.

18.1.2 The Receiver may from time to time delegate, by power of attorney or otherwise, to any person any of his powers and discretions, whether arising by statute, the provisions of this Debenture or otherwise, upon such terms and for such periods of time as he may in his discretion think fit. The Lender shall not be liable to the Borrower for any loss or damage arising from any act, default, neglect or misconduct of the Lender's delegates.

18.2   **Powers of Receiver**

The Receiver has all the powers to do or abstain from doing anything which the Borrower could do or abstain from doing in relation to the Charged Property including, without limitation the powers conferred by s 109 of the Law of Property Act 1925 (Appointment, powers, remuneration and duties of receivers) and, in the case of a Receiver who is an administrative receiver, the powers conferred by s 29 of the Insolvency Act 1986 (Definitions) and Sch 1 to the Insolvency Act 1986 (Powers of administrator or administrative receiver), and in particular the Receiver may:

18.2.1   *Carry on business*
carry on, manage or concur in carrying on managing the whole or any part of the business of the Borrower as he may in his discretion think fit;

18.2.2   *Protection of assets*
(a) manage, insure, repair, decorate, maintain, alter, improve, renew or add to the Charged Property or concur in so doing;
(b) commence or complete any building operations on the Property;
(c) apply for and maintain any planning permissions, building regulations, approvals and any other permissions, consents or licences,

in each case as he may in his discretion think fit;

18.2.3   *Realisation of assets*
sell, exchange, convert into money and realise the Charged Property or concur in so doing by public auction or private contract and generally in such manner and on such terms as he may in his discretion think fit. Without prejudice to the generality of the foregoing, he may do any of these things for any valuable consideration, including, without limitation, cash, shares, stock, debentures or other obligations. Any such consideration may be payable in a lump sum or by instalments spread over such period as he may in his discretion think fit;

18.2.4   *Let, hire or lease*
(a) let, hire or lease (with or without premium) and accept surrenders of leases or tenancies or concur in so doing;
(b) grant rights, options or easements over and otherwise deal with or dispose of, and exercise all rights, powers and discretions incidental to, the ownership of the Charged Property;
(c) exchange or concur in exchanging the Charged Property;

in each such case, in such manner and generally on such terms as he may in his discretion think fit, with all the powers of an absolute beneficial owner. The Receiver may exercise any such power by effecting such transaction in the name or on behalf of the Borrower or otherwise;

18.2.5 *Borrowing*

for the purpose of exercising any of the powers, authorities or discretions conferred on him by or pursuant to this Debenture or of defraying any Costs (including, without limitation, his remuneration) which are incurred by him in the exercise of such powers, authorities or discretions or for any other purpose, to raise and borrow money or incur any other liability either unsecured or secured on the Charged Property, either in priority to the security constituted by this Debenture or otherwise, and generally on such terms as he may in his discretion think fit. No person lending such money is to be concerned to enquire as to the propriety or purpose of the exercise of such power or as to the application of any money so raised or borrowed;

18.2.6 *Make calls*

make, or require the directors of the Borrower to make, such calls upon the shareholders of the Borrower in respect of any uncalled capital of the Borrower as the Receiver may in his discretion require and enforce payment of any call so made by action (in the name of the Borrower or the Receiver as the Receiver may in his discretion think fit) or otherwise;

18.2.7 *Compromise*

(a) settle or compromise any claim by, adjust any account with, refer to arbitration and dispute with, and deal with any question or demand from, any person who is, or claims to be, a creditor of the Borrower, as he may in his discretion think fit; and

(b) settle or compromise any claim, adjust any account, refer to arbitration any dispute and deal with any question or demand relating in any way to the Charged Property, as he may in his discretion think fit;

18.2.8 *Proceedings*

bring, prosecute, enforce, defend and abandon all such actions, suits and proceedings in relation to the Charged Property as he may in his discretion think fit;

18.2.9 *Subsidiaries*

(a) promote the formation of any Subsidiary of the Borrower with a view to such Subsidiary purchasing, leasing, licensing or otherwise acquiring an interest in the Charged Property;

(b) arrange for the purchase, lease, licence or acquisition of an interest in the Charged Property by any such Subsidiary for any valuable consideration, including, without limitation, cash, shares, debentures, loan stock, convertible loan stock or other securities, profits or a sum calculated by reference to profits, turnover, royalties, licence fees or otherwise, whether or not secured on the undertaking of assets of such Subsidiary and whether or not such consideration is payable or receivable in a lump sum or at any time or any number of times by instalments spread over such period, as the Receiver may in his discretion think fit; and

(c) arrange for such Subsidiary to trade or cease to trade as the Receiver may in his discretion think fit;

18.2.10 *Employees*
appoint and discharge any manager, officer, agent, professional adviser, employee and any other person, upon such terms as he may in his discretion think fit;

18.2.11 *Receipts*
give valid receipts for all monies and execute all assurances and things which he may in his discretion think proper or desirable for realising the Charged Property;

18.2.12 *Environment*
conduct and complete all investigations, studies, sampling and testing and all remedial, removal and other actions, whether required under Environmental Legislation or by the Lender or otherwise and comply with all lawful orders and directives of all authorities regarding Environmental Legislation; and

18.2.13 *General powers*
do all such other acts and things as the Receiver may in his discretion consider to be incidental or conducive to any of the matters or powers set out in this Debenture or otherwise incidental or conducive to the preservation, improvement or realisation of the Charged Property.

Purpose: *This is a comprehensive extension of the statutory powers which are themselves rather general and vary little between different security documents.*

Lender: *The lender's negotiating position tends to be that once the borrower is in default, the lender may exercise whatever powers it feels it needs in order to discharge all monies owing to it by the borrower.*

Borrower: *As the borrower would have to be in default for this clause to become operative at all, it is extremely unlikely that the lender will accept any amendments whatsoever. It is rarely negotiated, save perhaps for example, deleting as irrelevant a power to obtain planning permission in a charge over shares.*

18.3   **Receiver as agent of the Borrower**

The Receiver is at all times and for all purposes the agent of the Borrower. Subject to the provisions of the Insolvency Act 1986, the

Borrower is solely responsible for all the Receiver's acts, defaults, neglect and misconduct of any nature whatsoever and for his remuneration and Costs, to the exclusion of liability on the part of the Lender.

Lender: *This provision is of little value to the lender as the lender will have had to agree to indemnify the Receiver when appointing him in any event. The lender may reluctantly accept inclusion of liability where caused by the gross negligence or wilful default of the Receiver.*

Borrower: *That the Receiver is an agent of the borrower is non-negotiable and a matter of law,[21] but the Receiver's exclusion of liability can be narrowed down so as not to extend to any negligence or wilful default by the Receiver.*

18.4   **No obligation**

The Receiver is not obliged to exercise any of the powers set out in this Clause.

18.5   **Several power**

Where more than one Receiver is appointed, each Receiver has the power to act severally unless the Lender specifies otherwise in the appointment of such Receiver.

18.6   **Powers exercisable by the Lender**

18.6.1   The Lender may exercise all powers granted to the Receiver by this Debenture, whether as attorney or the Borrower or otherwise.

18.6.2   The powers of the Receiver set out above are in addition to, and without prejudice to, all statutory and other powers of the Lender as provided in Clause 17 (*Statutory power of sale*) or otherwise and so that, inter alia, such powers are and remain exercisable by the Lender in respect of that part of the Charged Property in respect of which no appointment of a Receiver by the Lender is from time to time subsisting.

18.7   **Application of proceeds**

The provisions of ss 99–109 inclusive of the Law of Property Act 1925 are varied and extended to the extent that all monies received by the Receiver be applied in the following order:

18.7.1   in full payment of his remuneration and the Costs of realisation including, without limitation, all Costs of, or incidental to, any exercise of any power referred to in this Debenture, including, without limitation, all outgoings paid by the Receiver;

---

21   Section 109(2) of the Law of Property Act 1925.

18.7.2   providing for the matters specified in paragraphs (i) to (iii) inclusive of s 109(8) of the Law of Property Act 1925 (Appointment, powers, remuneration and duties of receiver);

18.7.3   in or towards satisfaction of any debts or other imposts which are by statute made payable in preference to the Secured Liabilities to the extent to which such debts or imposts are made so payable;

18.7.4   if so required by the Lender in its discretion, in or towards satisfaction of the Secured Liabilities; and

18.7.5   to the person entitled to any surplus.

19   Protection of Third Parties

19.1   No person (including, without limitation, any purchaser, mortgagor or mortgagee) dealing with the Lender shall be concerned to enquire:

19.1.1   whether all or some part of the Secured Liabilities has become due; or

19.1.2   whether a demand for such Secured Liabilities has been duly made; or

19.1.3   whether any power which the Lender or the Receiver is purporting to exercise has become exercisable; or

19.1.4   whether any money remains due under the Finance Documents; or

19.1.5   how any money paid to the Lender or the Receiver is to be applied.

Purpose: A purchaser from a mortgagee is bound to investigate whether the power of sale has arisen and not whether it is exercisable.[22] Most security documents provide that the debt becomes due, demand may be made and the security becomes enforceable on an Event of Default. That is, most have express wording to provide that the power of sale arises upon a demand being served.

20   No Liability as Mortgagee in Possession

Neither the Lender nor the Receiver is, by virtue of entering into possession of any of the Charged Property, liable to account as mortgagee in possession in respect of the Charged Property or for any loss upon realisation or exercise of any power, authority or right of the Lender or the Receiver arising under this Debenture, not for any act, default, neglect, or misconduct of any nature whatsoever.

---

22   Sections 101(1), 104 and 109 of the Law of Property Act 1925.

21   Release and Reassignment

Following the date on which the Lender is satisfied that all the Secured Liabilities have been unconditionally and irrevocably paid and discharged in full the Lender shall, at the request and cost of the Borrower, take whatever action is necessary to release the Charged Property from the security constituted by this Debenture and shall reassign to the Lender all its interest in any property, contracts and collateral warranties assigned absolutely to the Lender under this Debenture.

Lender: Strictly speaking, this wording is unnecessary as the borrower retains its equity of redemption with a mortgage or charge. As an assignment is technically a transfer of title, this uncontroversial wording tends to give the borrower comfort that all its rights under a lease for example, will be passed back to it once the loan has been paid off. Some lenders may insist on inserting the following words, 'at the cost and expense of the borrower'.

Borrower: This clause is only relevant where assets have been assigned to the lender and, in those situations, is generally acceptable. It is not necessary to insert an equivalent 'discharge of security' wording as this is covered by the equity of redemption[23] anyway but many borrowers prefer to see it in the security document by way of comfort.

22   Power of Attorney

The Borrower irrevocably appoints, by way of security the Lender, each person deriving title from the Lender and the Receiver, jointly and severally to be its attorney (with full power to appoint substitutes and to sub-delegate) to do any act or thing which the Borrower is, or may become, obliged to do pursuant to this Debenture. The Borrower ratifies and confirms anything done or purported to be done by any attorney appointed pursuant to this Clause.

Lender: This clause is essential as the lender cannot guarantee the borrower's co-operation to tie up any loose ends and particularly cannot rely on it once a default has occurred and the lender wishes to enforce its security and, in particular, sell the Charged Property. It is vital, therefore, that the power be drafted as widely as possible. A power of attorney (and thus any document containing one) needs to be executed as a deed.[24]

Borrower: Given that the lender's rationale for wanting this power is likely to be to save time and because he cannot always rely on having the borrower's co-operation, it is worth arguing that the power should only be

---

23   Fisher and Lightwood *Law of Mortgage* 10th edn (Butterworths, 1995), at ch 27.
24   Section 1 of the Powers of Attorney Act 1971; s 1 of the Law of Property (Miscellaneous Provisions) Act 1989.

available following an Event of Default which is continuing. This is often accepted. For certain types of borrower, such as nationalised bodies and local government, there may be a 'constitutional' restriction on granting powers of attorney, and this should be investigated before a document comprising one is executed.

23   Cumulative and Continuing Security

23.1   This Debenture is a continuing security to the Lender regardless of any intermediate payment or discharge of the whole or any part of the Secured Liabilities and will not be prejudiced or affected by any act, omission or circumstance which, but for this Clause, might affect or diminish its effectiveness.

23.2   The security constituted by this Debenture is in addition to and is not in any way prejudiced by any rights whatsoever which the Lender may have in respect of the Secured Liabilities including, without limitation, any rights arising under any other Security Interest.

> **Purpose:** *The words 'continuing security' (particularly in an 'all monies' security document) where there is a running account between the borrower and lender, displace the implied legal position[25] and ensure that future drawdowns from the running account are secured. Otherwise, amounts paid in would be deemed to discharge amounts paid out in the order in which they were paid out: the 'first in, first out' rule. The non-prejudice wording in the second half of the clause is particularly important where the security is given as a means of guarantee, which could, by there having been a variation of the underlying debt, affect the validity of the security.*

> **Lender/Borrower:** *This is market standard both in content and in substance, protecting the lender's security rights.*

> **Borrower:** *It is extremely unlikely that any proposed deletion of any of this clause would be accepted.*

24   Avoidance of Payments

24.1   No assurance, security or payment which may be avoided under the law or subject to an order of the court made under any law relating to bankruptcy, insolvency, administration or winding-up, including, without limitation, the Insolvency Act, and no release, settlement or discharge given or made by the Lender on the faith of any such assurance, security or payment, prejudices or affects the right of the Lender:

---

25   *Devaynes v Noble (Clayton's case)* (1816) 1 Mer 529, [1814–1823] All ER Rep 1.

24.1.1   to recover any monies from the Borrower (including, without limitation, any monies which it is compelled to refund under Chapter X (Malpractice before and during liquidation; penalisation of companies and company officers; investigations and prosecutions) of the Insolvency Act and any Costs payable by it incurred in connection with such process); or

24.1.2   to enforce the security constituted by this Debenture to the full extent of the Secured Liabilities.

24.2   The Lender may at its discretion retain the security so created as security for the Secured Liabilities for a period of one month plus any statutory period within which any such assurance, security or payment can be avoided or invalidated notwithstanding any release, settlement, discharge or arrangement given or made by the Lender.

24.3   If at any time within the period referred to in Clause 24.2 any person takes any step whatsoever relating to (i) the winding-up or administration of the Borrower; or (ii) any arrangement with the creditors of the Borrower, the Lender may retain the whole or any part of the security constituted by this Debenture for such further period as the Lender may in its discretion think fit. Such security will be deemed to have been held and remained held by the Lender as security for the payment to the Lender of the Secured Liabilities.

> **Purpose:** *The lender is seeking protection against the possibility that a liquidator or administrator may attempt to recover money repaid to the lender on the grounds that such repayment constituted a preference or a transaction at an undervalue, or that the floating charge might be avoided.*

> **Lender:** *In a situation where the solvency of the borrower is in question, there may be a danger of a payment of the Secured Liabilities by the borrower being held to be a preference or a transaction at an undervalue. At the very least, Clause 24.2 should be retained so that the lender's basic entitlement to sue or prove for an unsecured debt remains if it has to repay any receipts to a liquidator or administrator in this situation. The lender should ensure that the retention of the security is not for an excessive period and does not in any way constitute 'a clog on the equity of redemption'. That is, it should not prohibit the borrower from successfully refinancing. To constitute a clog it would have to be unfair and unconscionable of the lender to retain the security if all amounts have been fully repaid.*

> **Borrower:** *Clauses 24.2 and 24.3 enable the lender to retain its security for up to 25 months after all the Secured Liabilities have been paid off and, as such, this could theoretically block any chance of the borrower refinancing and being able to grant security. The borrower should therefore try to delete this, arguing that it is extremely rare for such a preference or transaction at an undervalue to arise and that the costs of*

*any litigation by a liquidator or administrator to obtain such an order
would be extremely unattractive to a creditor reluctant to see further funds
drained from the assets of the borrower. On a refinancing the security
should be unconditionally released. Some lenders will agree to reduce the
period to a minimum, usually 6 months, and will also agree wording that
the release should be effected on a solvent refinancing.*

25   Prior Charges

At any time after this Debenture has become enforceable the
Lender may redeem any prior Security Interest or procure the
transfer of that Security Interest to itself and may settle and pass the
accounts of the person entitled to that Security Interest. Any
accounts which are settled and passed by the Lender are conclusive
and binding on the Borrower. The Borrower shall reimburse the
Lender for any monies paid out and Costs incurred by the Lender in
exercise of its rights under this Clause.

Purpose: *This is a market standard clause in wording and in substance,
designed to safeguard the lender's interests.*

Lender and Borrower: *It is inappropriate to delete this clause if the lender
is first ranking secured creditor, for after the date of this security
document, priority arrangements may be made expressly with any
subsequent mortgagee with the result that the lender no longer ranks first.*

26   Opening a New Account

If the Lender receives notice of any subsequent Security Interest
affecting the Charged Property the Lender may open a new account
for the Borrower in its books. If the Lender does not open a new
account then, unless the Lender gives express written notice to the
contrary to the Borrower, all payments by or on behalf of the
Borrower to the Lender will be treated from time of receipt of
notice of the subsequent Security Interest by the Lender as having
been credited to a new account of the Borrower and not as having
been applied in reduction of the amount of the Secured Liabilities
as at the time when the notice was received.

Purpose: *This is relevant to all lenders, not just banks as 'account' here
means ledger entry not bank account. The use of the terms 'all monies'
and 'continuing security' will not ensure that further advances made by
the lender after it receives notice of monies having been lent by a third
party and secured by a second charge will have priority for the further
advances over the second mortgagee.*[26] *Ruling off ensures the lender has
priority over the second mortgagee for the new advances, but this is
restricted to the limit of the original debt. In any event, the security*

---

26   *Devaynes v Noble (Clayton's Case)* (1816) 1 Mer 529, [1814–1823] All ER Rep 1.

granted to the lender should comprise a negative pledge against the creation of subsequent security and, in the case of a running account between lender and borrower, a condition of the lender giving consent to any further security will usually be that it retains priority for all monies pursuant to a Deed of Priority.

Lender: *This clause is only relevant where the security is 'all monies' or covers all amounts advanced under a running account such as an overdraft facility for example. It is not relevant to fixed sum security where there is no obligation to advance further funds, although a lender may choose to retain the clause in the event that the existing loan agreement is varied and/or supplemented to provide for further advances.*

Borrower: *The existence, form and substance of this clause is market standard and its deletion is rarely appropriate.*

27   Suspense Account

The Lender may hold in a suspense or impersonal account on whatever terms the Lender may think fit all monies received, recovered or realised by the Lender pursuant to this Debenture until the Secured Liabilities have been irrevocably paid in full.

Purpose: *This protects the lender's ability to prove and ensure it obtains the maximum return. If, for example, the lender receives £50 of the £100 it is owed and applies it to pay off the £100, its debt is then only £50 and it can only prove for that sum in the liquidation of the borrower. If the liquidation dividends are then only 50 pence in each pound, the lender will receive just £75 in total. If, however, on the same facts the lender pays the £50 into a suspense account its provable debt is still £100, which on a dividend of 50 pence brings it £50. Together with the suspense account balance, this means the lender incurs no loss.*

Lender/Borrower: *This is another clause which is market standard in form and substance and is generally only deleted by those who do not understand it. It does at first seem to benefit only the lender but its effect is that which is intended – that the lender receives all that is due to it. The borrower may request that interest should be reduced from that accruing on the outstanding debt to that amount less the amount paid into the suspense account.*

28   Payments and Withholding Taxes

The Borrower shall pay and discharge the Secured Liabilities without any deduction, withholding, set-off, counterclaim, restriction or condition and without regard to any equities between the Borrower and the Lender, except to the extent that the Borrower is required by law to deduct or withhold any amounts payable under this Debenture, in which case it shall pay to the Lender an additional amount sufficient to ensure that the net amount received by the Lender after the required deduction or withholding (including, without limitation, any required deduction or withholding on the additional amount) be equal to the amount that the Lender would have received had no deduction or withholding been made. Any additional amount paid under this Clause shall be treated as agreed compensation and not as interest.

Purpose: This is the market standard grossing up clause.

Lender/Borrower: Where there is a loan agreement this wording should be repeated in the security too as all interest and other payments under the security (after a default) are made in the same way.

29   Set-off

The Borrower agrees the Lender may at any time after this Debenture has become enforceable without notice or further demand combine or consolidate all or any of its then existing accounts including any accounts in the name of the Lender or of the Borrower jointly with others (whether current, deposit, loan or any other nature whatsoever whether subject to notice or not and whether in sterling or in any other currency) and set-off or transfer any sum standing to the credit of any one or more of those accounts in or towards satisfaction of the Secured Liabilities.

Purpose/Lender/Borrower: See Clause 28 in Document 1.

30   Assignment

Neither the Lender nor the Borrower may assign, transfer, novate or dispose of any of its rights and obligations under this Debenture except that the Lender may assign, transfer, novate or dispose of any of its rights and obligations under this Debenture to any person to whom it assigns, transfers, novates or disposes of any of its rights and obligations under the Finance Documents.

Purpose/Lender/Borrower: See Clauses 24 and 25 in Document 1.

31   Waivers

No failure or delay or other relaxation or indulgence on the part of the Lender to exercise any power, right or remedy shall operate as a waiver thereof nor shall any single or partial exercise or waiver of any power, right or remedy preclude its further exercise or the exercise of any other power, right or remedy.

Purpose/Lender/Borrower: See Clause 32 in Document 1.

32   **Severability**

Each of the provisions of this Debenture is distinct and severable from the others and if at any time one or more of such provisions is or becomes illegal, invalid or unenforceable the validity, legality and enforceability of the remaining provisions hereof shall not in any way be affected or impaired thereby.

Purpose/Lender/Borrower: See Clause 31 in Document 1.

33   **HM Land Registry**

The Borrower hereby applies to the Chief Land Registrar to enter a restriction in the Proprietorship Registers of the registered titles (if any) of the Scheduled Property or, in the case of the first registration of the whole or any part of the Scheduled Property, against the Scheduled Property, or both, of a restriction in the following form:

'Except under an order of the Registrar no disposition or dealing by the proprietor of the land is to be registered without the consent of the proprietor for the time being of the charge hereby created'.

Purpose: To 'top up' the strongest form of security over land, the legal mortgage, this is essential.

Lender/Borrower: The wording and existence of the clause and the restriction is very much standard and the only scope for negotiation is to question its relevance where real property is not a significant part of the borrower's assets.

34   **Notices**

34.1   Each party may give any notice, demand or other communication under or in connection with this Debenture by letter, telex, facsimile or comparable means of communication addressed to the other party at the address identified with its name below. Any such communication will be deemed to be given as follows:

34.1.1   if personally delivered, at the time of delivery;

34.1.2   if by letter, at noon on the Business Day following the day such letter was posted (or in the case of airmail, seven days after the envelope containing the same was delivered into the custody of the postal authorities); and

34.1.3   if by telex, facsimile transmission or comparable means of communication during the business hours of the addressee then on the day of transmission, otherwise on the next following Business Day.

Purpose/Lender/Borrower: See Clause 29 in Document 1.

34.2   In proving such service it shall be sufficient to prove that personal delivery was made or that such letter was properly stamped first class, addressed and delivered to the postal authorities or that the telex was transmitted with a correct answerback or in the case of facsimile transmission or other comparable means of communication, that a confirming hard copy was provided promptly after transmission.

35   Governing Law and Jurisdiction

35.1   This Debenture shall be governed by and construed in accordance with English law.

Purpose/Lender/Borrower: See Clause 34 in Document 1.

35.2   The Borrower agrees that any legal action or proceedings arising out of or in connection with this Debenture against the Borrower or any of its assets may be brought in the High Court of Justice in England, irrevocably and unconditionally submits to the jurisdiction of such Court and irrevocably designates, appoints and empowers [   ] at present of [   ] to receive for it and on its behalf, service of process issued out of such Court in any such legal action or proceedings. The submission to such jurisdiction shall not (and shall not be construed so as to) limit the right of the Lender to take proceedings against the Borrower in whatsoever jurisdictions it thinks fit, nor shall the taking of proceedings in any one or more jurisdiction preclude the taking of proceedings in any other jurisdiction, whether concurrently or not. The Borrower waives objection to such Court on the grounds of inconvenient forum or otherwise as regards proceedings in connection with this Debenture and agrees that the judgment or order of such Court in connection with this Debenture is conclusive and binding on it and may be enforced against it in the courts of any other jurisdiction.

IN WITNESS WHEREOF this Debenture has been executed and delivered as a deed on the date written at the beginning of this Debenture.

Purpose: A security document needs to be executed as a deed for several reasons:

(a)   if it is or contains a legal mortgage;[27]

(b)   if it is or contains an equitable charge;[28]

(c)   if it contains a power of attorney.[29]

---

27   Law of Property Act 1925, s 85(1).
28   Law of Property Act 1925, s 101.
29   Powers of Attorney Act 1971, s 1.

A security document containing security over land and a covenant for further assurance should be executed by both lender and borrower.[30]

Where executed by a company, a deed must be executed by two directors or one director and the company secretary.[31] *It is no longer a requirement for a company to execute a document under seal,*[32] *unless its constitutional documents require otherwise.*

---

30   Law Reform (Miscellaneous Provisions) Act 1971, s 2.
31   Companies Act 1985, s 35A.
32   Companies Act 1985, s 36A(4).

SCHEDULE 1

Scheduled Property

Description   Title Number and District Registry or London Borough

SCHEDULE 2

Form of notice to tenant

Part 1

Notice

[TO BE TYPED ON THE HEADED NOTEPAPER OF THE CHARGOR]

To: [The Tenant]
     [   ]
     [   ]   Date: [   ]

Dear Sirs,

Premises at [   ] (the 'Property')

We refer to a debenture dated [   ] (the **'Debenture'**) by which the Property has been charged to [   ] (the **'Lender'**) by us.

We hereby give you notice that by the Debenture we assigned by way of absolute assignment to the Lender all monies payable by yourselves by way of rent and other related payments (the **'Rent'**) (but excluding monies payable in respect of insurance, insurance rents, service charges and taxes on rental income (the **'Service Charges'**)) under the lease dated [   ] between yourselves and ourselves.

Until further notice from the Lender please pay all the Rent to account number [   ] [in the name of [   ], designated as [   ] or such other account as the Lender may notify to you in writing.

[[Managing Agents] are the managing agents in relation to the Property.]

Please acknowledge receipt of this notice by signing and delivering the attached acknowledgement to the Lender.

This notice shall be governed by and construed in accordance with English law.

Yours faithfully,

For and on behalf of
[   ]

Warning:

From the date of receipt of this notice you cannot obtain good discharge if you make any payment of Rent to us. You will remain liable to the Lender for payment of Rent **unless** it is made in accordance with the provisions of this notice.

Purpose: *The warning is essential, for with notice served the rent has been legally assigned and thus it is the lender who is its true legal owner. If a tenant continues to pay rent to the borrower or the managing agents therefore, the lender would still be entitled to sue for the same amount.*

Part 2

Acknowledgement

[TO BE TYPED ON THE HEADED NOTEPAPER OF THE TENANT]

To: [   ]
      [   ]

Dear Sirs,

Premises at [   ] (the 'Property')

We confirm receipt from you of a notice dated [   ] of an assignment of all Rent in relation to the Property (the **'Notice'**). Expressions defined in the Notice shall have the same meanings in this letter.

We confirm that we have not received notice of the interest of any third party to any of the Rent, including, without limitation, any assignment of any of the Rent, to any party other than the Lender.

We have no right of set-off, counterclaim or other deduction against the Rent and we undertake to pay the Rent and the Service Charges to the accounts specified in the Notice (or, as the case may be, such other account notified to us) without set-off, counterclaim or any other deduction.

This letter shall be governed by and construed in accordance with English law.

Yours faithfully,

For and on behalf of
[the Tenant]

SCHEDULE 3

Part 1

Notice to [Bank]

To: [Bank] plc

     [   ] Branch

     [

               ]

     Attention: [   ]

[Date]

Dear Sirs,

We hereby give you notice that by a Debenture dated the same date as this letter (the **'Debenture'**), we have charged to [   ] (the **'Lender'**) all our rights, title, interest and benefit in and to the following account held with yourselves and all amounts standing to the credit of such account from time to time:

Account No. [   ], sort code [   ] (the 'Blocked Account').

We have also assigned to the Lender all rental income in respect of our property at [   ] (the 'Rent'), which is the only cashflow into the Blocked Account.

Please acknowledge receipt of this letter by returning a copy of the attached letter on your own headed notepaper with a receipted copy of this notice forthwith, to the Lender at [   ].

Yours faithfully

for and on behalf of

[   ]

Purpose: This puts the bank at which the rent account is held on notice that the funds in the account have been charged to the lender and the income stream into the rent account has been assigned to the lender, which prevents the account holding bank from being able to set-off funds standing to the credit of the rent account with debit balances or other accounts post insolvency of the borrower.

Part 2

Acknowledgement from [Bank]

[TO BE TYPED ON THE HEADED NOTEPAPER OF [BANK]]

To: [   ] (the 'Lender')

Attention: [   ]

[Date]

Dear Sirs,

Re: [   ]

We refer to the notice, received today from [   ] (a copy of which we attach, receipted) (the **'Notice'**).

Terms not defined in this letter shall have the meanings given to them in the Notice.

We acknowledge that you have consented to the Blocked Account being held with us.

With respect to the Notice:

1	We hereby acknowledge:
1.1	that [ ] has charged to the Lender all of its rights, title, interest and benefit in and to the Blocked Account; and
1.2	that [ ] has absolutely and legally assigned (where assignable) or charged by way of fixed charge (where not assignable) to you all of its rights, title, interest and benefit in and to the Rent.
2	We hereby irrevocably undertake to you that until receipt by us of notice from you confirming that you no longer have any interest in the Blocked Account and the Rent, we shall:
2.1	not exercise any right of combination, consolidation, merger or set-off which we may have in respect of, or otherwise exercise any other right which we may have to apply any monies from time to time standing or accruing to the credit of the Blocked Account save for fees and charges payable to us for the operation of the Blocked Account;
2.2	promptly notify you of any renewal, renumbering or redesignation of the Blocked Account;
2.3	promptly send to you copies with respect to the Blocked Account of all statements together with copies of all credits, debits and notices given or made by us in connection with such account;

2.4   not permit or effect any withdrawal or transfer from the Blocked Account by or on behalf of [   ] save for withdrawals and transfers requested by you in writing to us pursuant to the terms of this letter;

2.5   comply with all instructions received by us from you from time to time with respect to the conduct of the Blocked Account provided that such instructions are given in accordance with the terms of this letter;

2.6   comply with all instructions received by us from you from time to time with respect to the movement of funds from the Blocked Account provided that:

(a)   all instructions are received in writing, by facsimile, to us at [Bank], facsimile number [   ], attention [   ]; and

(b)   all instructions must be received by 2 pm if they are to be complied with on the same Business Day. Instructions received outside such hours will be complied with on the next Business Day following such receipt. Facsimile instructions will be deemed received at the time of transmission;

(c)   all instructions are given in compliance with the mandate entered into by you stipulating who may give instructions to us; and

(d)   to the extent that an instruction is given which would in our opinion cause the Blocked Account to become overdrawn we will transfer the outstanding balance in the account;

2.7   we shall not be obliged to comply with any instructions received from you where:

(a)   due to circumstances not within our direct control we are unable to comply with such instructions; and

(b)   that to comply with such instructions will breach a Court Order or be contrary to applicable law;

and in each case we shall give notice thereof to [   ] and the Lender as well as reasons why we cannot comply with such instructions;

2.8   in the event that we are unable to comply with any instructions due to circumstances set out in paragraph 2.7 we shall not be responsible for any loss caused to you or to [   ] and in any event we shall not be liable for any consequential, special, secondary or indirect loss of or damage to goodwill, profits or anticipated savings (however caused); and

2.9   you acknowledge that we are obliged to comply with the terms of this letter and that we have no notice of the particulars of the charge granted to the Lender by [   ] other than as set out in the Notice and this letter.

We note that, for the purposes of this letter, all notices, copy notices, advices and correspondence to be delivered to you shall be effectively delivered if sent by facsimile to you at facsimile number [   ] or by post at the address at the top of this letter, in both cases marked for the attention of [   ].

This letter is governed by and shall be construed in accordance with English law.

Yours faithfully

for and on behalf of

[BANK]

We hereby acknowledge and accept the terms of this letter

for and on behalf of

[   ]

Debenture execution page

EXECUTED and DELIVERED as a DEED
for and on behalf of
[   ] by:

                         Director

                         Director/Secretary

Notice details

Address:

Telex No:

Fax No:

Telephone No:

Attention:

SIGNED for and on behalf of
[   ] by:

Notice details

Address:

Telex No:

Fax No:

Telephone No:

Attention:

DOCUMENT 3: THE GUARANTEE

CONTENTS

1	Definitions and Interpretation	167
3	Guarantee and Indemnity	170
3	Continuing Security	173
4	Protective Clauses	174
5	Powers of the Lender	177
6	Termination	178
7	Expenses	179
8	Set-off and Lien	180
9	Payments, Currencies and Taxes	180
10	Miscellaneous	181
11	Notices	183
12	Governing Law	184
13	Counterparts and Delivery	184

DOCUMENT 3: THE GUARANTEE

DATE

PARTIES

(1)   [   ] (the **'Guarantor'**); and

(2)   [   ] (the **'Lender'**).

Lender: *Caution should be shown where the guarantor has the same surname as the Principal Debtor as it may reveal the guarantor to be the Principal Debtor's spouse. This is an area fraught with danger for the Lender.*[1]

RECITALS

(A) The Lender has agreed to make available to the Principal Debtor a loan facility of up to £[   ] subject to and upon the terms and conditions contained in the Loan Agreement (as defined below).

(B) As a condition precedent to and pursuant to the provisions of the Loan Agreement the Guarantor has agreed to enter into this Guarantee for the purpose of providing security to the Lender for the Guaranteed Liabilities.

IT IS AGREED AS FOLLOWS:

1   Definitions and Interpretation

1.1   Definitions

In this Guarantee:

Purpose/Lender/Guarantor: *Terms defined in the loan and security documents should be defined here again if used here unless the guarantor is a party to the loan and security documents.*

| **'Business Day'** | means a day (other than a Saturday or Sunday) on which banks are open for general business in London; |

---

1   See *Barclays Bank v O'Brien* [1994] 1 AC 180; *CIBC Mortgages Plc v Pitt* [1994] AC 200.

'Collateral Instruments'	means notes, bills of exchange, certificates of deposit and other negotiable and non-negotiable instruments, guarantees, indemnities and other assurances against financial loss and any other documents or instruments which contain or evidence an obligation (with or without security) to pay, discharge or be responsible directly or indirectly for, any indebtedness or liabilities of the Principal Debtor or any other person liable and includes the Security Documents;
'Exchange Rate'	means the prevailing spot rate of exchange of the Lender (as conclusively determined by the Lender) at or around 11:00 am on the date on which any conversion of currency is to be effected pursuant to this Guarantee;
'Guarantee'	includes each separate or independent stipulation or agreement by the Guarantor contained herein;
'Guaranteed Liabilities'	means all monies, obligations and liabilities expressed to be guaranteed by the Guarantor in Clause 2.1;

Purpose: This definition will change depending on the nature of the underlying obligations and liabilities of the Principal Debtor.

'Incapacity'	in relation to a person, means the death, bankruptcy, unsoundness of mind, insolvency, liquidation, dissolution, winding up, administration, receivership, amalgamation, reconstruction or other incapacity of that person whatsoever (and, in the case of a partnership, includes the termination or change in the composition of the partnership);
'Loan Agreement'	means the Loan Agreement dated [ ] and made between the Principal Debtor and the Lender;
'Principal Debtor'	means [the Borrower];

Purpose: The Principal Debtor is the entity which has the primary obligation to the lender to repay the liabilities. It will usually be the borrower under a loan agreement, but may also be, for example, a tenant under a lease agreement or purchaser under a share sale agreement.

'Security Documents'	means documents or instruments creating or evidencing a mortgage, charge (whether fixed or floating), pledge, lien, hypothecation, assignment, trust arrangement or security interest of any kind; and
'Sterling' and '£'	means the lawful currency for the time being of the United Kingdom and in respect of all payments to be made hereunder in Sterling means immediately available, freely transferable cleared funds.

1.2   **Interpretation**

1.2.1   The index and clause headings are included for convenience only and do not affect the construction of this Guarantee, words denoting the singular include the plural and vice versa and words denoting one gender include each gender.

1.2.2   Unless the context otherwise requires, references herein to:

(a) persons include references to natural persons, firms, partnerships, companies, corporations, associations, organisations and trusts (in each case whether or not having a separate legal personality);

(b) documents, instruments and agreements are references to such documents, instruments and agreements as modified, amended, varied, supplemented or novated from time to time;

(c) the term 'Guarantor' includes every person liable hereunder including each of the partners, present and future, of a partnership and any one or more of them and their respective personal representatives and any other person lawfully acting on behalf of such person;

(d) a party hereto includes references to its successors, transferees and assigns;

(e) Clauses are references to clauses hereof;

(f) statutory provisions (where the context so admits and unless otherwise expressly provided) are construed as references to those provisions as respectively amended, consolidated, extended or re-enacted from time to time, and to any orders, regulations, instruments or other subordinate legislation made under the relevant statute; and

(g) a time of day is a reference to London time.

Purpose/Lender/Guarantor: As a general rule, a contract of guarantee will be construed like any other contract.[2]

2   Guarantee and Indemnity

2.1   In consideration of the Lender making or continuing loans or advances to, or otherwise giving credit or granting banking facilities or accommodation or granting time to, the Principal Debtor for so long as it may think fit, the Guarantor hereby guarantees to pay to the Lender on demand all monies and discharge all obligations and liabilities now or hereafter due, owing or incurred by the Principal Debtor to the Lender when the same become due for payment or discharge whether by acceleration or otherwise, and whether such monies, obligations or liabilities are express or implied, present, future or contingent, joint or several, incurred as principal or surety, originally owing to the Lender or purchased or otherwise acquired by it, denominated in Sterling or in any other currency, or incurred on any banking account or in any other manner whatsoever.

Purpose: This clause sets out the extent of the guarantor's obligations (ie the guaranteed liabilities) and the circumstances in which they will be payable.

For the guarantee to be effective, either there must be consideration or the document must be executed as a deed. The consideration should come from the lender rather than from the borrower. Normally, 'consideration' will be constituted by the provision of a loan facility to the borrower and to ensure that the guarantee is not provided before the loan facility is executed, most recital clauses will state that the provision of the gurantee is a condition precedent to the advance of the facility under the loan agreement.

Lender: From the lender's point of view this clause should be as extensive as possible, covering both payment and non-payment obligations of the principal debtor to the lender. Most guarantees are payable 'on demand' and therefore the limitation period (which is 6 years for an agreement and 12 years for a deed) will only commence once demand has been made. This is obviously for the benefit of the lender who clearly does not want the limitation period to commence as soon as the principal debtor has defaulted but before demand has been made.

Some lenders may try to incorporate indemnity type wording such as 'the guarantor hereby irrevocably and unconditionally guarantees as primary obligor'. If it is the lender's intention to obtain an indemnity and not a guarantee then the document should specifically state so. If the lender is actually seeking an unconditional primary obligation as is inherent in an

---

2   Where the wording is ambiguous the courts will apply the 'contra proferentem' rule. That is, the clause will be construed against the person relying upon it (usually the beneficiary). For further discussion, see Andrews and Millett *Law of Guarantees* 3rd edn (2000) at ch 4.

indemnity, then that is the document which should be drafted. It is clearly in both the lender's and guarantor's interest that both parties are aware of the obligations and the nature of the transaction. If the document is described as a guarantee, a court interpreting it may construe it as such and the onus of proof will be on the lender to establish that it is not in fact a guarantee but an indemnity. The name of the document will not of itself be conclusive.[3] There is also now a particular danger that any clause which has not been negotiated by a personal guarantor may be unenforceable if it is unfair.[4]

There has been a substantial amount of case-law on the meaning of the words 'as principal obligor and not merely as surety'. Some construe the document as a guarantee, others as an indemnity and some as a guarantee subsequently transforming into an indemnity.[5]

Guarantor: *The guarantor must ensure that this clause accurately reflects what its liability will be and no more and, in particular, whether the liability is to be primary or secondary. The guarantor will generally not wish to provide an indemnity and should therefore resist wording such as 'unconditionally', 'irrevocably' and 'as principal debtor'.*

If a guarantee is being sought, the guarantor should ensure that its liability will only crystallise on non-payment by the principal debtor. Where the guarantor is guaranteeing an amount under a loan agreement, the guarantor should ensure that the definition of 'Guaranteed Liabilities' reflects this and that the guarantee does not constitute an 'all monies' guarantee. This clause should be amended to limit the 'all monies' nature to a specific liability. That is, to 'all monies under the loan agreement dated [   ]'.

Most guarantee documents also contain clauses which oblige the guarantor to guarantee the performance of the borrower's other non-payment obligations. The guarantor must assess whether it can comply with such obligations.

2.2   The total amount recoverable from the Guarantor hereunder shall not exceed £[   ] together with a further sum for all interest, commission, fees and other charges and all legal and other costs, charges and expenses as stated in Clause 2.1 as shall have accrued or shall accrue due to the Lender at any time before or after the date of demand hereunder.

Purpose: *This clause sets out the limitation of the guarantor's liability under the guarantee. Not all guarantees will have a limit. It is important that the guarantor is aware of the extent of the liabilities under the*

---

3   *Re Denton's Estate* [1904] 2 Ch 178 at 188.
4   See Pitfalls: para 1 at p 187.
5   *Heald v O'Connor* [1971] 2 All ER 1105; *General Produce Co v United Bank Ltd* [1979] 2 Lloyd's Rep 255.

guarantee and whether it is to be limited or unlimited, either as to the amount of the liabilities or as to the duration for which it will be liable.

Lender: *It is important that this clause is expressed to be a guarantee of the whole of the liabilities albeit limited to an agreed lesser amount. In this way, the guarantor will not be able to argue that his obligation to pay is restricted to a particular part of the principal debt and therefore that the guarantee may be discharged before the principal obligations have been discharged in full. The phrasing of the limitation also prevents the guarantor from claiming in competition against the principal debtor until the lender has been paid in full, that is 'all of the liabilities'.*[6]

The lender will also seek to ensure that the guarantor will be liable not only for the principal amount (subject to a maximum) but also all interest, costs and charges incurred in respect thereof.

Guarantor: *The guarantor must be sure that the limitation clause accurately reflects the commercial agreement. The guarantor should try to limit the amount to a principal amount including interest, costs and charges, although it is unlikely that the lender will accept this. Furthermore, the guarantor should, if the liability is limited, try to ensure that the guarantee is for the agreed limit rather than the whole amount subject to the agreed limit. Guaranteeing a limited amount would allow the guarantor to exercise its rights of subrogation once it had paid the amount of the limit. If not, it would not be entitled to claim against the principal debtor until all amounts had been paid in full.*[7]

2.3   As a separate and independent stipulation, the Guarantor agrees that if any purported obligation or liability of the Principal Debtor which would have been the subject hereof had it been valid and enforceable is not or ceases to be valid or enforceable against the Principal Debtor on any ground whatsoever whether or not known to the Lender the Guarantor shall nevertheless be liable to the Lender in respect of that purported obligation or liability as if the same were fully valid and enforcable and the Guarantor were the Principal Debtor in respect thereof. The Guarantor hereby agrees to keep the Lender fully indemnified on demand against all damages, losses, costs and expenses arising from any failure of the Principal Debtor to perform or discharge any such purported obligation or liability.

Purpose: *The purpose of this clause is to prevent the guarantee from being discharged in the event that the principal debtor's obligations or liabilities are for any reason invalid or unenforceable. Without this express wording, the guarantor would not be liable if the principal liabilities were to fail.*[8]

---

6   *Ellis v Emmanuel* (1876) 1 Ex D 157.
7   Ibid.
8   *Heald v O'Connor* [1971] 2 All ER 1105.

Effectively, the clause upgrades the guarantee to an indemnity by removing the reliance on the underlying transaction.

Lender: *From the lender's point of view, it is important to state that this is a 'separate and independent stipulation' as without such wording it may be construed as a guarantee which would therefore be rendered ineffective if the underlying liability was invalid or unenforceable for any reason.*

2.4 Any statement of account of the Principal Debtor, signed as correct by an officer of the Lender, showing the amount of the Guaranteed Liabilities shall, in the absence of manifest error, be binding and conclusive on and against the Guarantor.

Purpose: *The purpose of this clause is to overcome any evidentiary difficulties regarding the proof of amounts owing by the principal debtor.*[9] *The guarantor may want to mitigate the effect of this clause by substituting 'prima facie' for 'conclusive', thus at least giving the opportunity to rebut this if it can. The LMA position is that accounts are considered prima facie evidence whilst certificates are conclusive.*

2.5 The Guarantor agrees to pay interest on each amount demanded of it hereunder from the date of such demand until payment (as well after as before judgment) at the rate of [   ] per cent per annum upon such days and upon such terms as the Lender may from time to time determine. Such interest shall be compounded in the event of it not being punctually paid with quarterly rests in accordance with the usual practice of the Lender but without prejudice to the Lender's right to require payment of such interest when due.

Purpose: *See Clause 8.4 in Document 1 at p 45.*

3   Continuing Security

3.1 This Guarantee shall:

3.1.1 secure the ultimate balance from time to time owing to the Lender by the Principal Debtor and shall, subject to Clause 6 (*Termination*) be a continuing security, notwithstanding any settlement of account or other matter whatsoever;

3.1.2 be in addition to any present or future Collateral Instrument, right or remedy held by or available to the Lender; and

3.1.3 not be in any way prejudiced or affected by the existence of any such Collateral Instrument, rights or remedies or by the same becoming wholly or partly void, voidable or unenforceable on any ground whatsoever or by the Lender dealing with, exchanging, varying or

---

9   *Bache and Co (London) Ltd v Banque Vernes et Commercial de Paris SA* [1973] 2 Lloyd's Rep 437.

failing to perfect or enforce any of the same or giving time for payment or indulgence or compounding with any other person liable.

3.2 If this Guarantee ceases to be continuing for any reason whatsoever the Lender may nevertheless continue any account of the Principal Debtor or open one or more new accounts and the liability of the Guarantor hereunder shall not in any manner be reduced or affected by any subsequent transactions or receipts or payments into or out of any such account.

Purpose: There is a distinction between a specific and continuing guarantee. The former is one which deals with a specific liability such as a specific amount under a specified invoice and the latter deals with liabilities which continue to arise such as amounts due under an overdraft loan facility.

Lender: The lender usually requires this clause to overcome the difficulties relating to guarantee obligations which arise from the 'first in, first out'[10] rule that the liability of the guarantor is reduced by successive payments to the lender by the borrower and hence subsequent drawings are no longer guaranteed. This clause is seldom contested other than to reflect the commercial terms of the transaction. It is most appropriate in overdraft facilities where amounts are being repaid and reborrowed.

4 Protective Clauses

4.1 The liability of the Guarantor shall not be affected nor shall this Guarantee be discharged or reduced by reason of:

4.1.1 the Incapacity or any change in the name, style or constitution of the Principal Debtor or any other person liable;

4.1.2 the Lender granting any time, indulgence or concession to, or compounding with, discharging, releasing or varying the liability of, the Principal Debtor or any other person liable or renewing, determining, varying or increasing any accommodation, facility or transaction or otherwise dealing with the same in any manner whatsoever or concurring in, accepting or varying any compromise, arrangement or settlement or omitting to claim or enforce payment from the Principal Debtor or any other person liable; or

4.1.3 any act or omission which would not have discharged or affected the liability of the Guarantor had it been a principal debtor instead of a guarantor or by anything done or omitted which but for this provision might operate to exonerate the Guarantor.

---

10   See Document 2 at p 148.

4.2   The Lender shall not be obliged to make any claim or demand on the Principal Debtor or to resort to any Collateral Instrument or other means of payment now or hereafter held by or available to the Lender before enforcing this Guarantee and no action taken or omitted by the Lender in connection with any such Collateral Instrument or other means of payment shall discharge, reduce, prejudice or affect the liability of the Guarantor hereunder nor shall the Lender be obliged to apply any money or other property received or recovered in consequence of any enforcement or realisation of any such Collateral Instrument or other means of payment in reduction of the Guaranteed Liabilities.

4.3   The Guarantor warrants that it has not taken or received, and undertakes that until all the Guaranteed Liabilities have been paid or discharged in full, it will not take or receive, the benefit of any security from the Principal Debtor or any other person in respect of its obligations hereunder.

> ***Purpose:*** *This clause is inserted to avoid certain legal presumptions which arise concerning guarantees.[11] The underlying rationale for these presumptions is that the guarantor should not be prejudiced where the underlying transaction changes after the date of the guarantee.[12] The effect of the presumptions is that where one of the circumstances occurs, the guarantor is released. This is obviously of great concern to lenders and the practice has arisen of inserting 'protective' clauses to combat and negate the effect of these presumptions.*

> ***Lender:*** *It is important that the guarantee continues notwithstanding any change to the underlying obligations. The lender can deal with this by ensuring that the guarantor agrees to these (often by countersigning the amendment documentation). In any event, this clause is not usually contested. It is implicit that the guarantor accepts all liabilities notwithstanding any variation of the underlying transaction, although where its principal liability is not capped, the guarantor may well insist that there is no material amendment to the underlying agreement which could increase its liability without its consent or at least without consultation.*

> *There is also a particular danger that any clause which has not been negotiated by a personal guarantor and which a guarantor later considers harsh may be unenforceable under the Unfair Terms in Consumer Contracts Regulations 1999.[13]*

> ***Guarantor:*** *The effect of these clauses is, to some extent, to impute indemnity language into what is a secondary obligation. The guarantor*

---

11   See *Perry v National Provincial Bank of England* [1910] 1 Ch 464, CA as to the effect of such clauses.

12   For more detail, see Lingard *Bank Security Documents* 3rd edn (Butterworths, 1993), at pp 226–242.

13   See Pitfalls: para 1 at p 187.

*can insist that notice should first be given to it if material changes are
made to the underlying transaction and, furthermore, its consent should
be obtained to such amendments. Obvious material matters would be an
increase in the amount of the loan facility or increase in the overdraft
limit.*[14]

4.4   Until all the Guaranteed Liabilities have been paid, discharged or
           satisfied in full (and notwithstanding payment of a dividend in any
           liquidation or bankruptcy or under any compromise or arrange-
           ment) the Guarantor agrees that, without the prior written consent
           of the Lender, it will not:

4.4.1   exercise its rights of subrogation, reimbursement and indemnity
           against the Principal Debtor;

4.4.2   demand or accept repayment in whole or in part of any indebted-
           ness now or hereafter due to the Guarantor from the Principal
           Debtor or from any other person liable or demand or accept any
           Collateral Instrument in respect of the same or dispose of the same;

4.4.3   take any step to enforce any right against the Principal Debtor or
           any other person liable in respect of any Guaranteed Liabilities; or

4.4.4   claim any set-off or counterclaim against the Principal Debtor or
           any other person liable or claim or prove in competition with the
           Lender in the bankruptcy or liquidation of the Principal Debtor or
           any other person liable or have the benefit of, or share in, any
           payment from or composition with, the Principal Debtor or any
           other person liable or any other Collateral Instrument now or
           hereafter held by the Lender for any Guaranteed Liabilities or for
           the obligations or liabilities of any other person liable but so that, if
           so directed by the Lender, it will prove for the whole or any part of its
           claim in the liquidation or bankruptcy of the Principal Debtor on
           terms that the benefit of such proof and of all money received by it
           in respect thereof shall be held on trust for the Lender and applied
           in or towards discharge of the Guaranteed Liabilities in such
           manner as the Lender shall deem appropriate.

4.5   If, contrary to Clauses 4.3 or 4.4, the Guarantor takes or receives the
           benefit of any security or receives or recovers any money or other
           property, such security, money or other property shall be held on
           trust for the Lender and shall be delivered to the Lender on
           demand.

           Purpose: *This clause aims to ensure that the lender shall be entitled to
           pursue the principal debtor without any competition or interference from
           the guarantor and that the amount guaranteed by the guarantor and*

---

14   See *Guinness Mahon & Co Ltd v Kensington and Chelsea Royal London Borough Council* [1998]
      3 WLR 829.

therefore recoverable from it is not in any way diminished or prejudiced. If the guarantor has paid off the principal debtor's liabilities in full, it is entitled to exercise all of the rights the creditors had against the principal debtor.[15] *This right, known as subrogation, will only arise once the debt is paid in full; there is no pro rata subrogation on part payments. Hence the importance of the wording of the limitation clause.*[16]

Lender: *This clause is seldom contested, being implicit that until all amounts have been paid to the lender the guarantor is not entitled to exercise any of its rights as a creditor against the principal debtor. The lender needs to ensure that it can claim against the guarantor the full amount stipulated in the guarantee and nothing should diminish or prejudice this right.*

In addition, the lender will ask the guarantor to pass on any amounts it has received from the principal debtor to the extent that it has breached the provisions of this clause and such amounts are deemed to be held on trust for the lender separate from the guarantor's other assets and thus 'safe' from a receiver or liquidator, for example. The lender will require the clause to be drafted to cover all situations so as to preserve its rights.

Guarantor: *Usually the guarantor will not have very much success in trying to negotiate this clause. At the very least the guarantor should understand the extent to which it is prohibited from competing against the lender (as against the principal debtor) and exercising any rights that it might have against the principal debtor. This may be pertinent where the guarantor is the holding company/shareholder of the principal debtor and there may be complex inter-company loan arrangements in place.*

5 Powers of the Lender

5.1 Any money received in connection herewith may be placed to the credit of a suspense account (with a view to preserving the rights of the Lender to prove for the whole of its claims against the Principal Debtor or any other person liable) or may be applied in or towards satisfaction of such of the Guaranteed Liabilities of the Principal Debtor as the Lender may from time to time conclusively determine in its absolute discretion.

5.2 The Lender shall be entitled to retain this Guarantee after as well as before the payment or discharge of all the Guaranteed Liabilities for such period as the Lender may determine.

Purpose/Lender/Guarantor: *See equivalent clause in Document 2 at page 151.*

---

15 The right of subrogation exists both in equity and under s 5 of the Mercantile Law Amendment Act 1856.

16 See Andrews and Millett *Law of Guarantees* pp 301–307.

5.3   Any release, discharge or settlement between the Guarantor and the Lender shall be conditional upon no security, disposition or payment to the Lender by the Principal Debtor or any other person liable being void, set aside or ordered to be refunded pursuant to any enactment or law relating to bankruptcy, liquidation, administration or insolvency or for any other reason whatsoever and if such condition shall not be fulfilled the Lender shall be entitled to enforce this Guarantee subsequently as if such release, discharge or settlement had not occurred and any such payment had not been made.

5.4   The Lender shall be entitled to retain this Guarantee after as well as before the payment or discharge of all the Guaranteed Liabilities for such period as the Lender may determine.

        Purpose/Lender/Guarantor: *See equivalent clause in Document 2 at page 148.*

6   Termination

        The Guarantor may at any time give the Lender notice in writing to determine this Guarantee with effect from the date (the 'Termination Date') specified in such a notice, being a date falling not less than three calendar months after such notice shall actually have been received by the Lender. Notwithstanding the giving of any such notice, the liability of the Guarantor hereunder shall continue in full force and effect in relation to:

6.1   all Guaranteed Liabilities which shall have become due at the Termination Date; and

6.2   all Guaranteed Liabilities which may become due, owing or incurred by the Principal Debtor to the Lender pursuant to any transaction, dealing, commitment or other engagement entered into or effected either (i) prior to the Termination Date; or (ii) on or after the Termination Date pursuant to any commitment, expressed or implied, assumed or undertaken by the Lender to the Principal Debtor prior to the Termination Date.

        Purpose: *This clause sets out when the guarantee terminates, thus making it a 'limited guarantee'.*

        Some guarantees provide for express termination by notice while others have no such provisions. Where the guarantee is silent, the ability of the guarantor to terminate or revoke its liability depends on whether the underlying transaction (the obligations which are being guaranteed) is divisible or complete. Divisible means that the guarantee covers a series of liabilities on a continuing basis; and complete (or indivisible) means that the guarantee is specific to particular liabilities.

        Generally, if the underlying or principal contract is divisible, the guarantor may revoke all future liability under the guarantee at any time

unless the contract provides to the contrary. Therefore, the guarantee of the principal debtor's obligations under an overdraft facility, where the lender has a continuing obligation to make further advances, would be revocable at any time by the guarantor in respect of future further advances. Where the underlying/principal contract is complete, such as a lease agreement, a guarantee for rent in respect of the lease agreement for a fixed period would not be capable of being revoked.

Revocation or cancellation of the guarantee will not affect the rights which have accrued up to the date of termination and the guarantor would normally be liable for all amounts outstanding as of that date.

Lender: *If the lender is prepared to agree to a termination provision, it will normally seek to ensure that all liabilities due as of the termination date, as well as liabilities which arise after the termination date but are caused by circumstances arising before the termination date, will still continue to be guaranteed.*

If the lender is not prepared to grant a termination provision, it should state specifically that the guarantee is irrevocable and not capable of being cancelled. If the underlying obligations are divisible it is sometimes more satisfactory to acknowledge that the guarantor has a right to revoke the guarantee and to include in the loan agreement an Event of Default if the guarantee is terminated.

Guarantor: *The guarantor must ensure that the commercial agreement is accurately reflected. Thus, if it is entitled to revoke/cancel the guarantee, this should be specifically stipulated together with the notice period requirements. An alternative to an indefinite guarantee might be one with a form of 'evergreen' or 'roll over' provision. Where the guarantor is an individual and the underlying contract is an indivisible one then, in the absence of an express clause, the guarantee will continue to bind the personal representatives of an individual guarantor if he or she dies. This should therefore be specifically excluded. This is not the case in respect of a divisible contract where the guarantor would be entitled to give notice terminating his/her liability. The death or insanity of the guarantor will not automatically revoke the guarantee but, depending on whether the underlying contract is divisible or not, it can be revoked on the provision of reasonable notice by the personal representative of a deceased guarantor.*

7 **Expenses**

The Guarantor agrees to reimburse the Lender on demand for all legal and other costs, charges and expenses on a full and unqualified indemnity basis which may be incurred by the Lender in relation to the enforcement hereof against the Guarantor.

Purpose/Lender/Guarantor: *See equivalent clause in Document 1 at page 61.*

8 **Set-off and Lien**

8.1 The Guarantor hereby agrees that the Lender may at any time without notice, notwithstanding any settlement of account or other matter whatsoever, combine or consolidate all or any of its then existing accounts wherever situate and any accounts in the name of the Lender or of the Guarantor jointly with others and set-off or transfer any sum standing to the credit or any one or more such accounts in or towards satisfaction of the Guaranteed Liabilities. Where such combination, set-off or transfer requires the conversion of one currency into another, such conversion shall be calculated at the Exchange Rate for purchasing the currency for which the Guarantor is liable, with the existing currency.

Purpose/Lender/Guarantor: See Clause 28 in Document 1 at page 93.

8.2 Until all the Guaranteed Liabilities have been paid, discharged or satisfied in full the Lender shall have a lien on all property and assets of the Guarantor from time to time in the possession of and a charge over all its stocks, shares and marketable or other securities from time to time registered in the name of the Lender or its nominees whether the same be held for safe custody or otherwise.

Purpose: It is quite standard for the guarantee to contain a clause giving the lender a lien on or over the stock and shares and other instruments of the guarantor which have been deposited with the bank.

Although arguably a security interest, this is not registrable at the Companies Registry as it does not fall within s 396 of the Companies Act 1985. There is, however, an argument that dividends may be regarded as Book Debts and are therefore registrable. If the clause extended to dividends therefore, the lien could be registrable.

The requirement for the lien is a commercial issue and usually most guarantors do not place any stocks or shares with the lender, rendering the clause irrelevant.

9 **Payments, Currencies and Taxes**

9.1 The obligation of the Guarantor shall be to make payment to the Lender in the currency in which, and at the time and place at which, the Guaranteed Liabilities are payable by the Principal Debtor.

Purpose: This clause is only relevant in an international transaction where currencies other than Sterling are involved. Usually, the lender will require payment by the guarantor to be in the currency which the lender has advanced to the borrower. Therefore, a UK company guaranteeing the liability of its US parent will be required to pay in dollars (if this is the currency it has borrowed in). The clause effectively ensures that the lender will not bear any exchange rate risk.

9.2   All payments to be made by the Guarantor hereunder shall be made in full, without any set-off, condition or counterclaim whatsoever and, subject as provided below, free and clear of any deductions or withholdings whatsoever. If at any time any applicable law, regulation or regulatory requirement or any governmental authority, monetary agency or central bank requires the Guarantor to make any deduction or withholding in respect of taxes, levies, duties, imposts or any charges whatsoever from any payment due hereunder for the account of the Lender, the sum due from the Guarantor in respect of such payment shall be increased to the extent necessary to ensure that, after the making of such deduction or withholding, the Lender receives on the due date for such payment (and retains, free from any liability in respect of such deduction or withholding) a net sum equal to the sum which it would have received had no such deduction or withholding been required to be made and the Guarantor shall indemnify the Lender against any losses or costs incurred by reason of any failure of the Guarantor to make any such deduction or withholding or by reason of any increased payment not being made on the due date for such payment. The Guarantor shall promptly deliver to the Lender any receipts, certificates or other proof evidencing the amount (if any) paid or payable in respect of any deduction or withholding as aforesaid.

Purpose/Lender/Guarantor: This is a condensed version of Clauses 27.3 and 13 in Document 1 at pages 92 and 53–58 respectively.

10   Miscellaneous

10.1   If this Guarantee is signed as guarantor by more than one person or is signed by one person for himself and on behalf of other persons (whether such person is signing on behalf of a partnership or otherwise) the expression the 'Guarantor' shall include all such persons and the liability of the Guarantor hereunder shall be the joint and several liability of all such persons and any demand for payment by the Lender on any one or more of such persons so jointly and severally liable shall be deemed to be a demand made to all such persons.

Purpose: It is important from both the lender's and the borrower's perspective that the nature of the liability is fully understood. There is a distinction between joint, several, and joint and several liability. If the guarantors are jointly liable for the entire debt, then they should all be joined as defendants by the lender in an action to recover the debt. If the guarantors are severally liable for a particular portion of their debt, they may be sued individually to recover that specific portion. If the guarantors are jointly and severally liable, the lender would be entitled to sue any of them in respect of the whole amount outstanding.

Joint and several liability is clearly the most beneficial for a lender. The guarantors would be able to seek contributions for co-guarantors in respect of amounts paid to the lender but would of course be running a credit risk on the co-guarantors.

10.2   Each person who shall have executed this Guarantee as guarantor or on whose behalf this Guarantee shall have been executed agrees to be bound hereby notwithstanding that any other person intended to execute or to be bound hereby may not do so or may not be effectually bound and notwithstanding that this Guarantee may be determined or be or become invalid or unenforceable against any other person, whether or not the deficiency is known to the Lender.

Purpose: *This clause is necessary if the guarantee is signed by more than one guarantor as, if for any reason it becomes invalid or unenforceable as against any one of the guarantors, it would otherwise be invalid as against all of them.*

10.3   No failure, delay or other relaxation or indulgence on the part of the Lender to exercise any power, right or remedy hereunder or at law shall operate as a waiver thereof nor shall any single or any partial exercise or waiver of any such power, right or remedy preclude its further exercise or the exercise of any other power, right or remedy.

10.4   This Guarantee shall remain binding on the Guarantor notwithstanding any change in the constitution of the Lender or its absorption in, or amalgamation with, or the acquisition of all of part of its undertaking or assets by, any other person, or any reconstruction or reorganisation of any kind, to the intent that this Guarantee shall remain valid and effective in all respects in favour of any assignee, transferee or other successor in title of the Lender in the same manner as if such assignee, transferee or other successor in title had been named herein as a party instead of, or in addition to, the Lender.

Purpose: *This is another protective clause for the lender. If the lender does change its identity, the guarantee will cease to be effective if this clause is not inserted.*

10.5   Each of the provisions hereof is severable and distinct from the others and if at any time one or more of such provisions is or becomes invalid, illegal or unenforceable the validity, legality and enforceability of the remaining provisions hereof shall not in any way be affected or impaired thereby.

Purpose/Lender/Guarantor: *See Clause 31 in Document 1 at page 96.*

10.6   This Guarantee shall not be determined or affected by the death of the Guarantor or any one or more of the persons constituting the Guarantor.

Purpose: *This clause ensures that the Guarantee continues notwithstanding the death of the guarantor, so that it will continue to bind the personal representatives of the guarantor who, depending on the type of the underlying transaction, would be entitled to determine it.*[17]

11   Notices

11.1   All notices, demands or other communications under or in connection herewith may be given by letter, telex or facsimile or other comparable means of communication addressed to the person at the address specified at the beginning of this Guarantee (or such other address as may be specified in writing from one party to the other). Any such communication will be deemed to be given as follows:

11.1.1   if personally delivered, at the time of delivery;

11.1.2   if by letter, at noon on the Business Day following the day such letter was posted (or in the case of airmail, seven days after the envelope containing the same was delivered into the custody of the postal authorities); and

1.1.3   if by telex, facsimile transmission or comparable means of communication during the business hours of the other party then on the day of transmission, otherwise on the next following Business Day.

11.2   In proving such service it shall be sufficient to prove that personal delivery was made or that such letter was properly stamped first class, addressed and delivered to the postal authorities or that the telex was transmitted with a correct answerback or in the case of facsimile transmission or other comparable means of communication, that a confirming hard copy was provided promptly after transmission.

Purpose: *See Clause 29 of Document 1 at page 93.*

If the guarantors are individuals it may be important from the lender's point of view to stipulate who the notice should go to in the event that one of the guarantors dies or becomes insane.

---

17   See notes to Clause 6 at pp 178 and 179.

12   Governing Law

This Guarantee shall be governed by and construed in accordance with English law.

Purpose: See Clause 34 of Document 1 at page 96.

13   Counterparts and Delivery

This Guarantee may be executed in any number of counterparts, each of which shall be deemed to be an original, and which together shall constitute one and the same agreement.

Purpose: See Clause 33 of Document 1 at page 96.

IN WITNESS OF WHICH this Guarantee has been executed and delivered as a deed on the date first above written.

Purpose/Lender/Guarantor: See note to execution clause of debenture at page 154.

EXECUTED and DELIVERED as a DEED
for and on behalf of THE GUARANTOR
by:

Director

Director/Secretary

OR

SIGNED, SEALED and DELIVERED by
THE GUARANTOR in the presence of:

Witness details

Witness:

Witness Name:

Witness Address:

EXECUTED and DELIVERED as a DEED
on behalf of THE LENDER by:

Director

Director/Secretary

PITFALLS

CONTENTS

1	Unfair Terms in Consumer Contracts Regulations 1999	187
2	Environmental Liability	189
3	Loans to Directors	190
4	Financial Assistance	194
5	Insolvency Act 1986	198
	5.1 Transactions at an undervalue	198
	5.2 Preferences	199
	5.3 Avoidance of certain floating charges	200
	5.4 Extortionate credit transactions	201
	5.5 Generally	201
6	Registration of Charges	201
	6.1 Charges created by English and Welsh companies	201
	6.2 Charges created by overseas companies	202
	6.3 Other forms of registration	203

PITFALLS

1   **Unfair Terms in Consumer Contracts Regulations 1999**[1]

1.1   These regulations, which came into force on 1 October 1999, extend the consumer protection afforded by the Unfair Contract Terms Act 1977 and revoke and replace the Unfair Terms in Consumer Contracts Regulations 1994. In the context of financing transactions these regulations may constitute a pitfall for lenders, as their effect could be to discharge a lender's security or invalidate its claim for repayment if the documentation contains an 'unfair term'.

1.2   Operating alongside the Unfair Contract Terms Act 1982 (but independently of it) the regulations apply to any term in a contract between a seller (or supplier) and a consumer where the term has not been individually negotiated.[2] They could, therefore, potentially affect any standard contract between a bank and a personal customer.

1.3   A lender will constitute a 'supplier' insofar as it supplies goods or services and the contract to which the regulations apply is made for purposes relating to the supplier's business. An individual borrower will constitute a 'consumer' for the purposes of the regulation where, as a 'natural person', it makes the contract in question for purposes outside its business. The regulations are therefore relevant to domestic mortgages, personal loans and personal guarantees.

1.4   A term is taken not to have been individually negotiated where it has been drafted in advance and the consumer has not been able to influence the substance of the term.[3] The burden of proof lies with the supplier.[4] It is possible for the regulations to apply to an entire contract even where a specific term has been individually negotiated if, on overall assessment, it is established that the contract is a pre-formulated standard contract.[5] Most 'standard forms' could therefore be in danger even where specific clauses have been negotiated.

---

1   SI 1999/2083 which restated SI 1994/3159 as from 1 October 1999.
2   Ibid, reg 5(2).
3   Ibid, reg 5(2).
4   Ibid, reg 5(4).
5   Ibid, reg 5(3).

1.5   Regulation 5 defines 'unfair term' with such breadth that it may
       permit sureties and mortgagors to challenge guarantees and
       security documents on more grounds than have been available to
       date. An unfair term is 'any term which contrary to the requirement
       of good faith causes a significant imbalance in the parties' rights
       and obligations under the contract to the detriment of the
       consumer'.[6] Unhelpfully, the regulations do not define 'significant
       imbalance' but regs 5(1) and 6(1) and Sch 2 give further guidance
       as to how to interpret the definition. Happily, the adequacy of the
       price of the contract as against the goods or services supplied in
       exchange cannot constitute an unfair term.[7]

1.6   The regulations set out an indicative list of terms which may be
       regarded as unfair,[8] the most relevant of which to lenders are the
       following:

       (a) any provision excluding the right to counterclaim or set-off;[9]
       (b) any provision irrevocably binding the consumer to a term with
            which he had no real opportunity of becoming acquainted
            before signing the contract;[10] and
       (c) any term having the effect or object of excluding the cus-
            tomer's right to take legal action or exercise any other legal
            remedy.[11]

1.7   If adjudged unfair by the Director General of Fair Trading or a
       'qualifying body',[12] the term will not bind the consumer; but the
       contract will continue to bind the parties if it is capable of
       continuing in existence without the unfair term.[13]

1.8   The 1999 regulations replace the 1994 regulations and give the
       adjudicator of a complaint certain additional powers. These
       include:

       (a) the power to obtain documents and information from the
            lender to facilitate consideration of any complaint;[14] and
       (b) the powers to publish in any form any information or advice
            given by a lender which appears expedient to the public.[15]

       The exercise of these powers would very likely be detrimental to a
       lender's business, image and reputation.

---

6   Ibid, reg 5(1).
7   Ibid, reg 6(2)(b).
8   Ibid, reg 5(5) and Sch 2.
9   Ibid, Sch 2, para 1(b).
10   Ibid, Sch 2, para 1(i).
11   Ibid, Sch 2, para 1(q).
12   Ibid, reg 3 and Sch 1.
13   Ibid, reg 8(1) and (2).
14   Ibid, reg 13(1) and (2).
15   Ibid, reg 15(3).

2   Environmental Liability

2.1   Borrowers and lenders involved in the finance of land acquisition and development should be aware of the growing issue of the environment.

2.2   The potential for a borrower to incur liability under environmental legislation is now very real[16] and the risks are now widely acknowledged. The scope of that liability, the means by which it arises and the remedial and preventative action which may be taken by a borrower are not, however, within the scope of this section. The principal environmental concerns to be addressed in the context of a financing transaction are the risks to a lender. Risk assessment is, after all, an integral part of any loan.

2.3   A lender may be exposed to both direct and indirect liability. Indirect risk under environmental laws may arise because the borrower to which it is exposed becomes directly liable to environmental costs and liabilities. This, in turn, may affect its ability to service a loan or may, if land becomes contaminated with toxic waste for example, devalue the lender's security. Direct liability is also a possibility, for although there is at the time of writing no domestic law rendering lenders who have not entered into possession of the mortgaged land liable for environmental damage, existing property legislation and the draft EC Directive for Civil Liability Caused by Waste[17] may either individually or jointly represent a potential risk area for a lender 'operating' or 'occupying' property whether or not it has enforced its security.

2.4   The EC Directive for Civil Liability Caused by Waste (unlike its American counterpart, the Comprehensive Environmental Response Compensation and Liability Act) does not incorporate a blanket exclusion from liability for secured lenders. A lender may face liability insofar as it is deemed to be in control of property. The EC Green Paper,[18] however, acknowledges the concerns of lenders regarding any EC legislation, particularly following the large amount of lobbying that has gone on, and it seems that any legislation flowing from the Green Paper will include a secured lender exclusion. Until such time as the European legislation is implemented in the United Kingdom, however, lenders should focus on the 'problematic' UK legislation.

2.5   Existing UK legislation relevant to a lender's potential liability before it enforces its security, includes the Environmental Protection Act 1990 ('EPA'),[19] the Insolvency Act 1986,[20] the Water

---

16   The Environmental Protection Act 1990 and the Environment Act 1995.
17   Official Journal no C251, 04/10/89 P3.
18   *Remedying Environmental Damage* (Com (93), 17 March 1993).
19   Section 157(1) and ss 79–82.
20   Section 251.

Resources Act 1991 ('WRA')[21] and the Environment Act 1995 ('EA') where a lender may be deemed the owner of the land in certain situations or regarded as purporting to act in the capacity of a director of the borrower. Broadly, it appears that to be liable before it takes any step of security enforcement, a lender would have to be exerting a certain influence on the management of the mortgaged land and, under the EA, would have to cause or knowingly permit contamination.[22] As at July 2001, the EA has not yet been brought into force owing to difficulties in finalising the guidance notes which would flesh out the meaning of these phrases. Without the guidance or any case-law on the subject as yet, it is not certain whether detailed environmental compliance covenants in loan and security documents constitute such control; it is hoped they would not. Such covenants should arguably only add to the onus of the borrower's existing good business practices and are unlikely to necessitate the lender being in day-to-day supervision of the land in question. One area of concern would be the lender's power to remedy, which is a common provision of security documents giving the lender a contractual right to cure environmental problems itself. Pending the issue of statutory guidance it is unclear whether this type of provision could extend liability to a lender before enforcement of its charge.

2.6   It appears that a lender may realistically face a greater risk of incurring environmental liability in enforcing its security if the lender can be construed as an owner, operator or occupier of the land in question (as those terms are defined in the relevant UK statutes). In particular, the EA, when in force, will confirm that the party who should have primary liability for remedying environmental contamination should be the person who has operated the site or process which caused it. This would seem to imply that a lender would realistically only face liability were it to go into possession. In addition, a lender may incur liability pursuant to the WRA,[23] the Occupiers Liability Act 1957, the Health and Safety at Work etc Act 1974 and the Mines and Quarries Act 1954[24] but, again, the risk seems limited to where the lender goes into possession or operates the site.

3   **Loans to Directors**

3.1   The Companies Act 1985[25] restricts the power of companies to grant loans and security to or on behalf of any of their directors or persons connected with any of their directors and any transaction or

---

21   Section 217(1).
22   Section 78F of the EPA (as inserted by s 57 of the EA).
23   Sections 85 and 161.
24   Section 181.
25   Companies Act 1985, s 330.

arrangement entered into in contravention of the restrictions may be voidable at the instance of the company.[26] There is a two-level statutory regime with basic limitations applying to all companies and wider limitations applying to public companies and private companies which are part of a group which also contains a public company (referred to in the statute as 'relevant companies'). There are also criminal penalties which may be imposed on relevant companies and their directors, and on any person procuring a 'relevant' company to enter into a transaction knowing it to breach these restrictions.[27] This could include a bank insisting on taking security which is in breach of these restrictions.

3.2   In general terms, these restrictions are unlikely to present a problem with most bank–borrower transactions, although there is always a possibility where a bank wishes to grant a residential mortgage to one of its directors, or guarantee his obligations in respect of his outside business interests, for example. These provisions should be borne in mind especially where an individual borrower intends to use assets held by his companies as security. The restrictions can also be very relevant in inter-company loan, security and guarantee situations and where non-bank companies advance funds to their board members. Companies which ordinarily lend money in their normal course of business are excluded from the prohibitions in s 330 subject to a statutory cap on the amount being lent (currently £100,000).[28]

3.3   It is worth remembering that the definition of 'director' extends beyond persons formally appointed as directors.[29]

3.4   Diagrams A and B are flow charts working through the relevant statutory provisions.[30] Using them with any given facts it should be possible to ascertain whether or not there appears initially to be a 'loan to director problem'. These charts are not intended to be definitive and they are certainly no substitute for detailed consideration of the relevant law, but from their first few levels, it is often possible to identify whether or not a potential problem exists. In any event, it should be clear that the distinction between private and 'relevant' companies (as defined in the statute) is paramount.

---

26   Ibid, s 341.
27   Ibid, s 342.
28   Ibid, s 338.
29   Ibid, s 744A.
30   Ibid, s 331(6).

3.5   **Diagram A: Loans to Directors – Private Companies**

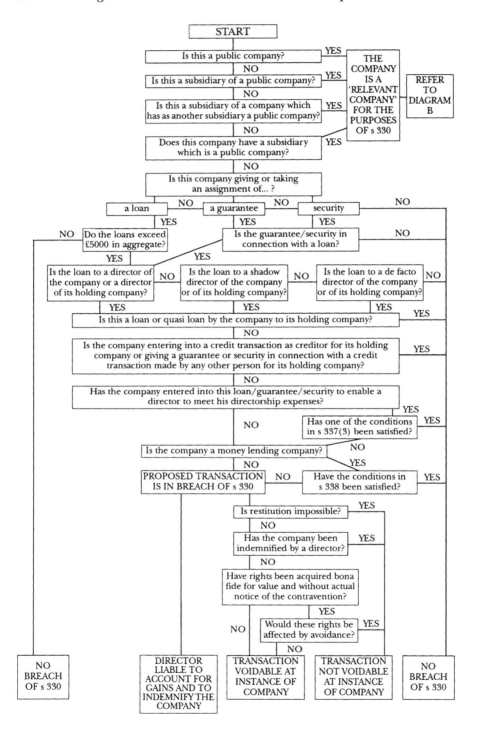

3.6 **Diagram B: Loans to Directors – Relevant Companies**

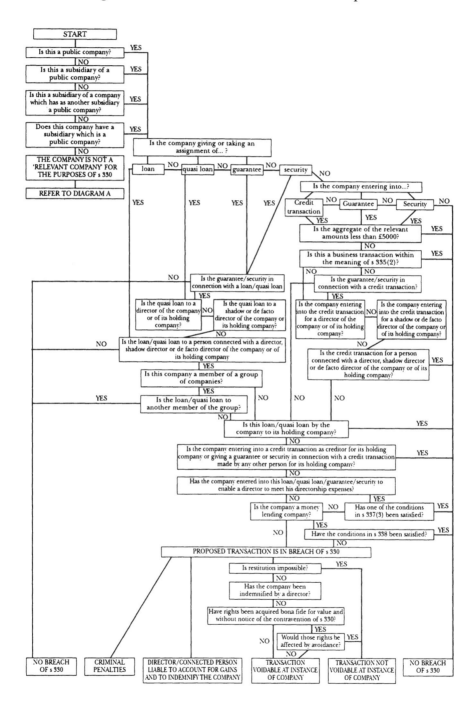

4   Financial Assistance

4.1   It is unlawful for a company to give financial assistance, either
            directly or indirectly for the purpose of the acquisition of its own
            shares or those of its holding company, either before or at the same
            time as the acquisition.[31] It is also unlawful for a company whose own
            or whose holding company's shares have been acquired, where a
            liability has been incurred for the purpose of that acquisition, to
            give financial assistance either directly or indirectly for the purpose
            of reducing or discharging that liability.[32] The key situations in
            which these sections are likely to be relevant are the granting of
            security by target companies for debt incurred to fund the
            acquisition and refinancing of such debt on the security of the
            target's assets. See paragraph 4.5 for more details.

4.2   The definition of financial assistance in the legislation[33] is very wide
            and can attach to transactions ranging from a loan by a company to
            an individual share subscriber, to a situation where the subsidiary of
            a target company in a share acquisition pays the purchaser's legal
            fees as a condition precedent to the purchaser's loan being drawn
            down at the time of the acquisition. The fundamental ingredient,
            however, is always an acquisition of shares and the transaction is not
            'safe' merely because that acquisition took place some time ago.
            There is no time-limit on the application of post-acquisition
            financial assistance. There is a likelihood that it will apply to the
            refinancing of acquisition debt no matter how long ago the
            acquisition took place. This is an area of the law that many
            practitioners would like to see reformed since it is drafted and
            interpreted in a way which extends some distance beyond the
            original intention of protecting shareholders.[34]

4.3   There are specific exclusions to the restrictions, in the form of nine
            types of authorised transaction.[35] Loans granted in the ordinary
            course of a money-lending business or for the purpose of employee
            share schemes are also excepted in certain situations.[36] Also of
            potential relevance are the 'wider purpose' provisions,[37] although
            practitioners tend to be loath to rely upon these since their scope is
            uncertain, choosing instead either to restructure the transaction or
            to work through the general exemption procedure available to

---

31   Ibid, s 151(1).
32   Ibid, s 151(2).
33   Ibid, s 152(1)(a).
34   See, generally, Department of Trade and Industry Consultation Paper, October 1993,
      Company Law Review; Proposals for reform of Sections 151 to 158 of the Companies Act 1985;
      Department of Trade and Industry Consultation Paper, September 1994, *Proposals for
      reform*; The Law Society Company Law Committee, October 1994, *Financial assistance by a
      company for the acquisition of its own shares, Memorandum No 310*.
35   Companies Act 1985, s 153(3).
36   Ibid, s 153(4).
37   Ibid, s 153(1) and (2).

private companies.[38] This procedure is commonly referred to as the 'whitewash' procedure and it consists of a statutory declaration by the directors and a report by the auditors as to the solvency of the assisting company. Public companies may find that they can re-register as private companies in order to be able to give financial assistance.

4.4   The legislation provides that breach of the prohibition on financial assistance is a criminal offence but does not prescribe any civil consequences of breach other than to describe financial assistance as 'unlawful'. Case-law on the identical wording of the former section[39] is probably applicable equally to s 151.[40] There is a very real danger of security constituting 'financial assistance' being held invalid,[41] together with any guarantee supplementing it. There is also the possibility that any underlying agreement (such as a share sale agreement), which cannot be severed properly from the financial assistance agreements, would be held invalid.[42] There is the additional possibility of a director acting in breach of s 151 being in breach of his fiduciary duty to the company and of anyone receiving funds in breach from the company, with actual or constructive notice of the breach, being liable to the company as a constructive trustee. The question of financial assistance is therefore a concern to both lenders and borrowers.

4.5   Diagrams C and D are further flow charts, this time providing a quick reference point to ascertain whether or not there appears initially to be a 'financial assistance' problem. Again, the distinction between the two diagrams is significant as it reflects the distinction between public and private companies by the statute. The diagrams have been drawn up as a 'first port of call' in a potential financial assistance situation and are not designed to replace thorough consideration of the relevant law in the context of the pertinent facts.

---

38   Ibid, s 155.
39   Companies Act 1948, s 54.
40   *Victor Battery Co Limited v Curry's Ltd* [1946] Ch 242; *Selangor United Rubber Estates Ltd v Craddock (No 3)* [1968] 1 WLR 1555; *Heald v O'Connor* [1971] 1 WLR 497; *South Western Mineral Water Co v Ashmore* [1967] 1 WLR 1110.
41   *Heald v O'Connor* [1971] 1 WLR 497.
42   *Carney v Herbert* [1985] BCLC 140, PC.

4.6 **Diagram C: Financial Assistance before or at the same time as the Acquisition**

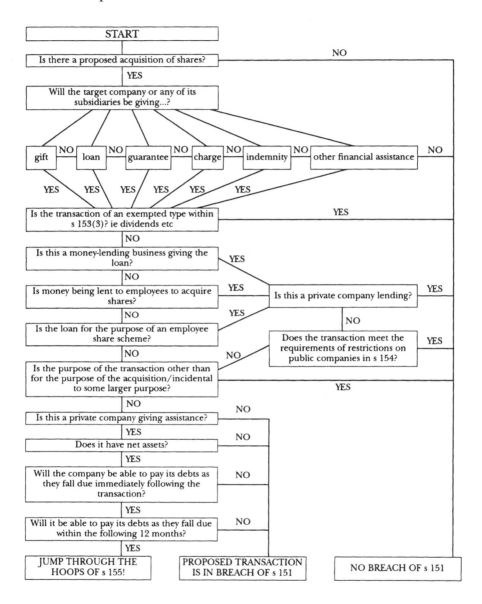

4.7   **Diagram D: Financial Assistance after the Acquisition**

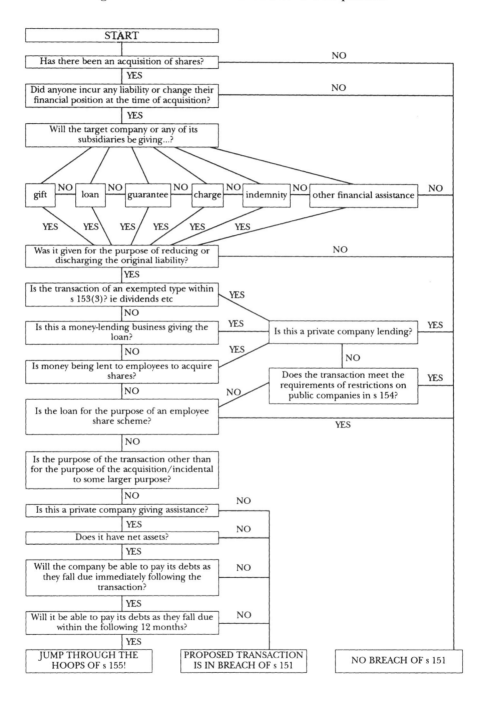

5   Insolvency Act 1986

Under the Insolvency Act 1986 there are a number of provisions
which may affect the enforcement of a lender's security if the
borrower is insolvent. Most security agreements will, however, often
contain an avoidance of payments clause in order to protect the
lender from the provisions of the Insolvency Act 1986.[43] The
underlying policy behind the avoidance provisions discussed below
is relatively simple. The debtor who is on the brink of insolvency
should not be allowed to prefer one creditor over another and,
further, should be prevented from removing assets from the
creditor's grasp and therefore diminishing the creditor's potential
return.

Examples of the avoidance provisions under the Insolvency Act
1986 are:

5.1   Transactions at an undervalue[44]

(a) Where a borrower enters into a transaction under which it
    receives significantly less value in money or money's worth than
    it gives, a liquidator or administrator can apply to the court for
    an order to set aside the transaction if, at the time, the borrower
    was (or, as a result of the transaction, becomes) 'unable to pay
    its debts'; and if liquidation commences or an administration
    petition is presented within two years of the transaction taking
    place.[45]

(b) The definition of 'unable to pay its debts' is contained in s 123
    of the Insolvency Act 1986 which provides two tests: first, that
    the company is unable to pay its debts as they fall due and,
    secondly, a balance sheet test whereby the company's assets are
    less than its liabilities. The first test is subdivided into five
    categories.[46] Therefore, a company which makes a gift, or
    enters into a transaction and receives either no value or the
    value received is less than that given may, if the following
    conditions are satisfied, have the transaction set aside or
    avoided.

    (i) The company must be insolvent at the date of the
         transaction or must become insolvent as a result of it.
         Where the transaction at an undervalue is entered into
         by a company with a person who is 'connected' with the
         company, the insolvency requirement referred to above
         is presumed unless the contrary is shown. A 'connected

---

43   See Document 2: Clause 24 at pp 148–149.
44   Insolvency Act 1986, s 238.
45   Ibid, s 240(2).
46   Ibid, s 123(1)(a) to (e).

person' includes any director, shadow director or anyone associated with the company.[47]

(ii)   The company must either go into liquidation or into administration. A receiver or administrative receiver does not have the ability to apply to have a transaction set aside.[48]

(iii) The transaction must have occurred at a 'relevant time'.[49] The 'relevant time' is if the company goes into liquidation or administration two years after the transaction is completed.[50] Thus any transaction before this two-year period would not be caught.

(c) Even if the above conditions are satisfied, the court will not make an order if the following defences apply:[51]

(i)   if the company transacts in good faith and for the purpose of carrying on its business;

(ii)   if there were reasonable grounds to believe that the transaction would benefit the company.

(d) If all the conditions referred to above are satisfied and the statutory defences do not apply then, on an application by the liquidator or administrator, the court is entitled to make an order restoring the position to what it would have been if the company had not entered into the transaction.[52] The court has discretion as to the particular form of order which may be granted and this includes the release or discharge of any security granted and repayment and retransfer respectively of payment and properties received.[53] The court's discretion even extends beyond the specific powers referred to in the statute.[54]

5.2   Preferences

(a) Where the company has, at a relevant time, given a preference to any person, the liquidator or administrator may apply to the court for an order under this section.[55]

(b) A company gives a preference to a person if that person is one of the company's creditors or a surety or guarantor for any of the company's debts or other liabilities and the company does anything or suffers anything which has the effect of putting that person into a position which, in the event of the company going into insolvent liquidation, would be better than the

---

47   Ibid, s 249.
48   Ibid, s 238(1)(a) and (b).
49   Ibid, s 240.
50   Ibid, s 240(1)(a).
51   Ibid, s 238(5)(a) and (b).
52   Ibid, s 238(3).
53   Ibid, s 241(1).
54   See Goode *Principles of Corporate Insolvency Law* 2nd edn (Sweet and Maxwell, 1990), at p 375.
55   Insolvency Act 1986, s 239.

position he would have been in if that thing had not been done.[56]

(c) For the section to apply the following conditions must be satisfied:

    (i)   the company must be insolvent at the date of the transaction or must become insolvent as a result of it. There is no presumption of insolvency for 'connected' persons as with transactions at an undervalue;

    (ii)   the company must have gone into either liquidation or administration; and

    (iii) the transaction must have occurred at the 'relevant time'. Note, however, that for preferences the 'relevant time' is six months which is then extended to a period of two years where the parties are 'connected'.[57]

(d) Although there are no formal defences available (in contrast to transactions at an undervalue), the court will not be entitled to make an order unless the company, in granting the preference, was influenced by the desire to put the recipient in a better position than he would have been in had the action not been done.[58] There is, however, a presumption to this effect where the preference is granted to a 'connected' party.[59]

(e) As with transactions at an undervalue, the court has discretion to make orders as it deems fit for restoring the status quo. The orders that the court may make are the same as those in respect of transactions at an undervalue.

5.3   **Avoidance of certain floating charges**

(a) These provisions[60] are similar to those dealing with preferences and transactions at an undervalue. An administrator or liquidator may challenge floating charges which are created within 12 months (two years if granted to a connected person)[61] of the commencement of a liquidation or the presentation of a petition for an administration order. Unless the floating charge is granted to a 'connected person', the borrower creating the floating charge must have been, or become unable to pay its debts as they fell due as a consequence of or at the time that the floating charge was granted.[62]

---

56   Ibid, s 239(4).
57   Ibid, s 240(1)(a) and (b).
58   Ibid, s 239(5).
59   Ibid, s 239(6).
60   Ibid, s 245.
61   Ibid, s 245(3).
62   Ibid, s 245(4).

(b) However, the security is valid to the extent of new monies advanced or the value of goods/services supplied or the discharge or reduction of any debt at the time of or after the creation of a floating charge.[63]

5.4   **Extortionate credit transactions**

A liquidator or administrator can apply for the setting aside of any transaction entered into during the period of three years before the date of the administration order (as opposed to the presentation of the petition) or the date of liquidation. The type of transaction relevant to the section is one which is such as to require grossly exorbitant payments to be made or otherwise grossly contravenes the ordinary principles of fair dealing.[64]

5.5   **Generally**

(a) There are equivalent provisions for individuals affecting trans-actions at an undervalue,[65] preferences[66] and extortionate credit transactions.[67] These provisions apply when the individual is bankrupt and it should be noted that the 'relevant time' is longer for transactions at an undervalue, namely five years.

(b) The effect of the avoidance provisions is primarily based on whether or not the borrower or individual is insolvent/bankrupt at the date of the transaction. From the lender's perspective, one way to avoid these insolvency pitfalls is to obtain assurance from the auditors of the borrower that the borrower is solvent within the meaning of s 123 of the Insolvency Act 1986 at the time of entering into the trans-action. Most auditors are reluctant to provide this, and lenders may have to rely on the directors' certificate instead.

6   **Registration of Charges**

6.1   **Charges created by English and Welsh companies**

(a) If the security for the advance is taken from a company incorporated in England and Wales over assets located in England and Wales, s 395 of the Companies Act 1985, which requires certain of such charges to be registered at the Companies Registry, may well be relevant.

(b) The charges which require registration include those securing an issue of debentures, charges over book debts, charges over land and floating charges.

---

63   Ibid, s 245(2).
64   Ibid, s 244.
65   Ibid, s 339.
66   Ibid, s 340.
67   Ibid, s 343.

(c) The particulars of the charge (a companies form number 395
available from Companies House, legal stationers and on some
software packages) together with the instrument by which the
charge is created must be delivered to the Registrar within 21
days after the date of the charge's creation. If this is not done,
the charge will be void as against the liquidator and any
creditor of the company. The Companies Act 1985 contains
provisions for registration of charges out of time with the leave
of the court.[68]

(d) The Companies Registry will provide a certificate of registration which is conclusive evidence of satisfactory
registration.[69]

(e) In practice, the form 396 is prepared by the lender although as
a matter of law it is the company's duty to register the charge.[70]

(f) Although s 396 lists the categories of charges which are
required to be registered, these are by no means certain. For
example, terms such as 'issue of debentures' and 'book debts'
are quite general.[71]

6.2   **Charges created by overseas companies**

(a) Overseas companies may be registered or unregistered.[72]
Companies incorporated outside Great Britain with a place of
business in Great Britain have a duty to register at Companies
House.[73]

(b) Section 409 of the Companies Act 1985 states that an overseas
company with an established place of business in England and
Wales must comply with the registration requirements in
respect of charges. In theory all such companies should have
registered with Companies House and therefore, again in
theory, it should be possible for third parties to identify them
simply by searching at Companies House.

(c) It was originally assumed by practitioners that the predecessor
to s 409 could not apply to companies which ought to have
registered under the predecessor of Part XXI of the Companies Act 1985 but had failed to do so because there was
nowhere to register the charges they created. However, in a
1980 case,[74] it was decided that charges created by overseas
companies that ought to have registered but had not would still
be invalid if no attempt was made to register the charge at
Companies House. This is not as odd as it may sound because

68   Companies Act 1985, s 404.
69   Ibid, s 401(2).
70   Ibid, s 399.
71   For further discussion see Lingard *Bank Security Documents* 3rd edn (Butterworths, 1993),
at pp 34–37.
72   For more details see, ibid, at pp 42–50.
73   Companies Act 1985, Pt XXI, s 691(1).
74   *Slavenburg's Bank NV v Intercontinental Natural Resources Ltd and Others* [1980] 1 WLR 1076.

the obligation to register charges is in fact an obligation to deliver the prescribed particulars of the charge and the original charging instrument to Companies House.

(d) The practical solution where an overseas company, whether registered or not as an overseas company, grants security is that it should comply with the registration of charges requirements and file particulars of the security within 21 days of the creation of charge in the correct form. This may often be 'tight' in terms of timing where the overseas jurisdiction may have a concurrent time-limit for registration. The solution to this is to execute sufficient originals to be able to file for registration concurrently in all relevant jurisdictions.

(e) As the unregistered company has no Companies House registered number the Registrar will be unable to register the particulars of the charge or issue the required registration certificate. Accordingly, the Registrar will issue a standard rejection letter now widely referred to as a 'Slavenburg letter' which constitutes proof that the charge has been presented for registration. As there is no conclusive certificate issued, which is sufficient to cure any deficiencies in the original application, it is necessary to be very careful to comply with the letter of the registration requirements in Slavenburg situations.

6.3   Other forms of registration

(a) Aside from registration under the relevant companies legislation (whether in the United Kingdom or abroad), additional registration may be required in a further registry, depending on the nature of the assets charged or mortgaged to the lender.

(b) Security over land may need to be perfected by registration at either HM Land Registry (in the case of registered land) or HM Land Charges Registry (in the case of unregistered land). Security over patents and other forms of intellectual property may require registration at the Patents Registry. Other forms of security such as 'bills of sale' have their own specific registration requirements.

(c) Each registry tends to have different procedures and time-limits. Most time-limits run concurrently with that for registration at the Companies Registry although some, such as that with the English Land Registry, may extend beyond 21 days.

(d) After a security interest has been created, the time within which it is registered at all the requisite registries is vital in determining the priority which that security interest has over other security interests created subsequently.

INDEX

References are to page numbers.

Acceleration 87–88
Account
  bank, *see* Bank account(s)
  ledger entry, new 150–151
Accounts 95
Acknowledgement by tenant 158
Address
  notices, for 94
Administrative receiver 122, 123
Administrator 85–86, 112
  preference or transaction at
      undervalue, claiming 149–150
Agent
  receiver, as, for borrower 144–145
  service of process, for 97, 100
Amendment costs 62
Amount of loan 38
Annual rental, projected 72
Arrangement fee 52
Arrears, *see* Default
Assets
  see also Charged property; Goodwill;
    Property
  assignment, *see* Assignment
  destruction of 137–138
  disposal of, *see* Permitted disposals
  floating charge on 122–123
  receiver's powers relating to 142
  repair 138
  security over, permitted, *see* Negative
    pledge; Permitted security
Assignment 88–91, 123–125
  borrower, by 89
  covenant against, *see* Negative pledge
  debenture rights and obligations
    152
  intellectual property, of, *see*
    Intellectual property
  legal or equitable 123, 124
  lender, by 88, 152
    consent of borrower 88, 90–91
    disclosure 89

  guarantee, clause in 182
    LMA guidelines 90
  notice to tenant 132, 157
  priority 124
  reassignment 147
  rent, of 131–132, 157
  rights and obligations
      distinguished 89
  sub-participation distinguished 89
Attachment 85
Attorney, power of 147–148
  event of default, making conditional
      on 147–148
Auditor
  certifications 70, 71
  report on compliance 69
Authorisations 65, 74, 98, 100
  environmental 139
Avoidance of payments
  see also Preference; Undervalue,
      transaction at
  lender's protection from 148–149,
      178, 198–201
    extortionate credit transaction
      201
    floating charge challenge 200–
      201

Bank
  see also Lender
  lead bank 7
  notice, to 159
    acknowledgement 160–162
Bank account(s) 49–52
  change, lender requesting 52
  information duty 52
  overdraft, *see* Overdraft facility
Bank of England
  compliance costs 103
Bankruptcy
  avoidance of transactions 201
Blue pencil test 96

Boilerplate clauses   15, 16, 96, 140
Book debts
    account   108, 129–131
    charge on   120, 129–131
        fixed or floating   130
        registration   201
        watering down clause   131
    definition   107–108
Borrower   98
    business of, no change to   78
    changes   40, 89
    concerns, general   15
    conditions precedent, *see* Conditions
        precedent
    construction of   34
    financial covenants   72–74
    foreign-incorporated   36, 100
    incapacity   174
    insolvent, *see* Insolvency
    representations and warranties, *see*
        Representations by borrower
    undertakings   69–72
Borrowing
    limit, borrower's constitutional   98
    receiver's powers   143
    total, *see* Financial indebtedness
Breach, *see* Event of default; Negative
    pledge; Representations by
    borrower
Break costs   42, 49
Business (borrower's)
    receiver carrying on   142
    undertaking not to change   78
Business (lender's)   91
Business day
    definition   22, 167
    non-business day,
        interest period ending on   47
        payment on   92

Cancellation   39–40, 42, 87
    guarantee   178–179
    voluntary   41
Capital, uncalled
    charge over   121
Certificate
    compliance   69
    evidence, as   95
    increased costs   59
    registration of charge   202
    share, deposit of   121, 128, 129,
        135

Charge   118–125
    book debts, on, *see* Book debts
    equitable   121
    fixed   119–122
    floating   120, 122–123, 130–131,
        201
        conversion/crystallisation   125–
        126
        lender's protection against
            avoidance   148–149, 200–
            201
    legal mortgage   118–119
    priority, *see* Priority or ranking
    registration   201–203
Charged property   108
    insurance monies, application of
        137–138
    no disposals   135
    ownership, representation as to
        135
    receiver for   141–144, *see also*
        Receiver
    release and reassignment   147
    repair   138
    representations as to   135–136
    sale by lender   140–141
    undertakings as to   136–138
Choice of law   65, 96
Collateral instruments   168, 173
Commission   95
Commitment, facility, *see* Facility
    commitment
Commitment fee   52
Compliance   74
    certificate   69, 70
    costs, lender's, *see* Mandatory cost
Compromise
    receiver's power   143
Conditions precedent   36–37, 98–100
    Consent
    assignment by lender, to   88, 90–91
Consolidation of loan   47, 48, 180
Continuing security, clause for   148,
    173–174
Control change, *see* Borrower
Costs   62, 100
    agreement, of   61
    amendment, of   62
    enforcement, of   62, 179
    fees   52, 61–62, 95, 99, 100
        banking supervision   104
    guarantor's liability   171–172, 179

Costs – *cont*
  increased costs   58–59, 61
    certificate confirming   59
    demand for   59
    exceptions   59
  indemnity   59–60, 139–140
Counterpart   96, 184
Court, *see* Jurisdiction
Covenant to pay   117
Covenants, *see* Covenant to pay; Financial
  covenants
Creditor
  process by, as event of default
    85–86
Cross-default   83–85, 88
Currency   38, 81, 101, 102
  change of   92–93, 102
  clause   92, 180–181
  Euro, change to   92–93, 95–96
  exchange rate   60, 92
    definition   168
    set-off, and   93, 180
  indemnity   60
  sterling   169
Current ratio   74

Date   21, 97, 107, 167
Death
  guarantor, of   179, 183
Debenture   4, 16, 22, 105–163
  see also specific entries
  deed, effect as   117, 154–155
  enforcement   117, 134–135, 140–
    146
  execution   117, 154–155, 163
  interpretation section   116–117
  security under   118–125
Debt service cover test   72–73
Deed
  debenture as   117, 154–155
  guarantee as   170, 184
  power of attorney   147
Default   22, 37
  see also Event of default
  continuing   37
  interest   45–46, 118
  investigating   60
  notification of   70, 94
Definitions   21–34, 107–116, 167–169
  glossary   1–14
Delivery
  notices, *see* Notice

Demand
  debenture, under, effect of   117
  guarantee payable on   170
Deposit of documents
  occupational lease   128
  share certificates   121, 128, 129,
    135
    guarantor's   180
  title deeds   99, 128–129
Designated Website   71
Director
  loan to, statutory restrictions   190–
    193
    bank-borrower transactions,
      relevance to   191
    contravening, effect of   190–191
    criminal penalties   191
    'director'   191
    exclusion   191
    flow charts   192–193
    private and public company
      distinctions   191
Disclosure, *see* Information
Disposal
  charged property, non   135
  permitted, *see* Permitted disposals
Dividends   134, 141
  lien over guarantor's   180
Division of loan   38, 47, 102
Document, *see* Counterpart;
    Information; Notices; Title to
    property
Double taxation agreement   54
Drawdown
  change in circumstances between
    agreement and   37
  meaning   5
  notice   38–39
  securing future drawdowns   148

Electronic information   71–72
Employee
  receiver's powers as to   144
  share scheme, loan for   194
Enforceable obligations
  warranty as to   64
Enforcement
  see also Event of default
  costs   62, 179
  debenture   117, 134–135, 140
  loan agreement   65, 97
    costs   62

Enforcement – *cont*
  loan agreement – *cont*
    discretion of lender   96
    jurisdiction and forum   97
Environmental issues
  clauses   136, 139
    receiver's powers   144
  liability of lender   189–190
    bases for   189–190
    contractual right to cure, and
      190
     indirect or direct   189
     possession of land, and   190
    risk assessment   189
Euro
  change to   93, 96
Event of default   23, 45–46, 81–88
  assignment of rent, and   132, 133
  cross-default clause   83–85
    dilutions to   84–85
  financial covenants breach   82
  grace period   82–83
  indemnity for loss from   60
  insolvency/insolvency proceedings
    85
  material adverse change clause   87
  materiality qualification   83
  misrepresentation   83
  non-payment   81–83
  obligations under agreement
    82–88
  remedying, period for   81, 82
  representation that none   66
  representation or warranty breach
    as   64, 65–66
  waiver   96
Evidence   95, 100
  admissibility, etc, of documents   65
  guaranteed liabilities, of   173
Exchange rate, *see* Currency
Execution
  debenture, of   117, 154–155, 163
  guarantee, of   184
    more than one signatory   181–
      182
Expenses, *see* Costs
Extortionate credit transaction   201

Facility   5, 35
  available, meaning   22
Facility commitment   23, 35

Fax   93, 94, 153, 183
Fees, *see* Costs
Filing
  representation that none required
    65, 68
Financial assistance for purchase of
    shares   194–197
  exclusions to restrictions   194–195
  'financial assistance'   194
  flow charts   196–197
  private company   194–195
  unlawful, scope   194
    breach, effect of   195
    key situations of relevance   194
    no time limit in legislation   194
    'wider purpose' provisions   194–
      195
Financial covenants   71, 72–74
  breach   82
  compliance certificate   69
Financial indebtedness   74, 77, 83–84
  definition   23–24, 84
Financial Services Authority
  compliance costs   103
Financial statements   69
  certification of   69–70
  preparation of   70
  representation as to   66
  requirements as to   70
  supply to lender, undertaking for
    69
Fixed charge, *see* Charge
Floating charge, *see* Charge
Foreign currency, *see* Currency
Foreign-incorporated borrower   36,
    100
Forfeiture, *see* Lease
Forum   97, 154
Further assurance clause   126–127

GAAP   24, 66, 70
Gearing covenant   74
General account   49, 50–51
Glossary   1–14
Goodwill
  charge over   122
Grossing-up clause   151–152
Group
  holding company
    definition   24
    guarantor as   177

Group – *cont*
  holding company – *cont*
    shares acquired incurring liability,
        restrictions   194
    material adverse change clause,
        and   87
    negative pledge, scope of   76
    permitted disposals   77
Guarantee   165–184
  change to lender   182
  collateral instruments   168, 173
  consideration   170
  construction of   171
  continuing   173–174
  deed, as   170, 184
  execution   181–182, 184
  indemnity distinguished   16–17,
      170–171
  legal presumptions, clause
      avoiding   174–175
  limited, clause making   178
  meaning   6
  principal debtor   168
  principal liabilities failing, liability
      continues   172–173
  'separate and independent
      stipulation'   172, 173
  protective clauses   174–177
  severability   182
  specific   174
  termination   178–179
  use   16–17
  waiver   182
Guaranteed liabilities   168, 170–173
  amount of, evidence of   173
  avoidance of payments   178
  joint and several liability   181–182
  payment   180–181
    no deductions, set-off or
        withholding   181
    retention of guarantees after
        177, 178
Guarantor   167
  costs and expenses, liability   171–
      172, 179
  death/insanity of   179, 183
  holding company or shareholder in
      debtor   177
  individual   183
  limitation on liability   171–172
  more than one   181–182
  notices   183

    material change in underlying
        transaction   175–176
    obligations, *see* Guaranteed liabilities
    revocation/cancellation right
        178–179
    subrogation right   176–177
    warranty   175

HM Land Registry   153, 203
  search   99
HM Land Charges Registry   203
Hedging, *see* Interest
Holding company, *see* Group

Illegality   35–36, 39–40, 61
  obligation becoming unlawful   86
  partial   96, 153, 182
Incapacity   174
Income, *see* Rental income
Increased costs, *see* Costs
Indemnity   60, 62, 170–171
  costs   58–59, 139–140
  currency   60
  guarantee distinguished   16–17,
      170
  tax, for   57–58
  various   60
Information
  accuracy, representation as to   66,
      69
  disclosure by lender
    assignment, on   89
    no obligation   91
  supply, undertakings as to   70
  undertakings   69–72
  websites   71–72
Insolvency   85, 198
  law reform   122–123
  preference or transaction at
      undervalue, lender's protection
      from   148–149, 178, 198–201
  bankruptcy, equivalent
      provisions   201
Insurance   80–81, 99, 136–137
Intellectual property   127–128
  'assigned'   107, 127
  assignment   125
  costs   128
  charge on   120–121
  registration   203
  debenture clause   127–128

Intellectual property – *cont*
  definition   110, 121
  reference to, need for   119
Interest   43–46, 118
  components of   43–44
  day-to-day accrual   95
  default   45–46, 118
    penalty, as   46
  guarantor's liability   171–172, 173
  hedging arrangement   24, 45, 50
  market disruption event   48–49
  payment   44, 50
    non-payment   81–82
  period   46–48, 102
    selection notice   46, 47
    separate for each drawing   48
  profit before interest and tax ratio
    74
  rate   43, 48
    change to   48–49
    extension of due date, where   92
    notification of   46
    swap   39, 45
Interest period, *see* Interest
Interest rate swap   39, 45
International transaction, *see* Choice of
  law; Currency; Jurisdiction; Overseas
  company
Interpretation clauses   34–35, 116–
  117, 169–170
Invalidity, *see* Illegality

Joint and several liability
  guarantors   181–182
Jurisdiction   97, 154, *see also* Choice
  of law

LIBOR   43–44, 47, 48, 59
Land, *see* Environmental issues;
  Registration of charges
Language, *see* Notices
Law, governing   65, 96, 154, 184
Lease
  documents   99
  forfeiture   86
  occupational
    definition   27, 111
    deposit of documents   128
    information duty   79
    insurance, and   81
    notice of assignment   132, 157

rent deposit, assignment of
    rights   125
  undertaking as to   78–79
  see also Rental account
  receiver's powers   142–143
  statutory power   140–141
Legal fees   62, *see also* Costs
Legal proceedings   66, *see also*
  Proceedings
Lender
  changes to   88–91, 182, *see also*
    Assignment
  concerns, general   15–16, 187–203
  construction of   34
  lien   180
  'qualifying'   53
Liabilities, *see* Guaranteed liabilities;
  Secured liabilities
Lien   76, 180
Limitation period
  date commences   117, 170
Limited guarantee, *see* Guarantee
Liquidation, *see* Insolvency; Liquidator
Liquidator
  appointment of   85
  extortionate credit transaction, setting
    aside   201
  floating charge, challenge to   200–
    201
  preference, transaction at undervalue,
    etc, setting aside   148–149,
    178, 198–201
Loan
  definition   25
Loan agreement   15–16, 21–104
  see also specific entries
  amount of loan   38
  construction   34–35
  enforcement, *see* Enforcement
  secured bilateral facility, for   15
Loan Market Association (LMA)   8,
  15, 90, 91
  website   8
Loan to director, *see* Director
Loan to value test   41
London Interbank Market   43–44, 92,
  95

MLA costs   44
Managing agents   79–80, 131
  duty of care agreement   80

Mandatory cost   43, 44, 48, 59
  formulae   103–104
Mandatory liquid asset costs   44
Margin   43, 48
Market disruption event   48–49
Material adverse change   87
Material adverse effect   25
Maximum loans   38
Merger
  undertaking not to enter   78
Minimum net worth   74
Misrepresentation   83
Mitigation
  lender, by   61
Monitoring   36
Mortgage, *see* Charge
Mortgagee in possession
  no liability of receiver or lender
    146–147

Negative pledge   74–75, 125
  breach   82, 126
  constructive notice of   76
  group facility, and scope of   76
Non-business day, *see* Business day
Non-payment   81–82, 95, *see also*
  Event of default
Notices   93–95, 153–154
  address   92
  bank, to   159
  delivery   94–95, 153, 183
  form of   93
  guarantor, to/by   176, 183–184
  language for   95
  selection notice   102
  service   94–95, 154, 183
  tenant, to   132, 157
  termination of guarantee   178, 179

Overdraft facility
  guarantee clauses
    continuing security appropriate
      174
    increase in, notice to guarantor
      176
    termination and future
      advances   179
Overseas company
  see also Foreign-incorporated borrower
  charge created by, registration
    202–203

Pari passu   67–68
Parties   21, 27, 34, 107, 167, *see also*
  Borrower; Guarantor; Lender
Patent, *see* Intellectual property
Payment
  see also Covenant to pay; Financial
    covenants; Interest; Non-payment;
    Prepayment; Repayment
  currency, *see* Currency
  guarantor's obligation   179–181
  mechanics of   91–93
  partial   91–92
  secured liabilities, of
    avoidance of, *see* Avoidance of
      payments
    irrevocable   147
  set-off   92, 93, 181
  unconditional   91
Permitted disposals   27–28, 77
  de minimis figure   77
  group, within   77
Permitted security   28–29, 75–77
  de minimis figure   76
Permitted security interest   111, 125
Plant and machinery
  fixed charge on   121
  insurance   80
  repair, undertaking as to   138
Preference   148–149, 199–200
Prepayment   39–43
  indemnity where not made following
    notice   60
  voluntary   42
Principal debtor   168
Priority or ranking   124
  assignment, of   124
  loan, of   67, 74–77, 119, 150
  payment obligations   67
  prior charges   119, 150
  registration of charge, and   203
  security   67, 74–77
  subsequent charges   150
Proceedings
  see also Enforcement; Process
  information on, supply of   70
  none outstanding/threatened   66
  receiver's power to take   143
Process
  agent for service   97, 100
  creditor, by   85–86
  service   97, 100, 154

Property   99
  'charged', *see* Charged property
  compulsory purchase   86
  definition   29, 111, 156
  insurance   80–81, 99
  lease of, *see* Lease, occupational
  major damage/destruction   86
  managing agents   79–80, 131
  monitoring, information
    undertaking   79
  searches and fees   99
  scheduled   114, 156
  survey   98
  title, *see* Title to property
  undertakings   78–81
  valuation, *see* Valuation
Purpose of loan   35–36

Qualifying lender, *see* Lender

Ranking, *see* Priority or ranking
Reassignment   147
Reborrowing   39, 43
Receiver   112
  agent of borrower   144
  application of monies   145–146
  appointment   85, 140, 141–142
  attorney, power of   147
  delegation by   141–142
  more than one   145
  negligence or misconduct   145
  powers   142–144
    lender exercising   145
    no obligation   145
    sale   142, 146
  removal   141
  remuneration   141
  statutory power of sale   141
Reduction of loan   41
Registration of charges   201–203
  Companies House
    certificate of registration   202
    overseas company, charge created
      by   202–203
    procedure   202
    relevant charges   201, 202
    time-limit   203
  HM Land Registry/Land Charges
    Registry   203
  Patents Registry   203
  priority   203

Release
  charged property from security
    147, 150
Remedy   81, 82, 96, *see also*
  Enforcement
  exclusion of consumer's right
    potentially 'unfair'   188
Rent
  see also Rental income
  application towards debt   133
  assignment   131–133, 157
  security over, form of   131–132
Rent account   29, 49, 50–51, *see also*
  Rental account
Rent deposit   125
Rental account   112, 114, 131–133
  fixed charge over   120
  lender's rights   133
  notice to bank   131, 159
    acknowledgement   160–162
  withdrawals   132
Rental income   29, 72, 112–113,
  132–133
  assignment of rights   125, 131–133
  income cover ratio   7
  payment to rental account   132
Repair
  undertakings   138
Repayment   39–40, 42
Representations by borrower
  debenture, in   135–136
    additional   136
    charged property, as to   135
  loan agreement, in   62–69, 83
    accuracy of information, etc   66,
      69
    authorisations   65
    binding and non-conflicting
      obligations   64
    breach   83
    choice of law   65
    default, that none   65–66
    extended life/repetition of
      31–32, 68–69, 83
    filing, that none required   65, 68
    financial statements, as to   66
    no pending proceedings   66
    power to enter transactions   65
    ranking, as to   67
    stamp duty, as to   65, 68
    status, as to   64
    tax deduction, none required
      65

Representations by borrower – *cont*
  loan agreement, in – *cont*
    title, as to   67
    valuation   68
Repudiation   86
Rescission   63
Restriction
  registering at HM Land Registry
    153
Revocation, *see* Cancellation;
  Termination

Sale, statutory power of   140–141
  receiver's   142, 146
Search   99
Secured bilateral facility   15
Secured liabilities
  avoidance of payments   148–149
  becoming due, deemed   140
  definition   114–115
  discharge   147
  not paid   140
  payment
    no deduction or withholding
      151–152
    final   147
Security   118–125
  see also Secured liabilities
  continuing, clause for   148, 173–
    174
  covenant against creating, *see* Negative
    pledge
  document   16, 99, *see also*
    Debenture
  enforcement, as event of default
    85
  permitted   28–29, 75, 77
  ranking of   67, 74–77
Security interest   115
Senior debt   12
Sequestration   85
Service
  notices   94–95, 153–154, 183
  process   97, 100
Set-off   92, 93, 151–152, 180, 181
  exclusion of right potentially
    'unfair'   188
Severability   96, 153, 182
Shareholder
  calls on   135, 143
  guarantor is   177

Shares
  calls on shareholders, receiver's
    powers   143
  charge on   121
    deposit of certificates   121, 128,
      129, 135
    enforcement   134–135
    equitable   121, 134
    stop notice procedure   121
  custody of certificates   135
  definition   116
  dividends, *see* Dividends
  guarantor, of, deposit with bank
    180
  receiver's powers   141
  transfer registration   129
  trustee powers of lender   134
  voting, etc, rights, exercise of
    134–135
Small company moratorium   122
Special purpose vehicle   12, 15
Spouse
  guarantor   167
Stamp duty   58, 65, 68, 99
Standard contract
  dangers of   187
Subordination deed   53, 99
Subrogation right
  guarantor, of   176–177
Subsidiary
  receiver's powers   143–144
Survey   98
Suspense account   151, 177
Syndicated loan   90

Tax   54–59, 99
  credit   53, 55, 57
  deduction   54, 55, 56, 60, 65
  gross-up   54–55, 61, 151–152
  indemnity   57–58
  payment   54
  stamp duty, *see* Stamp duty
  value added tax   58
  withholdings   55–56, 151–152, 181
Telex   93, 94, 153, 183
Tenant
  see also Lease
  notice of assignment to   132, 157
    acknowledgement   158
Termination   87–88, 178–179
Third party rights
  disapplication   35

Third party rights – *cont*
   receivership, protection during
      146
Title guarantee   118–119, 136
Title to property   67, 99
   deposit of deeds   99, 128–129
   restriction on Proprietorship
      Register   153
Transfer of loan, *see* Assignment
Treaty lender   53, 55

Undertakings
   breach   82, *see also* Event of default
   debenture, in   136–139
      information   136
      insurance   136–137
   loan agreement, in
      general   74–78
      information   70–71
      property   78–81
Undervalue, transaction at   148–149,
   198–199
Unfair term   96, 171, 175, 187–188
   'consumer'   187
   definition   188
   effect   188
   not individually negotiated term
      187
   powers of adjudicator   188
   scope of regulation   187
   'supplier'   187

Unlawfulness, *see* Illegality
Utilisation   33, 38–39
Utilisation request   34, 36–38, 101
   completion   38
   conditions precedent for   36–38,
      66, 98–100
   currency   101, *see also* Currency
   delivery   38
   form of   101

Validity of agreement   96, *see also*
   Illegality
Valuation
   condition precedent, as   36, 98
   definition   34
   loan to value test   41
   representation as to   68
Value added tax   58

Waiver   96, 152, 182
Warranty
   borrower   62–66, 83, *see also*
      Representations by borrower
   guarantor   175
Website   71–72
   LMA, for   8
Winding up   85, *see also* Insolvency;
   Liquidator
Withholding tax   56–57, 151–152, 181